# asian

# asian

Bath · New York · Singapore · Hong Kong · Cologne · Delhi · Melbourne

This edition published by Parragon in 2009

Parragon
Queen Street House
4 Queen Street
Bath BA1 1HE, UK

Copyright © Parragon Books Ltd 2009
Designed by Terry Jeavons & Company
Additional text by Linda Doeser

ISBN: 978-1-4075-4759-6

Printed in Indonesia

### Notes for the Reader

This book uses both metric and imperial measurements. Follow the same units of measurement throughout; do not mix metric and imperial. All spoon measurements are level: teaspoons are assumed to be 5 ml, and tablespoons are assumed to be 15 ml. Unless otherwise stated, milk is assumed to be full fat, eggs and individual vegetables are medium, and pepper is freshly ground black pepper.

The times given are an approximate guide only. Preparation times differ according to the techniques used by different people and the cooking times may also vary from those given. Optional ingredients, variations or serving suggestions have not been included in the calculations.

Recipes using raw or very lightly cooked eggs should be avoided by infants, the elderly, pregnant women, convalescents and anyone suffering from an illness. Pregnant and breastfeeding women are advised to avoid eating peanuts and peanut products. Sufferers from nut allergies should be aware that some of the ready-made ingredients used in the recipes in this book may contain nuts. Always check the packaging before use.

Vegetarians should be aware that some of the ready-prepared ingredients used in the recipes in this book may contain animal products. Always check the packaging before use.

# contents

# introduction

The continent of Asia includes nearly 30 per cent of the world's land mass and comprises many countries, billions of people, numerous languages, dialects and myriad cultures. Even if the focus, as here, is on only the eastern and south-eastern parts, the diversity is breathtaking – and this is as true of its culinary traditions as of everything else.

You have only to walk along the main streets of almost any Western city to see thriving restaurants serving Asian food, and preparing, say, Chinese or Thai dishes at home has become more and more popular and increasingly easy. The attraction is partly because of their great variety and partly because of what they have in common. Even in our modern global village, Asian food still has an air of the exotic, using ingredients such as lemon grass, wasabi, fermented shrimp paste and Szechuan pepper that have

never featured in traditional Western kitchens. From Kyoto to Kuala Lumpur and from Beijing to Bali, food is prepared with assiduous attention to balancing flavours, colours and textures, a subtle use of spices and other flavourings, an imaginative variety of ingredients and delightfully appetizing presentation that, in some cases, almost amounts to a work of art.

Nevertheless, the cuisine of each country – even different regions of the same country – is unique. As a result, there are recipes to suit all tastes, occasions and moods. If you love spicy food and hot chillies, look for the highly seasoned dishes of Chinese Szechuan or the colourful but very different curries of Thailand or Indonesia. Lovers of fish and seafood will be thrilled with Japanese and Vietnamese specialities, while poultry, especially chicken, features in a huge variety of dishes across the region because traditional peasant communities could rarely afford the luxury of other meats. This, in turn, means that recipes for beef or lamb, for example, were often created for special occasions or rich families and are ideal for entertaining. The high price of meat and the fact that many people in Asia are Buddhist means that the array of vegetable and vegetarian dishes is immense. Many

of them are based on the soya product tofu, created in China in the 2nd century BC and widely used in Japan since the 8th century. It took Westerners hundreds of years to catch up with this useful ingredient and the best recipes still come from Asia. An interesting misconception is that so-called fusion cooking is a modern Western fashion, but many classic dishes from Canton, Indonesia and Vietnam, in particular, have a remarkable cosmopolitan quality as a result of trade or conquest. For those new to cooking Asian food, these could be a good place to start.

In fact, most Asian cooking is not, as a rule, difficult, although Japanese sushi chefs are apprenticed for many years before reaching the highest level of their craft. Stir-frying and grilling – both quick-cooking techniques – are very common because in many places fuel was scarce, but other familiar ways of cooking,

such as braising and deep-frying, are also frequently used.

The most important thing, however, is to try to buy authentic ingredients, although, of course, many recipes also call for items that are already familiar. Nowadays, supermarkets stock the most commonly used storecupboard items, such as soy sauce, Thai fish sauce, Chinese five-spice powder, canned bamboo shoots, canned coconut milk and, of course, noodles and rice. They also offer a range of fresh ingredients, such as beansprouts, pak choi, Chinese leaves, mooli and shiitake mushrooms. It may be difficult to find some rather more unusual items, such as tamarind, spring roll wrappers, galangal and nori, but it is worth looking for Asian grocers and specialist shops.

When looking for authentic ingredients, make sure that you buy the right 'nationality'. For example, Chinese soy sauce has a much stronger flavour than Japanese and Thai basil is more pungent than the Western herb so they are not interchangeable. Although it's always best to use authentic ingredients, it may sometimes be necessary to use a substitute – lemon juice instead of tamarind, bottled lemon grass instead of fresh, or dry sherry instead of Chinese rice wine.

# soups, salads & vegetables

All these dishes may be served as part of a meal with a selection of other dishes, as they usually are in their countries of origin, or as a light lunch on their own. Soups, which range from delicately fragrant broths to more substantial bowlfuls, and salads also make great first courses if you want to serve them Western-style. You might even like to try serving miso soup for breakfast as they do in Japan.

We tend not to associate salads with Asian cuisine, but they are a revelation to the taste buds and to the eyes. They are characterized by fabulous contrasting flavours, exciting mixtures of texture, intriguing combinations of ingredients and often striking presentation.

Vegetables form an extremely important part of the diet in most Asian countries and so they are prepared and cooked with considerable care, attention and inventiveness. As a result, Asian vegetable dishes are among the most imaginative, interesting and delicious in the world. They are very often served with a dressing, usually of contrasting flavours such as hot and sour, rather like a warm salad. They may feature familiar vegetables, such as broccoli or potatoes, but are given a special Eastern treatment, or use

more exotic greens, such as choi sum, also known as Chinese flowering cabbage. While they are all great served as part of an Asian meal, they also make superb accompaniments to plainly grilled meat, chicken or fish – a clever way to encourage the family to eat more vegetables.

# mushroom & noodle soup

## ingredients

**SERVES 4**

1/2 cucumber

2 tbsp vegetable oil

2 spring onions, finely
    chopped

1 garlic clove, cut into thin
    strips

125 g/41/2 oz flat or open-cap
    mushrooms, thinly sliced

600 ml/1 pint water

25 g/1 oz Chinese rice noodles

3/4 tsp salt

1 tbsp soy sauce

## method

**1** Halve the cucumber lengthways. Scoop out the seeds using a teaspoon, then slice the flesh thinly.

**2** Heat the oil in a large preheated wok. Add the spring onions and garlic and stir-fry for 30 seconds. Add the mushrooms and stir-fry for 2–3 minutes.

**3** Stir in the water. Break the noodles into short lengths and add to the soup. Bring to the boil, stirring.

**4** Add the cucumber slices, salt and soy sauce and simmer for 2–3 minutes.

**5** Ladle the soup into warmed bowls, distributing the noodles and vegetables evenly.

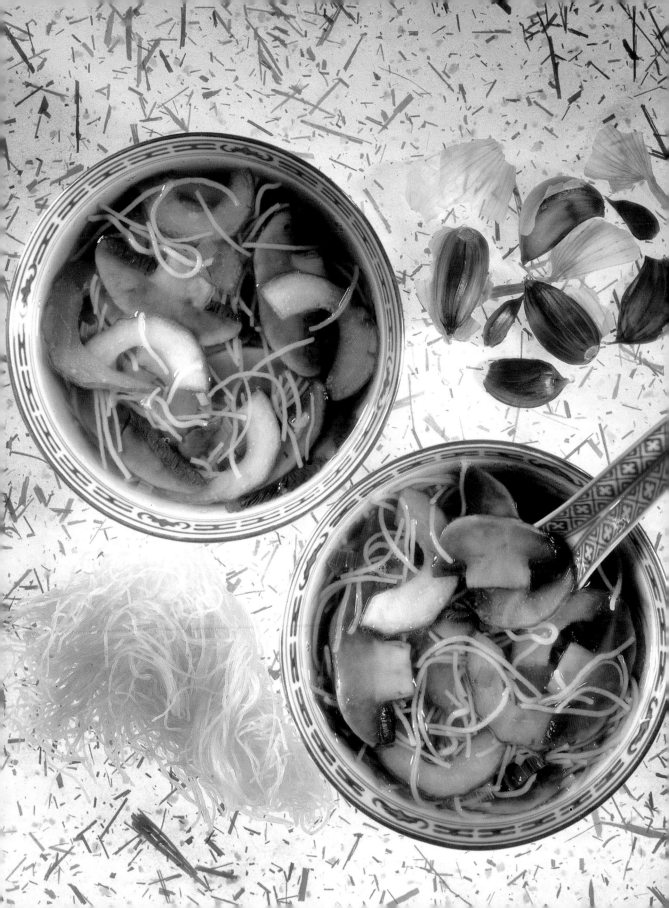

# rice noodles with tofu soup

## ingredients

**SERVES 4**

200 g/7 oz firm tofu, drained
vegetable or peanut oil,
    for deep-frying
1 litre/1³/₄ pints vegetable
    stock
5 spring onions, halved
1 yellow pepper, deseeded
    and sliced
2 celery stalks, sliced
1 small onion, sliced thinly
4 kaffir lime leaves
2 tbsp Thai soy sauce
1 tbsp Thai green curry paste
175 g/6 oz wide rice noodles,
    soaked and drained
chopped fresh coriander,
    to garnish

## method

**1** Using a sharp knife, cut the tofu into even cubes. Pour the oil into a wok to a depth of about 5 cm/2 inches and heat. Deep-fry the tofu, in batches, until browned all over. Remove with a slotted spoon, drain on kitchen paper and set aside.

**2** Pour the stock into a saucepan and bring to the boil. Add the spring onions, yellow pepper, celery, onion, lime leaves, soy sauce and curry paste and simmer for 4–5 minutes. Add the noodles and the tofu and simmer for 2–3 minutes. Ladle into warmed bowls and serve hot, topped with chopped coriander.

# tofu & beansprout soup

## ingredients

**SERVES 4–6**

280 g/10 oz spare ribs,
     cut into small pieces

1.2 litres/2 pints water

2 tomatoes, deseeded and
     roughly chopped

3 thin slices fresh ginger

140 g/5 oz beansprouts

2 tsp salt

200 g/7 oz soft tofu, cut into
     2.5-cm/1-inch cubes

## method

**1** Bring a saucepan of water to the boil and blanch the spare ribs for about 30 seconds. Skim the water, then remove the ribs and set aside.

**2** Bring the measured water to the boil in a large saucepan and add the spare ribs, tomatoes and ginger. After 10 minutes, remove the tomato skins from the water. Add the beansprouts and salt, then cover and simmer for 1 hour. Add the tofu cubes and simmer for a further 2 minutes, then serve.

# thai chicken-coconut soup

## ingredients

**SERVES 4**

115 g/4 oz dried cellophane
    noodles
1.25 litres/2 pints chicken or
    vegetable stock
1 lemon grass stalk, crushed
1-cm/$\frac{1}{2}$-inch piece fresh
    ginger, peeled and very
    finely chopped
2 fresh kaffir lime leaves,
    thinly sliced
1 fresh red chilli, or to taste,
    deseeded and thinly sliced
2 skinless, boneless chicken
    breasts, thinly sliced
225 g/8 oz coconut cream
2 tbsp nam pla (Thai fish
    sauce)
about 1 tbsp fresh lime juice
55 g/2 oz beansprouts
green part of 4 spring onions,
    finely sliced
fresh coriander leaves,
    to garnish

## method

**1** Soak the dried noodles in a large bowl with enough lukewarm water to cover for 20 minutes, until soft. Alternatively, cook according to the packet instructions. Drain well and set aside.

**2** Meanwhile, bring the stock to the boil in a large saucepan over high heat. Lower the heat, add the lemon grass, ginger, lime leaves and chilli and simmer for 5 minutes. Add the chicken and continue simmering for a further 3 minutes, or until the flesh is poached. Stir in the coconut cream, nam pla and most of the lime juice and continue simmering for 3 minutes. Add the beansprouts and spring onions and simmer for a further 1 minute. Taste and gradually add extra nam pla or lime juice at this point, if you like. Remove and discard the lemon grass stalk.

**3** Divide the noodles between 4 bowls. Bring the soup back to the boil, then add the soup to each bowl. The heat of the soup will warm the noodles. Serve garnished with coriander leaves.

# chinese mushroom soup

## ingredients

**SERVES 4**

115 g/4 oz dried thin Chinese
   egg noodles
15 g/¹⁄₂ oz dried Chinese
   wood ear mushrooms,
   soaked in boiling water
   for 20 minutes
2 tsp arrowroot or cornflour
1 litre/1³⁄₄ pints vegetable
   stock
5-cm/2-inch piece fresh
   ginger, peeled and sliced
2 tbsp dark soy sauce
2 tsp mirin or sweet sherry
1 tsp rice vinegar
4 small pak choi, each cut
   in half
salt and pepper
snipped fresh Chinese or
   ordinary chives, to garnish

## method

**1** Boil the noodles for 3 minutes or according to the packet instructions, until soft. Drain well, rinse with cold water to stop the cooking, and set aside.

**2** Strain the mushrooms through a sieve lined with a tea towel and reserve the liquid. Leave the mushrooms whole or slice them, depending on how large they are. Put the arrowroot in a wok or large saucepan and gradually stir in the reserved mushroom liquid. Add the vegetable stock, sliced ginger, soy sauce, mirin, rice vinegar, mushrooms and pak choi and bring the mixture to the boil, stirring constantly. Lower the heat and simmer for 15 minutes.

**3** Add salt and pepper, but remember that soy sauce is salty so you might not need any salt at all – taste first. Use a slotted spoon to remove the pieces of ginger.

**4** Divide the noodles between 4 bowls, then spoon the soup over and garnish with chives.

# chinese vegetable soup

## ingredients

**SERVES 4–6**

115 g/4 oz Napa cabbage

2 tbsp peanut oil

225 g/8 oz firm marinated
    tofu, cut into 1-cm/1/2-inch
    cubes

2 garlic cloves, thinly sliced

4 spring onions, thinly sliced
    diagonally

1 carrot, thinly sliced

1 litre/13/4 pints vegetable
    stock

1 tbsp Chinese rice wine

2 tbsp light soy sauce

1 tsp sugar

salt and pepper

## method

**1** Shred the Napa cabbage and set aside. Heat the oil in a large preheated wok or frying pan over a high heat. Add the tofu cubes and stir-fry for 4–5 minutes until browned. Remove from the wok with a slotted spoon and drain on kitchen paper.

**2** Add the garlic, spring onions and carrot to the wok and stir-fry for 2 minutes. Pour in the stock, rice wine and soy sauce, then add the sugar and shredded Napa cabbage. Cook over a medium heat, stirring, for a further 1–2 minutes until heated through.

**3** Season with salt and pepper and return the tofu to the wok. Ladle the soup into warmed bowls and serve.

# szechuan pumpkin soup

## ingredients

### SERVES 4–6

1 litre/1³/₄ pints chicken stock

450 g/1 lb pumpkin, peeled
and cut into small cubes

1 tbsp chopped preserved
vegetables

1 tsp white pepper

115 g/4 oz any leafy green
Chinese vegetable,
shredded

salt (optional)

## method

**1** Bring the stock to the boil in a large saucepan, then stir in the pumpkin and simmer for 4–5 minutes.

**2** Add the preserved vegetables with the pepper and stir. Finally, add the green vegetable. Season with salt, if liked. Simmer for a further minute and serve.

# vegetable & noodle soup

## ingredients

**SERVES 4**

2 tbsp vegetable or peanut oil

1 onion, sliced

2 garlic cloves, chopped finely

1 large carrot, cut into thin
  sticks

1 courgette, cut into thin sticks

115 g/4 oz head of broccoli,
  cut into florets

1 litre/1¾ pints vegetable
  stock

400 ml/14 fl oz coconut milk

3–4 tbsp Thai soy sauce

2 tbsp Thai red curry paste

55 g/2 oz wide rice noodles

115 g/4 oz mung or soy
  beansprouts

4 tbsp chopped fresh
  coriander

## method

**1** Heat the oil in a wok or large frying pan and stir-fry the onion and garlic for 2–3 minutes. Add the carrot, courgette and broccoli and stir-fry for 3–4 minutes, until just tender.

**2** Pour in the stock and coconut milk and bring to the boil. Add the soy sauce, curry paste and noodles and simmer for 2–3 minutes, until the noodles have swelled. Stir in the beansprouts and coriander and serve immediately.

# monk's soup

## ingredients

**SERVES 4**

1 litre/1¾ pints vegetable
   stock

1 stalk lemon grass, centre
   part only, finely chopped

1 tsp tamarind paste

pinch of dried red pepper
   flakes, or to taste

140 g/5 oz thin green beans,
   cut into 2.5-cm/1-inch
   pieces

1 tbsp light soy sauce

1 tsp brown sugar

juice of ½ lime

250 g/9 oz firm tofu, drained
   and cut into small cubes

2 spring onions, sliced
   diagonally

55 g/2 oz enoki mushrooms,
   hard end of the stalks
   cut off

400 g/14 oz fresh udon
   noodles or thick Chinese
   egg noodles

## method

**1** Put the stock in a large pan with the lemon grass, tamarind paste and red pepper flakes and bring to the boil, stirring until the tamarind dissolves. Lower the heat, add the green beans and simmer for 6 minutes. Add the soy sauce, brown sugar and lime juice. Taste and stir in more sugar, lime juice or red pepper flakes if liked.

**2** Stir in the tofu and spring onions and continue simmering for just 1–2 minutes longer, or until the green beans are tender, but still with a bit of bite, and the tofu is warm. Add the enoki mushrooms.

**3** Pour boiling water over the udon noodles to separate them, then divide them between 4 large bowls and divide the soup between the bowls. The heat of the soup will warm the noodles.

# spicy beef & noodle soup

## ingredients

### SERVES 4

1 litre/1¾ pints beef stock

150 ml/5 fl oz vegetable or
   peanut oil

85 g/3 oz rice vermicelli
   noodles

2 shallots, sliced thinly

2 garlic cloves, crushed

2.5-cm/1-inch piece fresh
   ginger, sliced thinly

225-g/8-oz piece fillet steak,
   cut into thin strips

2 tbsp Thai green curry paste

2 tbsp Thai soy sauce

1 tbsp fish sauce

chopped fresh coriander,
   to garnish

## method

**1** Pour the stock into a large saucepan and bring to the boil. Meanwhile, heat the oil in a wok or large frying pan. Add a third of the noodles and cook for 10–20 seconds, until they have puffed up. Lift out of the oil with tongs, drain on kitchen paper and set aside. Discard all but 2 tablespoons of the oil.

**2** Add the shallots, garlic and ginger to the wok or frying pan and stir-fry for 1 minute. Add the beef and curry paste and stir-fry for a further 3–4 minutes, until tender.

**3** Add the beef mixture, the uncooked noodles, soy sauce and fish sauce to the pan of stock and simmer for 2–3 minutes, until the noodles have swelled. Serve hot, garnished with the chopped coriander and the reserved crispy noodles.

# beef mince & coriander soup

## ingredients

**SERVES 4–6**

225 g/8 oz beef mince

1.7 litres/3 pints chicken stock

3 egg whites, lightly beaten

1 tsp salt

$1/2$ tsp white pepper

1 tbsp finely chopped fresh
    ginger

1 tbsp finely chopped spring
    onion

4–5 tbsp finely chopped
    coriander, tough stems
    discarded

marinade

1 tsp salt

1 tsp sugar

1 tsp Shaoxing rice wine

1 tsp light soy sauce

## method

**1** Combine all the ingredients for the marinade in a bowl and add the beef. Allow to marinate for 20 minutes.

**2** Bring the stock to the boil in a large saucepan. Add the beef, stirring to break up any clumps, and simmer for 10 minutes.

**3** Slowly add the egg whites, stirring rapidly so that they form into fine shreds. Add the salt and pepper and taste to check the seasoning.

**4** To serve, place the ginger, spring onion and coriander in the base of each individual bowl and pour the soup on top.

# clear soup with mushrooms & chicken

## ingredients

**SERVES 4–6**

25 g/1 oz dried cèpes or other
    mushrooms
1 litre/1¾ pints water
2 tbsp vegetable or peanut oil
115 g/4 oz mushrooms, sliced
2 garlic cloves, chopped
    coarsely
5-cm/2-inch piece fresh
    galangal, sliced thinly
2 chicken breast portions
    (on the bone, skin on)
225 g/8 oz baby chestnut
    or white mushrooms,
    quartered
juice of ½ lime
sprigs fresh flat-leaf parsley,
    to garnish

## method

**1** Place the dried mushrooms in a small bowl and pour over hot water to cover. Set aside to soak for 20–30 minutes. Drain the mushrooms, reserving the soaking liquid. Cut off and discard the stalks and chop the caps coarsely.

**2** Pour the reserved soaking water into a saucepan with the measured water and bring to the boil. Reduce the heat to a simmer.

**3** Meanwhile, heat the oil in a wok and stir-fry the soaked mushrooms, sliced fresh mushrooms, garlic and galangal for 3–4 minutes. Add to the pan of hot water with the chicken breasts. Simmer for 10–15 minutes, until the meat comes off the bones easily.

**4** Remove the chicken from the pan. Peel off and set aside the skin. Remove the meat from the bones, slice and set aside. Return the skin and bones to the stock and simmer for a further 30 minutes.

**5** Remove the pan from the heat and strain the stock into a clean pan through a cheesecloth-lined sieve. Bring back to the boil and add the chestnut or white mushrooms, sliced chicken and lime juice. Reduce the heat and simmer for 8-10 minutes. Ladle into warmed bowls, garnish with parsley sprigs and serve at once.

# whole chicken soup

## ingredients

### SERVES 6–8

100 g/3¹/₂ oz Yunnan ham or
  ordinary ham, chopped
2 dried Chinese mushrooms,
  soaked in warm water for
  20 minutes
85 g/3 oz fresh or canned
  bamboo shoots, rinsed
  (if using fresh shoots,
  boil in water first for
  30 minutes)
1 whole chicken
1 tbsp slivered spring onion
8 slices fresh ginger
225 g/8 oz lean pork, chopped
2 tsp Shaoxing rice wine
2.8 litres/5 pints water
2 tsp salt
300 g/10¹/₂ oz Chinese
  cabbage, cut into large
  chunks

sesame & spring
  onion dipping
  sauce
2 tbsp light soy sauce
¹/₄ tsp sesame oil
2 tsp finely chopped spring
  onion

## method

**1** To make the dipping sauce, combine all the ingredients in a small bowl and set aside.

**2** Blanch the Yunnan ham in boiling water for 30 seconds. Skim the surface, then remove the ham and set aside. Squeeze out any excess water from the mushrooms, then finely slice, discarding any tough stems. Chop the bamboo shoots into small cubes.

**3** Stuff the chicken with the spring onion and ginger. Put all the ingredients, except the cabbage and dipping sauce, in a casserole. Bring to the boil, then lower the heat and simmer, covered, for 1 hour. Add the cabbage and simmer for a further 3 minutes.

**4** Remove the chicken skin before serving, then place a chunk of chicken meat in each individual bowl, adding pieces of vegetable and the other meats, and pour the soup on top. Serve with the dipping sauce.

# chicken noodle soup

## ingredients

**SERVES 4–6**

1 sheet dried egg noodles from a 250 g/9 oz packet

1 tbsp corn oil

4 skinless, boneless chicken thighs, diced

1 bunch of spring onions, sliced

2 garlic cloves, chopped

2-cm/³⁄₄-inch piece fresh ginger, finely chopped

850 ml/1¹⁄₂ pints chicken stock

175 ml/6 fl oz coconut milk

3 tsp Thai red curry paste

3 tbsp peanut butter

2 tbsp light soy sauce

salt and pepper

1 small red pepper, deseeded and chopped

55 g/2 oz frozen peas

## method

**1** Place the noodles in a shallow heatproof dish and soak in boiling water according to the packet directions.

**2** Meanwhile, heat the oil in a preheated wok. Add the chicken and stir-fry for 5 minutes, or until lightly browned. Add the white part of the spring onions, the garlic and ginger and stir-fry for 2 minutes.

**3** Add the stock, coconut milk, curry paste, peanut butter and soy sauce. Season to taste with salt and pepper. Bring to the boil, stirring constantly, then simmer for 8 minutes, stirring occasionally. Add the pepper, peas and green spring onion tops and cook for a further 2 minutes.

**4** Drain the noodles, then add them to the wok and heat through. Spoon into warmed serving bowls and serve immediately.

# hot-&-sour soup

## ingredients

**SERVES 4–5**

3 dried Chinese mushrooms,
    soaked in warm water for
    20 minutes
115 g/4 oz pork loin
55 g/2 oz fresh or canned
    bamboo shoots, rinsed
    (if using fresh shoots,
    boil in water first for
    30 minutes)
225 g/8 oz firm tofu
850 ml/1$^1$/$_2$ pints chicken
    stock
1 tbsp Shaoxing rice wine
1 tbsp light soy sauce
1$^1$/$_2$ tbsp white rice vinegar
1 tsp salt
1 tsp white pepper
1 egg, lightly beaten

## method

**1** Squeeze out any excess water from the mushrooms, then finely slice, discarding any tough stems. Finely slice the pork, bamboo shoots and tofu, all to a similar size.

**2** Bring the stock to the boil in a large saucepan. Add the pork and boil over a high heat for 2 minutes. Add the mushrooms and bamboo shoots and boil for a further 2 minutes. Next, add the Shaoxing, light soy sauce, rice vinegar, salt and pepper. Bring back to the boil and simmer, covered, for 5 minutes. Add the tofu and boil, uncovered, for 2 minutes.

**3** To serve, rapidly stir in the egg until it has formed fine shreds. Serve immediately.

# wonton soup

## ingredients

**SERVES 6**

30 square wonton skins

1 egg white, lightly beaten

2 tbsp finely chopped spring
onion, to serve

1 tbsp chopped coriander
leaves, to garnish

filling

175 g/6 oz pork mince,
not too lean

225 g/8 oz raw prawns,
peeled, deveined and
chopped

1/2 tsp finely chopped fresh
ginger

1 tbsp light soy sauce

1 tbsp Shaoxing rice wine

2 tsp finely chopped spring
onion

pinch of sugar

pinch of white pepper

dash of sesame oil

soup

2 litres/31/2 pints chicken
stock

2 tsp salt

1/2 tsp white pepper

## method

**1** Mix together the filling ingredients and stir well until the texture is thick and pasty. Set aside for at least 20 minutes.

**2** To make the wontons, place a teaspoon of the filling in the centre of a skin. Brush the edges with a little egg white. Bring the opposite points towards each other and press the edges together, creating a flower-like shape. Repeat with the remaining skins and filling.

**3** To make the soup, bring the stock to the boil in a large saucepan and add the salt and pepper. Boil the wontons in the stock for about 5 minutes, or until the skins begin to wrinkle around the filling.

**4** To serve, put the spring onion in individual bowls, then spoon in the wontons and soup and top with the coriander.

# duck with spring onion soup

## ingredients

**SERVES 4**

2 duck breasts, skin on
2 tbsp Thai red curry paste
2 tbsp vegetable or peanut oil
bunch of spring onions,
    chopped
2 garlic cloves, crushed
5-cm/2-inch piece fresh
    ginger, grated
2 carrots, sliced thinly
1 red pepper, deseeded and
    cut into strips
1 litre/1¾ pints chicken stock
2 tbsp sweet chilli sauce
3–4 tbsp Thai soy sauce
400 g/14 oz canned straw
    mushrooms, drained

## method

**1** Slash the skin of the duck 3 or 4 times with a sharp knife and rub in the curry paste. Cook the duck breasts, skin side down, in a wok over high heat for 2–3 minutes. Turn over, reduce the heat and cook for a further 3–4 minutes, until cooked through. Lift out and slice thickly. Set aside and keep warm.

**2** Meanwhile, heat the oil in a wok and stir-fry half the spring onions, the garlic, ginger, carrots and red pepper for 2–3 minutes. Pour in the stock and add the chilli sauce, soy sauce and mushrooms. Bring to the boil, reduce the heat and simmer for 4–5 minutes.

**3** Ladle the soup into warmed bowls, top with the duck slices and garnish with the remaining spring onions. Serve immediately.

# thai-style seafood soup

## ingredients

**SERVES 4**

1.25 litres/2¼ pints fish stock

1 lemon grass stalk, split
   lengthways

pared rind of ½ lime or
   1 fresh kaffir lime leaf

2.5-cm/1-inch piece fresh
   ginger, sliced

¼ tsp chilli paste, or to taste

4–6 spring onions

200 g/7 oz large or medium
   raw prawns, peeled

salt

250 g/9 oz scallops (16–20)

2 tbsp coriander leaves

finely chopped red pepper or
   fresh red chilli rings,
      to garnish

## method

**1** Place the stock in a wok with the lemon grass, lime rind, ginger and chilli paste. Bring just to the boil, then reduce the heat and simmer, covered, for 10–15 minutes.

**2** Cut the spring onions in half lengthways, then slice crossways very thinly. Cut the prawns almost in half lengthways, keeping the tails intact. Devein if necessary.

**3** Pour the stock through a sieve, then return to the wok and bring to a simmer, with bubbles rising at the edges and the surface trembling. Add the spring onions and cook for 2–3 minutes. Taste and season with salt, if needed. Stir in a little more chilli paste if wished.

**4** Add the scallops and prawns and poach for 1 minute, or until they turn opaque and the prawns curl.

**5** Drop in the coriander leaves, then ladle the soup into warmed serving bowls, dividing the shellfish evenly, and garnish with pepper or chilli rings.

# spicy thai soup with prawns

## ingredients

**SERVES 4**

2 tbsp tamarind paste

4 fresh red Thai chillies, very finely chopped

2 garlic cloves, crushed

2.5-cm/1-inch piece fresh galangal, very finely chopped

4 tbsp Thai fish sauce

2 tbsp palm sugar or caster sugar

8 fresh kaffir lime leaves, roughly torn

1 litre/1¾ pints fish stock

115 g/4 oz very thinly sliced carrots

175 g/6 oz diced sweet potato

100 g/3½ oz baby corn cobs, halved

3 tbsp coriander, coarsely chopped

100 g/3½ oz cherry tomatoes, halved

225 g/8 oz cooked fantail prawns

## method

**1** Place the tamarind paste, chillies, garlic, galangal, fish sauce, sugar, lime leaves and stock in a large, preheated wok. Bring to the boil, stirring constantly.

**2** Reduce the heat and add the carrots, sweet potato and baby corn cobs to the mixture in the wok.

**3** Simmer the soup for 10 minutes or until the vegetables are just tender.

**4** Stir the coriander, cherry tomatoes and prawns into the soup and heat through for 5 minutes.

**5** Transfer the soup to warmed serving bowls and serve hot.

# crab & sweetcorn soup

## ingredients

**SERVES 4**

115 g/4 oz fresh or frozen
    crabmeat
600 ml/1 pint water
425 g/15 oz canned
creamed sweetcorn, drained
1/2 tsp salt
pinch of pepper
2 tsp cornflour, dissolved in
    2 tbsp water (optional)
1 egg, beaten

## method

**1** If using frozen crabmeat, blanch the flesh in boiling water for 30 seconds. Remove with a slotted spoon and set aside.

**2** In a large saucepan, bring the water to the boil with the crab and sweetcorn and simmer for 2 minutes. Season with the salt and pepper. Stir in the cornflour, if using, and continue stirring until the soup has thickened. Rapidly stir in the egg and serve.

# miso soup

## ingredients

**SERVES 4**

1 quantity dashi stock

175 g/6 oz firm tofu, cut into
   1-cm/$1/2$-inch cubes

4 shiitake or white
   mushrooms, sliced

4 tbsp miso paste

2 spring onions, finely sliced

2 tsp white sesame seeds,
   toasted

## method

**1** Put the dashi stock into a pan and heat through. Add the cubed tofu and sliced mushrooms and simmer gently for 3 minutes. Add the miso and stir until it has dissolved completely.

**2** Turn off the heat, add the spring onions and divide the soup between 4 serving bowls. Scatter $1/2$ teaspoon of the toasted sesame seeds over each serving.

# thai prawn & scallop soup

## ingredients

**SERVES 4**

1 litre/1³/4 pints fish stock

juice of ¹/2 lime

2 tbsp rice wine or sherry

1 leek, sliced

2 shallots, finely chopped

1 tbsp grated fresh ginger

1 fresh red chilli, deseeded
and finely chopped

225 g/8 oz raw prawns, peeled
and deveined

225 g/8 oz live scallops,
shucked and cleaned

1¹/2 tbsp chopped fresh
flat-leaf parsley, plus extra
to garnish

salt and pepper

## method

**1** Put the stock, lime juice, rice wine, leek, shallots, ginger and chilli in a large saucepan. Bring to the boil over a high heat, then reduce the heat, cover and simmer for 10 minutes.

**2** Add the prawns, scallops and parsley, season with salt and pepper and cook for 1–2 minutes.

**3** Remove the pan from the heat and ladle the soup into warmed serving bowls. Garnish with chopped parsley and serve.

# prawn & papaya salad

## ingredients

**SERVES 4**

1 papaya, peeled
350 g/12 oz large cooked
    prawns, shelled
assorted baby salad leaves

dressing

4 spring onions, chopped
    finely
2 fresh red chillies, deseeded
    and chopped finely
1 tsp fish sauce
1 tbsp vegetable or peanut oil
juice of 1 lime
1 tsp jaggery or soft light
    brown sugar

## method

**1** Scoop the seeds out of the papaya and slice thinly. Stir gently together with the prawns.

**2** Mix the spring onions, chillies, fish sauce, oil, lime juice and sugar together.

**3** Arrange the salad leaves in a bowl and top with the papaya and prawns. Pour the dressing over the salad and serve immediately.

# crab & coriander salad

## ingredients

**SERVES 4**

350 g/12 oz canned white
    crabmeat, drained
4 spring onions, finely
    chopped
handful of fresh coriander,
    chopped
1 iceberg lettuce, shredded
7.5-cm/3-inch piece
    cucumber, chopped

dressing

1 garlic clove, crushed
2.5-cm/1-inch piece fresh
    ginger, peeled and grated
2 lime leaves, torn into pieces
juice of 1 lime
1 tsp fish sauce

## method

**1** Put the crabmeat into a bowl and stir in the spring onions and coriander. Mix the ingredients for the dressing together.

**2** Place the lettuce leaves on a serving platter and sprinkle with the cucumber.

**3** Arrange the crab salad over the leaves and drizzle the dressing over the salad. Serve immediately.

# tuna & tomato salad with ginger dressing

## ingredients

**SERVES 4**

1/2 cup shredded Napa
    cabbage
3 tbsp rice wine or dry sherry
2 tbsp Thai fish sauce
1 tbsp finely shredded fresh
    root ginger
1 garlic clove, finely chopped
1/2 small fresh red Thai chilli,
    finely chopped
2 tsp brown sugar
2 tbsp lime juice
400 g/14 oz fresh tuna steak
corn oil, for brushing
125 g/41/2 oz cherry tomatoes
fresh mint leaves and mint
    sprigs, coarsely chopped,
    to garnish

## method

**1** Place a small pile of shredded Napa cabbage on a large serving plate. Place the rice wine or dry sherry, fish sauce, ginger, garlic, chilli, sugar and 1 tablespoon of lime juice in a screw-top jar and shake well to combine.

**2** Using a sharp knife, cut the tuna into strips of an even thickness. Sprinkle with the remaining lime juice.

**3** Brush a wide frying pan or ridged griddle pan with oil and heat until very hot. Arrange the tuna strips in the pan and cook until just firm and light golden, turning them over once. Remove the tuna strips from the pan and reserve.

**4** Add the tomatoes to the pan and cook over high heat until lightly browned. Spoon the tuna and tomatoes over the Napa cabbage, then spoon over the dressing. Garnish with fresh mint and serve warm.

# seaweed salad

## ingredients

**SERVES 4**

20 g/³/4 oz assorted dried
    seaweed, such as wakame,
    hijiki and arame
1 cucumber
2 spring onions, shredded
1 box of salad cress, snipped

### sesame dressing

2 tbsp rice vinegar
2 tsp Japanese soy sauce
1 tbsp mirin
2 tsp sesame oil
1 tsp white miso

## method

**1** Soak the different seaweeds in separate bowls of cold water – the wakame will need 10 minutes and the others 30 minutes. Drain.

**2** Cook the wakame only in a pan of boiling water for 2 minutes, then drain and cool. Put all the seaweeds in a serving bowl.

**3** Halve the cucumber lengthways. Reserve half for another recipe, scoop the seeds out of the remaining half and finely slice the flesh. Add to the seaweeds with the chopped spring onions and the snipped salad cress.

**4** Place all the ingredients for the dressing in a small jug and stir to combine. Add to the bowl and toss the salad before serving.

# sea bass & mango salad

## ingredients

**SERVES 2**

2 small sea bass, cleaned

1 tbsp Thai red curry paste

small handful of fresh
    coriander, chopped

150 ml/5 fl oz coconut milk

2 tbsp sweet chilli sauce

6-8 Thai basil leaves, chopped

$\frac{1}{2}$ tsp fish sauce

1 tsp rice wine vinegar

1 mango, deseeded, peeled
    and sliced

selection of mixed salad leaves

## method

**1** Place the fish on a board. Mix the curry paste and coriander together and stuff inside each fish cavity. Cover and marinate for 1–2 hours.

**2** Place the fish in a roasting pan. Mix the coconut milk, chilli sauce, basil, fish sauce and vinegar and pour over the fish. Arrange the mango slices in the pan as well. Cover with foil and cook in a preheated oven, 200°C/ 400°F/ Gas Mark 6, for 15 minutes.

**3** Remove the foil and cook uncovered for a further 10–15 minutes, until cooked.

**4** Place the fish on 2 warmed serving plates, drizzle with the cooking sauces and serve with the mixed salad leaves.

# seared swordfish salad

## ingredients

**SERVES 4**

85 g/3 oz daikon (long white radish)

55 g/2 oz carrot

1/2 cucumber

250 g/9 oz fresh swordfish steak, skinned

2 tsp peanut oil

2 tsp white sesame seeds, toasted

### sesame dressing

1 tbsp Japanese soy sauce

2 tbsp sesame oil

1/2 tsp wasabi paste

1 tsp rice vinegar

## method

**1** Place all the ingredients for the sesame dressing in a small bowl and stir to combine. Refrigerate until needed.

**2** Shred the daikon and carrot using the finest setting on a mandolin. Alternatively, cut into long thin slices and then cut each slice along its length as finely as possible. Rinse, drain and then place in the refrigerator until needed. Shred the cucumber, discarding the seeded parts. Add to the daikon and carrot.

**3** Trim the swordfish steak. Heat the oil in a frying pan until very hot, then sear the swordfish for 30–60 seconds on both sides and the edges. Allow to cool.

**4** Cut the seared swordfish into 8-mm/1/3-inch thick pieces, using a wet, very sharp knife and slicing across the grain. Wipe your knife on a damp cloth between each cut.

**5** Arrange the fish slices on 4 serving plates and place a mound of the shredded salad vegetables alongside. Drizzle the salad vegetables with the sesame dressing and sprinkle with the toasted sesame seeds.

# chinese prawn salad

## ingredients

**SERVES 4**

250 g/9 oz dried thin Chinese
   egg noodles

3 tbsp sunflower oil

1 tbsp sesame oil

1 tbsp sesame seeds

175 g/6 oz beansprouts

1 mango, peeled, pitted and
   sliced

6 spring onions, sliced

75 g/2³/₄ oz radishes, sliced

350 g/12 oz cooked peeled
   prawns

2 tbsp light soy sauce

1 tbsp sherry

## method

**1** Put the noodles in a large, heatproof bowl and pour over enough boiling water to cover. Set aside for 10 minutes, then drain thoroughly and pat dry with kitchen paper.

**2** Heat the sunflower oil in a large, preheated wok. Add the noodles and stir-fry for 5 minutes, tossing frequently.

**3** Remove the wok from the heat and add the sesame oil, sesame seeds and beansprouts, tossing to mix well.

**4** Mix the mango, spring onions, radishes, prawns, soy sauce and sherry together in a separate bowl. Toss the prawn mixture with the noodles. Alternatively, arrange the noodles around the edge of a serving plate and pile the prawn mixture into the centre. Serve immediately.

# prawn & rice salad

## ingredients

**SERVES 4**

175 g/6 oz mixed long-grain
  and wild rice
350 g/12 oz cooked peeled
  prawns
1 mango, peeled, stoned and
  diced
4 spring onions, sliced
25 g/1 oz flaked almonds
1 tbsp finely chopped fresh
  mint
salt and pepper

### dressing

1 tbsp extra virgin olive oil
2 tsp lime juice
1 garlic clove, crushed
1 tsp honey
salt and pepper

## method

**1** Bring a large saucepan of lightly salted water to the boil. Add the rice, return to the boil and cook for 35 minutes or until tender. Drain, then transfer to a large bowl and stir in the prawns.

**2** To make the dressing, combine the olive oil, lime juice, garlic and honey in a large jug, season to taste with salt and pepper and whisk until well blended. Pour the dressing over the rice and prawn mixture and cool.

**3** Add the mango, spring onions, almonds and mint to the salad and season to taste with pepper. Stir thoroughly, transfer to a large serving dish and serve.

# peppered beef salad

## ingredients

**SERVES 4**

4 x 115-g/4-oz fillet steaks

2 tbsp black peppercorns, crushed

1 tsp Chinese five spice powder

115 g/4 oz beansprouts

2.5-cm/1-inch piece fresh ginger, chopped finely

4 shallots, sliced finely

1 red pepper, deseeded and sliced thinly

3 tbsp Thai soy sauce

2 fresh red chillies, deseeded and sliced

$1/2$ lemon grass stalk, chopped finely

3 tbsp vegetable or peanut oil

1 tbsp sesame oil

## method

**1** Wash the steaks and pat dry on kitchen paper. Mix the peppercorns with the five spice powder and press onto all sides of the steaks. Cook on a griddle pan or under a grill for 2–3 minutes each side, or until cooked to your liking.

**2** Meanwhile mix the beansprouts, half the ginger, the shallots and pepper together and divide between 4 plates. Mix the remaining ginger, soy sauce, chillies, lemon grass and oils together.

**3** Slice the beef and arrange on the vegetables. Drizzle with the dressing and serve immediately.

# grilled beef salad

## ingredients

**SERVES 4**

50 g/1¾ oz dried oyster
  mushrooms
600 g/1 lb 5 oz rump steak
1 red pepper, deseeded and
  thinly sliced
55 g/2 oz roasted cashew nuts
red and green lettuce leaves
fresh mint leaves, to garnish

### dressing

2 tbsp sesame oil
2 tbsp Thai fish sauce
2 tbsp sweet sherry
2 tbsp oyster sauce
1 tbsp lime juice
1 fresh red chilli, deseeded
  and finely chopped

## method

**1** Put the mushrooms in a heatproof bowl, cover with boiling water and let stand for 20 minutes. Drain, then cut into slices.

**2** Preheat the grill to medium or heat a ridged griddle pan. To make the dressing, place all the ingredients in a bowl and whisk to combine.

**3** Cook the steak under the preheated grill or on the hot griddle pan, turning once, for 5 minutes, or until browned on both sides but still rare in the centre. Cook the steak longer if desired.

**4** Slice the steak into thin strips and place in a bowl with the mushrooms, pepper and nuts. Add the dressing and toss together.

**5** Arrange the lettuce on a large serving platter and place the beef mixture on top. Garnish with mint leaves. Serve at room temperature.

# red chicken salad

## ingredients

### SERVES 4

4 boneless chicken breasts

2 tbsp Thai red curry paste

2 tbsp vegetable or peanut oil

1 head Napa cabbage,
    shredded

175 g/6 oz pak choi, torn into
    large pieces

1/2 savoy cabbage, shredded

2 shallots, chopped finely

2 garlic cloves, crushed

1 tbsp rice wine vinegar

2 tbsp sweet chilli sauce

2 tbsp Thai soy sauce

## method

**1** Slash the flesh of the chicken several times and rub the curry paste into each cut. Cover and chill overnight.

**2** Cook in a heavy-based frying pan over medium heat or on a griddle pan for 5-6 minutes, turning once or twice, until cooked through. Keep warm.

**3** Heat 1 tablespoon of the oil in a wok or large frying pan and stir-fry the Napa cabbage, pak choi and savoy cabbage until just wilted. Add the remaining oil, shallots and garlic and stir-fry until just tender but not browned. Add the vinegar, chilli sauce and soy sauce. Remove from the heat.

**4** Arrange the leaves on 4 serving plates. Slice the chicken, arrange on the salad leaves and drizzle the hot dressing over. Serve immediately.

# gingered chicken & vegetable salad

## ingredients

**SERVES 4**

4 skinless, boneless chicken breasts

4 spring onions, chopped

2.5-cm/1-inch piece fresh ginger, chopped finely

4 garlic cloves, 2 crushed and 2 chopped

3 tbsp vegetable or peanut oil

1 onion, sliced

2 garlic cloves, chopped

115 g/4 oz baby corn, halved

115 g/4 oz mangetout, halved lengthways

1 red pepper, deseeded and sliced

7.5-cm/3-inch piece cucumber, peeled, deseeded and sliced

4 tbsp Thai soy sauce

1 tbsp soft light brown sugar

few Thai basil leaves

175 g/6 oz fine egg noodles

## method

**1** Cut the chicken into large cubes, each about 2.5 cm/1 inch. Mix the spring onions, ginger, crushed garlic and 2 tablespoons of the oil together in a shallow dish and add the chicken. Cover and marinate for at least 3 hours. Lift the meat out of the marinade and set aside.

**2** Heat the remaining oil in a wok or large frying pan and cook the onion for 1–2 minutes. Add the garlic, baby corn, mangetout and pepper and cook for 2–3 minutes, until just tender. Add the cucumber, half the soy sauce, the sugar and the basil and mix gently.

**3** Soak the noodles for 2–3 minutes (check the packet instructions) or until tender, and drain well. Sprinkle the remaining soy sauce over them and arrange on plates. Top with the cooked vegetables.

**4** Add a little more oil to the wok if necessary and cook the chicken over fairly high heat until browned on all sides. Arrange the chicken cubes on top of the salad and serve hot or warm.

# rice & turkey salad

## ingredients

### SERVES 4

1 litre/1¾ pints chicken stock

200 g/7 oz mixed long-grain
   and wild rice

2 tbsp corn oil

225 g/8 oz skinless, boneless
   turkey breast, trimmed of
   all visible fat and cut into
   thin strips

115 g/4 oz mangetout

115 g/4 oz oyster mushrooms,
   torn into pieces

25 g/1 oz shelled pistachio
   nuts, finely chopped

2 tbsp chopped fresh
   coriander

1 tbsp snipped fresh
   garlic chives

salt and pepper

1 tbsp balsamic vinegar

fresh garlic chives, to garnish

## method

**1** Set aside 3 tablespoons of the chicken stock and bring the remainder to the boil in a large saucepan. Add the rice and cook for 30 minutes or until tender. Drain and cool slightly.

**2** Meanwhile, heat 1 tablespoon of the oil in a preheated wok or frying pan. Stir-fry the turkey over medium heat for 3–4 minutes or until cooked through. Using a slotted spoon, transfer the turkey to a dish. Add the mangetout and mushrooms to the wok and stir-fry for 1 minute. Add the reserved stock, bring to the boil, then reduce the heat, cover and simmer for 3–4 minutes. Transfer the vegetables to the dish and cool slightly.

**3** Thoroughly mix the rice, turkey, mangetout, mushrooms, nuts, coriander and garlic chives together, then season to taste with salt and pepper. Drizzle with the remaining corn oil and the vinegar and garnish with fresh garlic chives. Serve warm.

# duck salad

## ingredients

**SERVES 4**

4 boneless duck breasts,
   skin on
1 lemon grass stalk, broken
   into three and each cut in
   half lengthways
3 tbsp vegetable or peanut oil
2 tbsp sesame oil
1 tsp fish sauce
1 fresh green chilli, deseeded
   and chopped
2 tbsp Thai red curry paste
1/2 fresh pineapple, peeled
   and sliced
7.5-cm/3-inch piece
   cucumber, peeled,
   deseeded and sliced
3 tomatoes, cut into wedges
1 onion, sliced thinly

### dressing
juice of 1 lemon
2 garlic cloves, crushed
1 tsp jaggery
2 tbsp vegetable or peanut oil

## method

**1** Unwrap the duck and let the skin dry out overnight in the refrigerator.

**2** The following day, slash the skin side 5–6 times. Mix the lemon grass, 2 tablespoons of the vegetable oil, all the sesame oil, fish sauce, chilli and curry paste together in a shallow dish and place the duck breasts in the mixture. Turn to coat and to rub the marinade into the meat. Chill for 2–3 hours.

**3** Heat the remaining oil in a wok or large frying pan and cook the duck, skin-side down, over medium heat for 3–4 minutes until the skin is browned and crisp and the meat cooked most of the way through.

**4** Turn the breasts over and cook until browned and the meat is cooked to your liking.

**5** Meanwhile, arrange the pineapple, cucumber, tomatoes, and onions on a platter. Mix the dressing ingredients together and pour over the top.

**6** Lift the duck out of the wok and slice thickly. Arrange the duck slices on top of the salad and serve while still hot.

# chinese tomato salad

## ingredients

**SERVES 4–6**

2 large tomatoes

dressing

1 tbsp finely chopped spring
  onions

1 tsp finely chopped garlic

$1/2$ tsp sesame oil

1 tbsp white rice vinegar

$1/2$ tsp salt

pinch of white pepper

pinch of sugar

## method

**1** Mix together all the ingredients for the dressing and set aside.

**2** Thinly slice the tomatoes. Arrange on a plate and pour the dressing over the top. Serve immediately.

# aubergine & onion salad

## ingredients

**SERVES 4**

4 tbsp vegetable or peanut oil

1 onion, sliced

4 shallots, chopped finely

4 spring onions, sliced

350 g/12 oz aubergines,
      cubed

2 tbsp Thai green curry paste

2 tbsp Thai soy sauce

1 tsp jaggery or soft light
      brown sugar

115 g/4 oz block creamed
      coconut, chopped

3 tbsp water

small handful of fresh
      coriander, chopped

few Thai basil leaves, chopped

small handful of fresh parsley,
      chopped

115 g/4 oz rocket leaves

2 tbsp sweet chilli sauce

## method

**1** Heat half the oil in a wok or large frying pan and cook all the onions together for 1–2 minutes, until just softened but not browned. Lift out and set aside.

**2** Add the aubergine cubes, in batches if necessary, adding more oil as needed, and cook until they are crisp and golden brown.

**3** Return the onions to the wok and add the curry paste, soy sauce and sugar. Add the creamed coconut and water and cook until dissolved. Stir in most of the coriander, the basil and the parsley.

**4** Toss the rocket in the sweet chilli sauce and serve with the aubergine and onion salad. Garnish with the remaining herbs.

# daikon & cucumber salad

## ingredients

**SERVES 4**

20-cm/8-inch piece of daikon
    (long white radish)
1 cucumber
handful of baby spinach
    leaves, chopped
3 red radishes, sliced into thin
    rounds
a few leaves of Chinese
    cabbage, cut into thin
    strips
1 tbsp sunflower seeds
2 tsp white sesame seeds,
    toasted

### wasabi dressing

4 tbsp rice vinegar
2 tbsp grapeseed oil
1 tsp light soy sauce
1 tsp wasabi paste
1/2 tsp sugar
salt, to taste

## method

**1** Shred the daikon using the finest setting on a mandolin or a very sharp knife. If you are using a knife, then cut the daikon into long, thin slices and cut each slice along its length as finely as you can. Rinse under cold water, then drain well.

**2** Halve the cucumber lengthways, reserve half for another recipe, and use a teaspoon to scoop the seeds out of the remaining half. Peel and shred in the same way as the daikon.

**3** Place the sliced daikon and cucumber in a salad bowl with the chopped spinach leaves. Add the sliced radishes and Chinese cabbage.

**4** Place the ingredients for the dressing in a small jug and stir to mix. Pour the dressing over the salad, toss gently to mix and sprinkle with the sunflower seeds and the toasted sesame seeds.

# julienne vegetable salad

## ingredients

**SERVES 4**

4 tbsp vegetable or peanut oil

225 g/8 oz tofu with herbs, cubed

1 red onion, sliced

4 spring onions, cut into 5-cm/2-inch lengths

1 garlic clove, chopped

2 carrots, cut into short, thin sticks

115 g/4 oz fine green beans, trimmed

1 yellow pepper, deseeded and cut into strips

115 g/4 oz head of broccoli, cut into florets

1 large courgette, cut into short, thin sticks

55 g/2 oz beansprouts

2 tbsp Thai red curry paste

4 tbsp Thai soy sauce

1 tbsp rice wine vinegar

1 tsp jaggery or soft light brown sugar

few Thai basil leaves

350 g/12 oz rice vermicelli noodles

## method

**1** Heat the oil in a wok and cook the tofu cubes for 3–4 minutes, until browned on all sides. Lift the cubes out of the oil and drain on kitchen paper.

**2** Add the onions, garlic and carrots to the hot oil and cook for 1–2 minutes before adding the rest of the vegetables, except for the beansprouts. Stir-fry for 2–3 minutes. Add the beansprouts, then stir in the curry paste, soy, vinegar, sugar and basil leaves. Cook for 30 seconds.

**3** Soak the noodles in boiling water or stock for 2–3 minutes (check the packet instructions) or until tender and drain well.

**4** Pile the vegetables onto the noodles, and serve topped with the tofu cubes. Garnish with extra basil if desired.

# buckwheat noodle salad with smoked tofu

## ingredients

### SERVES 2

200 g/7 oz buckwheat noodles

250 g/9 oz firm smoked tofu, drained weight

200 g/7 oz white cabbage, finely shredded

250 g/9 oz carrots, finely shredded

3 spring onions, diagonally sliced

1 fresh red chilli, deseeded and finely sliced into circles

2 tbsp sesame seeds, lightly toasted

### dressing

1 tsp grated fresh ginger

1 garlic clove, crushed

175 g/6 oz silken tofu, drained weight

4 tsp tamari (wheat-free soy sauce)

2 tbsp sesame oil

4 tbsp hot water

salt

## method

**1** Cook the noodles in a large saucepan of lightly salted boiling water according to the packet instructions. Drain and refresh under cold running water.

**2** To make the dressing, blend the ginger, garlic, silken tofu, tamari, oil and water together in a small bowl until smooth and creamy. Season with salt.

**3** Place the smoked tofu in a steamer. Steam for 5 minutes, then cut into thin slices.

**4** Meanwhile, put the cabbage, carrots, spring onions and chilli into a bowl and toss to mix. To serve, arrange the noodles on serving plates and top with the carrot salad and slices of tofu. Spoon over the dressing and sprinkle with sesame seeds.

# hot-&-sour vegetable salad

## ingredients

**SERVES 4**

2 tbsp vegetable or peanut oil

1 tbsp chilli oil

1 onion, sliced

2.5-cm/1-inch piece fresh
　ginger, grated

1 small head of broccoli,
　cut into florets

2 carrots, cut into short thin
　sticks

1 red pepper, deseeded and
　cut into squares

1 yellow pepper, deseeded
　and cut into strips

55 g/2 oz mangetout, trimmed
　and halved

55 g/2 oz baby corn, halved

## dressing

2 tbsp vegetable or peanut oil

1 tsp chilli oil

1 tbsp rice wine vinegar

juice of 1 lime

$1/2$ tsp fish sauce

## method

**1** Heat the oils in a wok or large frying pan and sauté the onion and ginger for 1–2 minutes until they start to soften. Add the vegetables and stir-fry for 2–3 minutes until they have softened slightly. Remove from the heat and set aside.

**2** Mix the dressing ingredients together. Transfer the vegetables to a serving plate and drizzle the dressing over. Serve warm immediately, or let the flavours develop and serve cold.

# cabbage & cucumber in a vinegar dressing

## ingredients

**SERVES 4–6**

225 g/8 oz Chinese cabbage, very finely shredded

1 tsp salt

1 cucumber, peeled, deseeded and finely chopped into short thin sticks

1 tsp sesame oil

2 tbsp white rice vinegar

1 tsp sugar

## method

**1** Sprinkle the cabbage with the salt and set aside for at least 10 minutes. Drain the cabbage if necessary, then mix with the cucumber pieces.

**2** Whisk together the sesame oil, vinegar and sugar and toss the vegetables in it. Serve immediately.

# curried egg salad

## ingredients

**SERVES 4**

6 eggs

1 tbsp vegetable or peanut oil

1 onion, chopped

1 tbsp Thai yellow curry paste

4 tbsp plain yogurt

$1/2$ tsp salt

handful of fresh coriander, chopped finely

bunch of watercress or rocket

2 courgettes, cut into short thin sticks

1 fresh green chilli, deseeded and chopped finely

1 tsp fish sauce

1 tsp rice wine vinegar

3 tbsp vegetable or peanut oil

## method

**1** Put the eggs in a saucepan, cover with cold water and bring to the boil. Simmer for 10 minutes, then drain and rinse in cold water. Shell and halve.

**2** Meanwhile, heat the oil in a medium frying pan and sauté the onion gently until softened but not browned. Remove from the heat and stir in the curry paste. Let cool slightly before stirring in the yogurt, salt and half the coriander. Set the mixture aside.

**3** Arrange the watercress and courgettes on a platter. Mix the chilli, fish sauce, vinegar and oil together and pour the dressing over the leaves.

**4** Arrange the eggs on top and spoon the yogurt mixture over each one. Garnish with the remaining coriander and serve immediately.

# classic stir-fried vegetables

## ingredients

**SERVES 4**

3 tbsp sesame oil

6 spring onions, finely
chopped, plus 2 spring
onions, finely chopped,
to garnish

1 garlic clove, crushed

1 tbsp grated fresh ginger

1 head of broccoli, cut into
florets

1 orange or yellow pepper,
roughly chopped

125 g/4$^{1}/_{2}$ oz red cabbage,
shredded

125 g/4$^{1}/_{2}$ oz baby corn

175 g/6 oz portobello or large
cup mushrooms, thinly
sliced

200 g/7 oz fresh beansprouts

250 g/9 oz canned water
chestnuts, drained

4 tsp soy sauce, or to taste

cooked wild rice, to serve

## method

**1** Heat 2 tablespoons of the oil in a large frying pan or wok over a high heat. Stir-fry the 6 chopped spring onions with the garlic and ginger for 30 seconds.

**2** Add the broccoli, pepper and red cabbage and stir-fry for 1–2 minutes. Mix in the baby corn and mushrooms and stir-fry for a further 1–2 minutes.

**3** Finally, add the beansprouts and water chestnuts and cook for 2 minutes. Pour in the soy sauce and stir well.

**4** Serve immediately over cooked wild rice, garnished with the remaining spring onions.

# cabbage & cucumber in a vinegar dressing

## ingredients

**SERVES 4–6**

225 g/8 oz Chinese cabbage, very finely shredded

1 tsp salt

1 cucumber, peeled, deseeded and finely chopped into short thin sticks

1 tsp sesame oil

2 tbsp white rice vinegar

1 tsp sugar

## method

**1** Sprinkle the cabbage with the salt and set aside for at least 10 minutes. Drain the cabbage if necessary, then mix with the cucumber pieces.

**2** Whisk together the sesame oil, vinegar and sugar and toss the vegetables in it. Serve immediately.

# stir-fried french beans with red pepper

## ingredients

**SERVES 4–6**

280 g/10 oz French beans, cut
    into 6-cm/2$^1$/$_2$-inch lengths
1 tbsp vegetable or peanut oil
1 red pepper, slivered
pinch of salt
pinch of sugar

## method

**1** Blanch the beans in a large saucepan of boiling water for 30 seconds. Drain and set aside.

**2** In a preheated wok or deep saucepan, heat the oil and stir-fry the beans for 1 minute over a high heat. Add the pepper and stir-fry for a further 1 minute. Sprinkle the salt and sugar on top and serve.

# spicy french beans

## ingredients

**SERVES 4**

200 g/7 oz French beans,
 trimmed and cut diagonally
 into 3–4 pieces
2 tbsp vegetable or peanut oil
4 dried chillies, cut into
 2–3 pieces
1/2 tsp Szechuan peppers
1 garlic clove, finely sliced
6 thin slices of fresh ginger
2 spring onions, white part
 only, cut diagonally into
 thin pieces
pinch of sea salt

## method

**1** Blanch the beans in a large saucepan of boiling water for 30 seconds. Drain and set aside.

**2** In a preheated wok or deep saucepan, heat 1 tablespoon of the oil. Over a low heat, stir-fry the beans for about 5 minutes, or until they are beginning to wrinkle. Remove from the wok and set aside.

**3** Add the remaining oil and stir-fry the chillies and peppers until they are fragrant. Add the garlic, ginger and spring onions and stir-fry until they begin to soften. Throw in the beans and toss, then add the sea salt and serve immediately.

# green beans with sesame dressing

## ingredients

**SERVES 4**

200 g/7 oz green beans

pinch of salt

1 tbsp sesame paste

1 tsp caster sugar

1 tsp miso paste

2 tsp Japanese soy sauce

## method

**1** Cook the beans in a pan of simmering water for 4–5 minutes, until tender. Remove from the heat and drain.

**2** Mix the remaining ingredients to a paste in a bowl that is large enough to take the beans. Toss the beans in the paste, then let them cool before serving.

# stir-fried broccoli

## ingredients

**SERVES 4**

2 tbsp vegetable oil

2 medium heads of broccoli,
    cut into florets

2 tbsp soy sauce

1 tsp cornflour

1 tbsp caster sugar

1 tsp grated fresh ginger

1 garlic clove, crushed

pinch of hot chilli flakes

1 tsp toasted sesame seeds,
    to garnish

## method

**1** In a large frying pan or wok, heat the oil until almost smoking. Stir-fry the broccoli for 4–5 minutes.

**2** In a small bowl, combine the soy sauce, cornflour, sugar, ginger, garlic and hot chilli flakes. Add the mixture to the broccoli. Cook over gentle heat, stirring constantly, for 2–3 minutes until the sauce thickens slightly.

**3** Transfer to a serving dish, garnish with the sesame seeds and serve immediately.

# stir-fried chinese greens

## ingredients

**SERVES 4**

1 tbsp vegetable or peanut oil
1 tsp finely chopped garlic
225 g/8 oz leafy Chinese
    greens, roughly chopped
$1/2$ tsp salt

## method

**1** In a preheated wok or deep saucepan, heat the oil and stir-fry the garlic until fragrant.

**2** Over a high heat, toss in the Chinese greens and salt and stir-fry for 1 minute maximum. Serve immediately.

# choi sum in oyster sauce

## ingredients

**SERVES 4–6**

300 g/10$\frac{1}{2}$ oz choi sum

1 tbsp vegetable or peanut oil

1 tsp finely chopped garlic

1 tbsp oyster sauce

## method

**1** Blanch the choi sum in a large saucepan of boiling water for 30 seconds. Drain and set aside.

**2** In a preheated wok or deep saucepan, heat the oil and stir-fry the garlic until fragrant. Add the choi sum and toss for 1 minute. Stir in the oyster sauce and serve.

# hot-&-sour cabbage

## ingredients

**SERVES 4**

450 g/1 lb firm white cabbage

1 tbsp vegetable or peanut oil

10 Szechuan peppers or
    more, to taste

3 dried chillies, roughly
    chopped

$1/2$ tsp salt

1 tsp white rice vinegar

dash of sesame oil

pinch of sugar

## method

**1** To prepare the cabbage, discard the outer leaves and tough stems. Chop the cabbage into 3-cm/1$1/4$-inch squares, breaking up the chunks. Rinse thoroughly in cold water.

**2** In a preheated wok or deep saucepan, heat the oil and cook the peppers until fragrant. Stir in the chillies. Throw in the cabbage, a little at a time, together with the salt, and stir-fry for 2 minutes.

**3** Add the vinegar, sesame oil and sugar and cook for a further minute, or until the cabbage is tender. Serve immediately.

# chunky potatoes with coriander leaves

## ingredients

**SERVES 6–8**

4 potatoes, peeled and cut into large chunks

vegetable or peanut oil, for frying

100 g/3½ oz pork, not too lean, finely chopped or minced

1 green pepper, finely chopped

1 tbsp finely chopped spring onions, white part only

2 tsp salt

½ tsp white pepper

pinch of sugar

2–3 tbsp cooking water from the potatoes

2 tbsp chopped coriander leaves

## method

**1** Boil the potatoes in a large saucepan of boiling water for 15–25 minutes, or until cooked. Drain, reserving some of the water.

**2** In a wok or deep saucepan, heat plenty of the oil and cook the potatoes until golden. Drain and set aside.

**3** In the clean preheated wok or saucepan, heat 1 tablespoon of the oil and stir-fry the pork, pepper and spring onions for 1 minute. Season with the salt, pepper and sugar and stir-fry for a further 1 minute.

**4** Stir in the potato chunks and add the water. Cook for 2–3 minutes, or until the potatoes are warmed through. Turn off the heat, then stir in the coriander and serve warm.

# szechuan fried aubergine

## ingredients

**SERVES 4**

vegetable or peanut oil,
    for frying

4 aubergines, halved
    lengthways and cut
    diagonally into 5-cm/2-inch
    pieces

1 tbsp chilli bean sauce

2 tsp finely chopped fresh
    ginger

2 tsp finely chopped garlic

2–3 tbsp chicken stock

1 tsp sugar

1 tsp light soy sauce

3 spring onions, finely
    chopped

## method

**1** In a preheated wok or deep pan, heat 2 tablespoons of oil and cook the aubergine pieces for 3–4 minutes, or until lightly browned. Drain on kitchen paper and set aside.

**2** In the clean wok or deep saucepan, heat 2 tablespoons of the oil. Add the chilli bean sauce and stir-fry rapidly, then add the ginger and garlic and stir until fragrant. Add the stock, sugar and light soy sauce. Toss in the fried aubergine pieces and simmer for 2 minutes. Stir in the spring onions and serve.

# aubergine with red peppers

## ingredients

### SERVES 4

3 tbsp vegetable or peanut oil

1 garlic clove, finely chopped

3 aubergines, halved
   lengthways and cut
   diagonally into 2.5-cm/
   1-inch pieces

1 tsp white rice vinegar

1 red pepper, finely sliced

2 tbsp light soy sauce

1 tsp sugar

1 tbsp finely chopped
   coriander leaves, to garnish

## method

**1** In a preheated wok or deep saucepan, heat the oil. When it begins to smoke, toss in the garlic and stir-fry until fragrant, then add the aubergine. Stir-fry for 30 seconds, then add the vinegar. Turn down the heat and cook, covered, for 5 minutes, stirring occasionally.

**2** When the aubergine pieces are soft, add the pepper and stir. Add the light soy sauce and sugar and cook, uncovered, for 2 minutes.

**3** Turn off the heat and rest for 2 minutes. Transfer to a dish, then garnish with coriander and serve.

# aubergine with miso

## ingredients

**SERVES 4**

2 aubergines

oil, for stir-frying

1 fresh red chilli, sliced

2 tbsp sake

4 tbsp mirin

2 tbsp shoyu (Japanese
   soy sauce)

3 tbsp hatcho miso

2 tbsp water

## method

**1** Cut the aubergines into wedges.

**2** Preheat a wok over high heat. Add a little oil and heat until very hot. Stir-fry the aubergine, in batches, for 4 minutes, or until browned and cooked through.

**3** Return all the aubergine to the wok together with the chilli and stir together. Add the remaining ingredients and toss everything together. Cook, stirring, until the sauce thickens. Serve immediately.

# braised straw mushrooms

## ingredients

### SERVES 4

1 tbsp vegetable or peanut oil

1 tsp finely chopped garlic

175 g/6 oz straw mushrooms,
    washed but left whole

2 tsp fermented black beans,
    rinsed and lightly mashed

1 tsp sugar

1 tbsp light soy sauce

1 tsp dark soy sauce

## method

**1** Heat the oil in a small claypot or saucepan. Cook the garlic until fragrant, then add the mushrooms and stir well to coat in the oil.

**2** Add the beans, sugar and soy sauces, then lower the heat and simmer, covered, for about 10 minutes, or until the mushrooms are soft.

# bamboo shoots with tofu

## ingredients

**SERVES 4–6**

3 dried Chinese mushrooms,
    soaked in warm water for
    20 minutes
55 g/2 oz baby pak choi
vegetable or peanut oil,
    for deep-frying
450 g/1 lb firm tofu, cut into
    2.5-cm/1-inch squares
55 g/2 oz fresh or canned
    bamboo shoots, rinsed and
    finely sliced (if using fresh
    shoots, boil in water first for
    30 minutes)
1 tsp oyster sauce
1 tsp light soy sauce

## method

**1** Squeeze out any excess water from the mushrooms and finely slice, discarding any tough stems. Blanch the pak choi in a large saucepan of boiling water for 30 seconds. Drain and set aside.

**2** Heat enough oil for deep-frying in a wok, deep-fat fryer, or large heavy-based saucepan until it reaches 180–190°C/350–375°F, or until a cube of bread browns in 30 seconds. Cook the tofu cubes until golden brown. Remove, then drain and set aside.

**3** In a preheated wok or deep saucepan, heat 1 tablespoon of the oil, then toss in the mushrooms and pak choi and stir. Add the tofu and bamboo shoots with the oyster and soy sauces. Heat through and serve.

# stir-fried beansprouts

## ingredients

**SERVES 4**

1 tbsp vegetable or peanut oil

225 g/8 oz beansprouts,
   trimmed

2 tbsp finely chopped spring
   onions

$1/2$ tsp salt

pinch of sugar

## method

**1** In a preheated wok or deep saucepan, heat the oil and stir-fry the beansprouts with the spring onions for about 1 minute. Add the salt and sugar and stir.

**2** Remove from the heat and serve immediately.

# edamame

## ingredients

**SERVES 4**

500 g/1 lb 2 oz frozen soya
    beans, in their pods
sea salt flakes

## method

**1** Bring a large pan of water to the boil. Add the beans and cook for 3 minutes, or until tender.

**2** Drain well, sprinkle with salt flakes to taste, and toss together. Serve warm or cold.

# mixed vegetables with quick-fried basil

## ingredients

**SERVES 4**

2 tbsp vegetable or peanut oil

2 garlic cloves, chopped

1 onion, sliced

115 g/4 oz baby corn cobs, cut in half diagonally

1/2 cucumber, peeled, halved, deseeded and sliced

225 g/8 oz canned water chestnuts, drained and rinsed

55 g/2 oz mangetout, trimmed

115 g/4 oz shiitake mushrooms, halved

1 red pepper, deseeded and sliced thinly

1 tbsp jaggery or soft light brown sugar

2 tbsp Thai soy sauce

1 tbsp fish sauce

1 tbsp rice vinegar

boiled rice, to serve

vegetable or peanut oil, for cooking

8–12 sprigs fresh Thai basil

## method

**1** Heat the oil in a wok and stir-fry the garlic and onion for 1–2 minutes. Add the corn cobs, cucumber, water chestnuts, mangetout, mushrooms and red pepper and stir-fry for 2–3 minutes, until starting to soften.

**2** Add the sugar, soy sauce, fish sauce and vinegar and gradually bring to the boil. Simmer for 1–2 minutes.

**3** Meanwhile, heat the oil for the basil in a wok and, when hot, add the basil sprigs. Cook for 20–30 seconds, until crisp. Remove with a slotted spoon and drain on kitchen paper.

**4** Garnish the vegetable stir-fry with the crispy basil and serve immediately, with the boiled rice.

# cauliflower & beans with cashew nuts

## ingredients

**SERVES 4**

1 tbsp vegetable or peanut oil

1 tbsp chilli oil

1 onion, chopped

2 garlic cloves, chopped

2 tbsp Thai red curry paste

1 small cauliflower, cut into
    florets

175 g/6 oz runner beans,
    cut into 7.5-cm/3-inch
    lengths

150 ml/5 fl oz vegetable stock

2 tbsp Thai soy sauce

50 g/1$^3$/$_4$ oz toasted cashew
    nuts, to garnish

## method

**1** Heat both the oils in a wok and stir-fry the onion and garlic until softened. Add the curry paste and stir-fry for 1–2 minutes.

**2** Add the cauliflower and beans and stir-fry for 3–4 minutes, until softened. Pour in the stock and soy sauce and simmer for 1–2 minutes. Serve immediately, garnished with the cashew nuts.

# starters & accompaniments

In most Asian countries several dishes are served together at everyday meals rather than as separate courses so, strictly speaking, there are neither appetizers nor accompaniments except at banquets and formal occasions. However, all sorts of tasty snacks are served to guests, often with cups of tea, in the morning and afternoon and these also make an ideal first course.

Small parcels of meat, chicken, seafood or vegetables in a crisp coating, succulent bite-sized dumplings, miniature skewers, spicy little meatballs or fishcakes, mini wraps and rolls, many of them served with individual bowls of dipping sauce, are a delight to the eye as well as the taste buds. Other enticing treats include pickles, fritters, toasts and, of course, that Japanese picture on a plate, sushi. Asian cooks have perfected the art of tempting the appetite by appealing to all the senses with fragrant, colourful, utterly delicious miniature culinary masterpieces that surprise and please with their contrasting or melt-in-the-mouth textures.

Rice is an integral part of virtually every Asian meal, although we tend to think of it as an accompaniment. Perfectly cooked steamed rice goes with everything, but there are lots of different ways to cook rice to add extra flavour and interest. Asian cooks are expert at matching the type of grain to the style of dish, from gently clinging sushi rice to sweetly fragrant jasmine rice.

Last but not least, there are recipes for dipping sauces. Whether sweet and sticky or warm and spicy, these add the final flourish and finishing touch to make any Asian meal special.

# spring rolls

## ingredients

**MAKES 25**

6 dried Chinese mushrooms, soaked in warm water for 20 minutes

1 tbsp vegetable or peanut oil

225 g/8 oz pork mince

1 tsp dark soy sauce

100 g/3$^{1/2}$ oz fresh or canned bamboo shoots, rinsed and julienned (if using fresh shoots, boil in water first for 30 minutes)

pinch of salt

100 g/3$^{1/2}$ oz raw prawns, peeled, deveined and chopped

225 g/8 oz beansprouts, trimmed and roughly chopped

1 tbsp finely chopped spring onions

25 spring roll skins

1 egg white, lightly beaten

vegetable or peanut oil, for deep-frying

## method

**1** Squeeze out any excess water from the mushrooms and finely slice, discarding any tough stems.

**2** In a preheated wok or deep saucepan, heat the tablespoon of oil and stir-fry the pork until it changes colour. Add the dark soy sauce, bamboo shoots, mushrooms and a little salt. Stir over a high heat for 3 minutes.

**3** Add the prawns and cook for 2 minutes, then add the beansprouts and cook for a further minute. Remove from the heat, stir in the spring onions and set aside to cool.

**4** Place a tablespoon of the mixture towards the bottom of a skin. Roll once to secure the filling, then fold in the sides to create a 10-cm/ 4-inch piece and continue to roll up. Seal with egg white.

**5** Heat enough oil for deep-frying in a wok, deep-fat fryer or large heavy-based saucepan to 180–190°C/350–375°F, or until a cube of bread browns in 30 seconds. Without overcrowding the pan, fry the rolls for about 5 minutes until golden brown and crispy. Drain well on kitchen paper and serve immediately.

# vegetarian spring rolls

## ingredients

**MAKES 20**

6 dried Chinese mushrooms,
   soaked in warm water for
   20 minutes
55 g/2 oz beanthread noodles,
   soaked in warm water for
   20 minutes
2 tbsp vegetable or peanut oil
1 tbsp finely chopped fresh
   ginger
100 g/3$\frac{1}{2}$ oz carrot, julienned
100 g/3$\frac{1}{2}$ oz finely shredded
   cabbage
1 tbsp finely sliced spring
   onions
1 tbsp light soy sauce
85 g/3 oz soft tofu, cut into
   small cubes
$\frac{1}{2}$ tsp salt
pinch of white pepper
pinch of sugar
20 spring roll skins
1 egg white, lightly beaten
vegetable or peanut oil,
   for deep-frying
soy sauce, for dipping

## method

**1** Squeeze out any excess water from the mushrooms and finely chop, discarding any tough stems. Drain the beanthread noodles and roughly chop.

**2** In a preheated wok or deep saucepan, heat the oil, then toss in the ginger and cook until fragrant. Add the mushrooms and stir for about 2 minutes. Add the carrot, cabbage and spring onions and stir-fry for 1 minute. Add the beanthread noodles and light soy sauce and stir-fry for 1 minute. Add the tofu and cook for a further 1 minute. Season with the salt, pepper and sugar and mix well. Continue cooking for 1–2 minutes, or until the carrot is soft. Remove from the heat and allow to cool.

**3** Place a level tablespoon of the mixture towards the bottom of a skin. Roll once to secure the filling, then fold in the sides to create a 10-cm/4-inch width and continue to roll up. Seal with egg white.

**4** Heat enough oil for deep-frying in a wok, deep-fat fryer or large, heavy-based saucepan to 180–190°C/350–375°F, or until a cube of bread browns in 30 seconds. Without overcrowding the pan, cook the rolls in batches for about 5 minutes, or until golden brown and crispy. Serve with a good soy sauce for dipping.

# soft-wrapped pork & prawn rolls

## ingredients

**MAKES 20**

115 g/4 oz firm tofu

3 tbsp vegetable or peanut oil

1 tsp finely chopped garlic

55 g/2 oz lean pork, shredded

115 g/4 oz raw prawns, peeled
and deveined

1/2 small carrot, cut into short
thin sticks

55 g/2 oz fresh or canned
bamboo shoots, rinsed and
shredded (if using fresh
shoots, boil in water first for
30 minutes)

115 g/4 oz very finely sliced
cabbage

55 g/2 oz mangetout,
julienned

1-egg omelette, shredded

1 tsp salt

1 tsp light soy sauce

1 tsp Shaoxing rice wine

pinch of white pepper

20 soft spring roll skins

chilli bean sauce, to serve

## method

**1** Slice the tofu into thin slices horizontally and cook in 1 tablespoon of the oil until it turns golden brown. Cut into thin strips and set aside.

**2** In a preheated wok or deep saucepan, heat the remaining oil and stir-fry the garlic until fragrant. Add the pork and stir for about 1 minute, then add the prawns and stir for a further minute. One by one, stirring well after each addition, add the carrot, bamboo shoots, cabbage, mangetout, tofu and, finally, the shredded omelette. Season with the salt, light soy sauce, Shaoxing rice wine and pepper. Stir for one more minute, then turn into a serving dish.

**3** To assemble each roll, smear a skin with a little chilli bean sauce and place a heaped teaspoon of the filling towards the bottom of the circle. Roll up the bottom edge to secure the filling, turn in the sides, and continue to roll up gently. Serve accompanied by a bowl of chilli bean sauce.

# crispy egg rolls

## ingredients

**SERVES 4**

2 tbsp vegetable or peanut oil

6 spring onions, cut into
    5-cm/2-inch lengths

1 fresh green chilli, deseeded
    and chopped

1 carrot, cut into thin sticks

1 courgette, cut into thin sticks

1/2 red pepper, deseeded and
    thinly sliced

115 g/4 oz beansprouts

115 g/4 oz canned bamboo
    shoots, drained and rinsed

3 tbsp Thai soy sauce

1–2 tbsp chilli sauce

8 egg roll skins

vegetable or peanut oil,
    for deep-frying

## method

**1** Heat the oil in a wok and stir-fry the spring onions and chilli for 30 seconds. Add the carrot, courgette and red pepper and stir-fry for 1 minute more. Remove the wok from the heat and stir in the beansprouts, bamboo shoots, soy sauce and chilli sauce. Taste and add more soy sauce or chilli sauce if necessary.

**2** Place an egg roll skin on a work surface and spoon some of the vegetable mixture diagonally across the centre. Roll one corner over the filling and flip the sides of the skin over the top to enclose the filling. Continue to roll up to make an enclosed package. Repeat with the remaining skins and filling to make 8 egg rolls.

**3** Heat the oil for deep-frying in a wok or large frying pan. Deep-fry the egg rolls, 3–4 at a time, until they are crisp and golden brown. Remove with a slotted spoon, drain on kitchen paper while you cook the remainder, then serve immediately.

# salmon & prawn spring rolls with plum sauce

## ingredients

**SERVES 4**

125 g/4¹/₂ oz salmon fillet, skinned, boned and cut into 3-mm/¹/₈-inch cubes

60 g/2¹/₄ oz beansprouts

60 g/2¹/₄ oz Chinese cabbage, finely shredded

25 g/1 oz spring onion, finely chopped

60 g/2¹/₄ oz red pepper, deseeded and finely sliced into strips

¹/₄ tsp five-spice powder

60 g/2¹/₄ oz cooked peeled prawns

4 spring roll wrappers, halved widthways

vegetable oil spray

¹/₄ tsp sesame seeds

plum sauce

100 ml/3¹/₂ fl oz water

50 ml/2 fl oz orange juice

¹/₂ tsp chopped red chilli

1 tsp grated fresh ginger

200 g/7 oz red plums, pitted weight

1 tsp chopped spring onion

1 tsp chopped fresh coriander

¹/₄ tsp sesame oil

## method

**1** To make the sauce, put the water, orange juice, chilli, ginger and plums into a saucepan and bring to the boil. Reduce the heat, cover and simmer for 10 minutes. Remove from the heat, blend with a hand-held electric blender, or use a food processor, then stir in the spring onion, coriander and sesame oil. Let cool.

**2** Heat a non-stick wok over a high heat, add the salmon, and stir-fry for 1 minute. Remove from the wok with a slotted spoon onto a plate. Using the cooking juices from the salmon, stir-fry the vegetables with the five-spice powder until just tender, drain in a colander, then stir in the cooked salmon and prawns – the mixture should be quite dry to prevent the rolls from becoming soggy.

**3** Divide the salmon and vegetable mixture into 8 portions. Spoon a portion along one short edge of each spring roll wrapper and roll up, tucking in the sides.

**4** Lay the spring rolls on a non-stick baking sheet and spray lightly with vegetable oil, sprinkle with sesame seeds and bake in a preheated oven, 200°C/400°F/Gas Mark 6, for 12–15 minutes, or until golden brown. Serve the spring rolls, and hand round the cold plum sauce separately.

# omelette rolls

## ingredients

**SERVES 4**

4 large eggs

2 tbsp water

1 tbsp Thai soy sauce

6 spring onions, chopped
    finely

1 fresh red chilli, deseeded
    and chopped finely

1 tbsp vegetable or peanut oil

1 tbsp Thai green curry paste

bunch of fresh coriander,
    chopped

## method

**1** Put the eggs, water and Thai soy sauce in a bowl. Set aside. Mix together the spring onions and chopped chilli to form a paste.

**2** Heat half the oil in a 20-cm/8-inch frying pan and pour in half the egg mixture. Tilt to coat the bottom of the pan evenly and cook until set. Lift out and set aside. Heat the remaining oil and make a second omelette in the same way.

**3** Spread the spring onion and chilli paste and the curry paste in a thin layer over each omelette and sprinkle the coriander on top. Roll up tightly. Cut each one in half and then cut each piece on the diagonal in half again. Serve immediately, while still warm.

# soba noodle rolls

## ingredients

**MAKES 24 PIECES**

115 g/4 oz sashimi-grade tuna
     or piece of tuna fillet
1 tbsp vegetable oil (if using
     tuna fillet)
100 g/3½ oz soba noodles,
     broken into pieces
1 spring onion, green part
     only, thinly sliced
1 tbsp light soy sauce
½ tbsp rice wine vinegar
wasabi paste
1 tbsp finely chopped pickled
     ginger, plus extra to serve
6 sheets of toasted nori
½ cucumber, peeled and
     finely shredded, seeds
     removed
Japanese soy sauce, to serve

## method

**1** If using sashimi-grade tuna, cut into strips. If cooking the fish, use the fillet and heat the oil in a frying pan. Sear the tuna for 30–60 seconds on all sides, so that the edges are sealed but the fish is rare in the middle. Allow to cool, then cut into strips.

**2** Cook the soba noodles in a pan of boiling water until they are just cooked through, drain, then rinse under cold running water. Drain again thoroughly. Gently mix the soba noodles with the spring onion, light soy sauce, rice wine vinegar, a pinch of wasabi and the pickled ginger.

**3** Put a sheet of nori smooth-side down on to a rolling mat with one of the long ends in front of you. Spread a sixth of the noodle mixture over the bottom third of the nori. Lay a line of cucumber across the centre of the noodles, then add a layer of tuna strips.

**4** Pick up the nearest edge of the rolling mat. Slowly roll the mat away from you to wrap the nori around the filling. Use gentle, even pressure until you have finished the roll, and lift the mat out of the way as you go.

**5** Transfer the roll to a chopping board, seam-side down. Cut it into 4 even-sized pieces with a wet, very sharp knife. Repeat with the remaining ingredients. Serve with soy sauce, pickled ginger and extra wasabi paste.

# pork & ginger dumplings

## ingredients

**MAKES ABOUT 50**

450 g/1 lb pork mince,
 not too lean

1 tbsp light soy sauce

1½ tsp salt

1 tsp Shaoxing rice wine

½ tsp sesame oil

100 g/3½ oz very finely
 chopped cabbage

2 tsp minced fresh ginger

2 tsp finely chopped spring
 onions

½ tsp white pepper

50 round wonton skins,
 about 7 cm/2¾ inches
 in diameter

ginger & garlic
 dipping sauce

1 tbsp soy sauce

1 tbsp vinegar

½ tsp sugar

1 tsp chopped fresh ginger

1 tsp chopped garlic

## method

**1** To make the dipping sauce, stir all the ingredients together and set aside.

**2** For the filling, mix the pork with the light soy sauce and ½ teaspoon salt. Stir carefully, always in the same direction, to create a thick paste. Add the Shaoxing and sesame oil and continue mixing in the same direction. Cover and let rest for at least 20 minutes.

**3** Meanwhile, sprinkle the cabbage with the remaining salt to help draw out the water. Add the ginger, spring onions and white pepper and knead for at least 5 minutes into a thick paste. Combine with the filling.

**4** To make the dumplings, place about 1 tablespoon of the filling in the centre of each skin, holding the skin in the palm of one hand. Moisten the edges with water, then seal the edges with 2–3 pleats on each side and place on a lightly floured board.

**5** To cook the dumplings, bring 1 litre/1¾ pints of water to a rolling boil in a large saucepan. Drop in about 20 dumplings at a time, stirring gently with a chopstick to prevent them sticking together. Cover, then bring back to the boil and cook for 2 minutes. Uncover and add about 225 ml/7 fl oz of cold water. Bring back to the boil, cover and cook for a further 2 minutes. Serve the dumplings with individual bowls of dipping sauce.

# dumplings in a cold spicy sauce

## ingredients

**MAKES 20**

20 square wheat skins

filling

1 tsp vegetable or peanut oil

200 g/7 oz pork mince, not too
   lean

1 tsp salt

1/2 tsp white pepper

sauce

100 ml/3 1/2 fl oz vegetable or
   peanut oil

1 tbsp dried chilli flakes

1 tsp sesame oil

1 tsp sugar

1 tbsp light soy sauce

1/2 tsp white pepper

1 tsp salt

1 garlic clove, finely chopped

## method

**1** To prepare the filling, heat the oil in a small saucepan and stir-fry the pork with the salt and pepper for 3–4 minutes, stirring to break up any meat clumps and letting the juices begin to come out.

**2** To prepare the sauce, heat the oil until smoking in a wok or deep saucepan and pour over the chilli flakes. Allow to cool, then stir in all the other ingredients.

**3** To make the dumplings, hold a skin in the palm of one hand and place a scant teaspoon of the filling in the centre. Wet the edges and fold over to create a triangle, then, with the point facing towards you at the bottom of your index finger, cross the edges behind your finger, sealing with a little water. Take the point facing towards you and turn up to form a wonton.

**4** Drop the dumplings into a large saucepan of boiling water and cook for 5 minutes.

**5** To serve, assemble 4–5 pieces per serving on a small plate and pour over a generous amount of the sauce.

# crispy pork dumplings

## ingredients

**SERVES 4**

350 g/12 oz ground pork

2 tbsp finely chopped fresh
    coriander

1 garlic clove, crushed

1 fresh green chilli, deseeded
    and chopped

3 tbsp cornflour

1 egg white

$1/2$ tsp salt

16 wonton skins

1 tbsp water

vegetable or peanut oil,
    for cooking

chilli sauce, to serve

## method

**1** Put the pork in a bowl and beat in the coriander, garlic, chilli, 1 tablespoon of the cornflour, the egg white and salt. Beat together to a thick, smooth texture. With damp hands shape into 16 equal portions and roll into balls.

**2** Put a pork ball in the centre of each wonton skin. Make a paste by mixing the remaining cornflour with 1 tablespoon of water. Brush the edges of the skins with the cornflour paste and gather them up around the filling to make half into small, sack-like parcels, and the rest into triangular shapes.

**3** Arrange the dumplings in a single layer (in batches if need be) in the top of a steamer and cook over boiling water for 10–15 minutes, until the meat is cooked through.

**4** Heat the oil in a wok and carefully drop the parcels into it. Deep-fry for 2–3 minutes, until golden brown and crisp. Drain on kitchen paper.

**5** Serve hot with chilli sauce.

# pork & crab meatballs

## ingredients

**SERVES 6**

225 g/8 oz pork fillet, chopped
    finely
170 g/5¾ oz canned
    crabmeat, drained
3 spring onions, chopped
    finely
1 garlic clove, chopped finely
1 tsp Thai red curry paste
1 tbsp cornflour
1 egg white
vegetable or peanut oil,
    for deep-frying
boiled rice, to serve

s a u c e
1 tbsp vegetable or peanut oil
2 shallots, chopped
1 garlic clove, crushed
2 large fresh red chillies,
    deseeded and chopped
4 spring onions, chopped
3 tomatoes, chopped coarsely

## method

**1** Put the pork and crabmeat into a bowl and mix together. Add the spring onions, garlic, curry paste, cornflour and egg white, and beat well to make a thick paste. With damp hands, shape the mixture into walnut-size balls.

**2** Heat the oil in a wok and deep-fry the balls, in batches, for 3–4 minutes, turning frequently, until golden brown and cooked. Drain on kitchen paper and keep warm.

**3** To make the sauce, heat the oil in a wok and stir-fry the shallots and garlic for 1–2 minutes. Add the chillies and spring onions and stir-fry for 1–2 minutes, then add the tomatoes. Stir together quickly, then spoon the sauce over the pork and crab balls. Serve immediately with rice.

# beef satay with peanut sauce

## ingredients

**SERVES 4**

500 g/1 lb 2 oz lean beef
    fillet, cut into 1-cm/$\frac{1}{2}$-inch
    cubes

2 garlic cloves, crushed

2-cm/$\frac{3}{4}$-inch piece fresh
    ginger, finely grated

1 tbsp brown sugar

1 tbsp dark soy sauce

1 tbsp lime juice

2 tsp sesame oil

1 tsp ground coriander

1 tsp ground turmeric

$\frac{1}{2}$ tsp chilli powder

chopped cucumber and red
    pepper pieces, to garnish


peanut sauce

300 ml/10 fl oz coconut milk

8 tbsp chunky peanut butter

$\frac{1}{2}$ small onion, grated

2 tsp brown sugar

$\frac{1}{2}$ tsp chilli powder

1 tbsp dark soy sauce

## method

**1** Place the beef cubes in a large bowl. Add the garlic, ginger, sugar, soy sauce, lime juice, sesame oil, coriander, turmeric and chilli powder. Mix well to coat the pieces of meat evenly. Cover and marinate in the refrigerator for at least 2 hours or overnight.

**2** Preheat the grill to high. To make the peanut sauce, place all the ingredients in a small saucepan and stir over medium heat until boiling. Remove the pan from the heat and keep warm.

**3** Thread the beef cubes onto presoaked bamboo skewers. Cook the skewers under the hot grill for 3–5 minutes, turning frequently, until golden. Alternatively, barbecue over hot coals. Transfer to a large serving plate, then garnish with chopped cucumber and red pepper pieces and serve with the peanut sauce.

# soy chicken wings

## ingredients

**SERVES 3–4**

250 g/9 oz chicken wings,
    defrosted if frozen
250 ml/9 fl oz water
1 tbsp sliced spring onion
2.5-cm/1-inch piece of fresh
    ginger, cut into 4 slices
2 tbsp light soy sauce
1/2 tsp dark soy sauce
1 star anise
1 tsp sugar

## method

**1** Wash and dry the chicken wings. In a small saucepan, bring the water to the boil, then add the chicken, spring onion and ginger and bring back to the boil.

**2** Add the remaining ingredients, then cover and simmer for 30 minutes.

**3** Remove the chicken wings from any remaining liquid and serve hot.

# kara-age chicken

## ingredients

**SERVES 4**

6 skinless, boneless chicken
  thighs, about 100 g/3½ oz
  each
4 tbsp shoyu (Japanese
  soy sauce)
4 tbsp mirin
2 tsp finely grated fresh ginger
2 garlic cloves, crushed
oil, for deep-frying
70 g/2½ oz potato flour or
  cornflour
pinch of salt
lemon wedges, to serve

## method

**1** Cut the chicken into large cubes and put in a bowl. Add the soy sauce, mirin, ginger and garlic and turn the chicken to coat well. Cover with clingfilm and marinate in a cool place for 20 minutes.

**2** Preheat a wok, then fill one-third full with oil, or use a deep-fryer. Heat the oil to 180–190°C/ 350–375°F, or until a cube of bread browns in 30 seconds.

**3** Meanwhile, mix the potato flour with the salt in a bowl. Lift the chicken out of the marinade and shake off any excess. Drop it into the potato flour and coat well, then shake off any excess.

**4** Add the chicken to the oil, in batches, and cook for 6 minutes, or until crisp and brown. Remove, drain on kitchen paper and keep hot while you cook the remaining chicken.

**5** Serve with lemon wedges.

# lemon grass chicken skewers

## ingredients

**SERVES 4**

2 long or 4 short lemon grass
   stems
2 large skinless, boneless
   chicken breasts, about
   400 g/14 oz in total
1 small egg white
1 carrot, finely grated
1 small fresh red chilli,
   deseeded and chopped
2 tbsp snipped fresh garlic
   chives
2 tbsp chopped coriander
salt and pepper
1 tbsp corn oil
coriander sprigs and lime
   slices, to garnish
mixed salad leaves, to serve

## method

**1** If the lemon grass stems are long, cut them in half across the centre to make 4 short lengths. Cut each stem in half lengthways, so that you have 8 sticks.

**2** Coarsely chop the chicken pieces and place them in a food processor with the egg white. Process to a smooth paste, then add the carrot, chilli, chives, coriander and salt and pepper to taste. Process for a few seconds to mix well. Transfer the mixture to a large bowl. Cover and chill in the refrigerator for 15 minutes.

**3** Preheat the grill to medium. Divide the mixture into 8 equal-size portions and use your hands to shape the mixture around the lemon grass 'skewers'.

**4** Brush the skewers with oil and cook under the hot grill for 4–6 minutes, turning them occasionally, until golden brown and thoroughly cooked. Alternatively, barbecue over medium–hot coals.

**5** Transfer to serving plates. Garnish with coriander sprigs and lime slices and serve hot with salad leaves.

# chicken satay

## ingredients

**SERVES 4**

2 tbsp vegetable or peanut oil

1 tbsp sesame oil

juice of $1/2$ lime

2 skinless, boneless chicken
    breasts, cut into small
    cubes

dip

2 tbsp vegetable or peanut oil

1 small onion, chopped finely

1 small fresh green chilli,
    deseeded and chopped

1 garlic clove, chopped finely

125 ml/4 fl oz crunchy peanut
    butter

6–8 tbsp water

juice of $1/2$ lime

## method

**1** Combine both the oils and the lime juice in a non-metallic dish. Add the chicken cubes, cover with clingfilm and chill for 1 hour.

**2** To make the dip, heat the oil in a frying pan and sauté the onion, chilli and garlic over low heat, stirring occasionally, for about 5 minutes, until just softened. Add the peanut butter, water and lime juice and simmer gently, stirring constantly, until the peanut butter has softened enough to make a dip – you may need to add extra water to make a thinner consistency.

**3** Meanwhile, drain the chicken cubes and thread them onto 8–12 wooden skewers – soak the skewers in cold water for 45 minutes before threading the meat to help stop them burning during cooking. Put under a hot grill or on a barbecue, turning frequently, for about 10 minutes, until cooked and browned. Serve hot with the warm dip.

# whitebait with green chilli

## ingredients

**SERVES 4**

175 g/6 oz whitebait

sauce

1 tbsp vegetable or peanut oil

1 large fresh green chilli

2 drops of sesame oil

1 tbsp light soy sauce

pinch of salt

pinch of sugar

1 garlic clove, finely chopped

## method

**1** In a large saucepan of boiling water, cook the fish for 30 seconds–2 minutes, or until the flesh is turning soft but not breaking up. Drain, then set aside to cool.

**2** To prepare the sauce, first heat the oil in a small saucepan and, when smoking, cook the chilli until the skin blisters. Remove the skin and finely chop the chilli. When cool, mix with all the other ingredients.

**3** To serve, pour the sauce over the fish and serve immediately.

# prawn toasts

## ingredients

**MAKES 16**

100 g/3½ oz raw prawns,
   peeled and deveined

2 egg whites

2 tbsp cornflour

½ tsp sugar

pinch of salt

2 tbsp finely chopped
   coriander leaves

2 slices day-old white bread

vegetable or peanut oil,
   for deep-frying

## method

**1** Pound the prawns to a pulp in a mortar and pestle or with the base of a cleaver.

**2** Mix the prawns with one of the egg whites and 1 tablespoon of the cornflour. Add the sugar and salt and stir in the coriander. Mix the remaining egg white with the remaining cornflour.

**3** Remove the crusts from the bread and cut each slice into 8 triangles. Brush the top of each piece with the egg white and cornflour mixture, then add 1 teaspoon of the prawn mixture. Smooth the top.

**4** Heat enough oil for deep-frying in a wok, deep-fat fryer or large heavy-based saucepan to 180–190°C/350–375°F, or until a cube of bread browns in 30 seconds. Without overcrowding the wok, cook the toasts prawn-side up for about 2 minutes. Turn and cook for a further 2 minutes, or until beginning to turn golden brown. Drain and serve warm.

# crispy wrapped prawns

## ingredients

**SERVES 4**

16 large, unpeeled cooked
    prawns
juice of 1 lime
4 tbsp chilli sauce
16 wonton skins
vegetable or peanut oil,
    for deep-frying
plum sauce, to serve

## method

**1** Remove the heads and shell the prawns, but leave the tails intact. Place them in a non-metallic bowl, add the lime juice, and toss lightly to coat. Set aside in a cool place for 30 minutes.

**2** Spread a little chilli sauce over a wonton skin. Place a prawn diagonally across it, leaving the tail protruding. Fold the bottom corner of the skin over the prawn, fold the next corner up over the head end, and then roll the prawn up in the skin so that the body is encased, but the tail is exposed. Repeat with the remaining skins, chilli sauce and prawns.

**3** Heat the oil in a wok or frying pan and deep-fry the prawns, in batches, until crisp and browned. Serve hot with plum sauce for dipping.

# crispy sesame prawns

## ingredients

**SERVES 4**

115 g/4 oz self-raising flour

3 tbsp sesame seeds, toasted
    or dry-fried

1 tsp Thai red curry paste

1 tbsp fish sauce

150 ml/5 fl oz water

vegetable or peanut oil,
    for deep-frying

20 large, uncooked prawns,
    peeled with tails intact

chilli sauce, for dipping

## method

**1** Combine the flour and sesame seeds in a bowl. Stir the curry paste, fish sauce and water together in a jug until mixed. Gradually pour the liquid into the flour, stirring constantly, to make a thick batter.

**2** Heat the oil for deep-frying in a wok. Holding the prawns by their tails, dip them into the batter, one at a time, then carefully drop into the hot oil. Cook for 2–3 minutes, until crisp and brown. Drain on kitchen paper.

**3** Serve immediately with chilli sauce.

# crab parcels

## ingredients

**SERVES 4**

350 g/12 oz canned white
    crabmeat, drained
1 fresh red chilli, deseeded
    and chopped
4 spring onions, sliced finely
1 tbsp Thai red curry paste
juice of 1/2 lime
1/2 tsp salt
20 wonton skins
oil for cooking

d i p

55 g/2 oz caster sugar
2 tbsp water
2 tbsp rice wine vinegar
3 pieces preserved ginger,
    sliced
1 tbsp ginger syrup from
    the jar

## method

**1** Put the crabmeat into a bowl and add the chilli, spring onions and curry paste. Stir together with the lime juice and salt.

**2** Put the skins in a pile and put 1 portion of the crabmeat in the centre of the top skin. Brush the edges with a little water and roll up the edges to make a small cigar-shaped parcel. Continue to make parcels with the skins – you need at least 20.

**3** Heat the oil in a wok and cook the parcels, a few at a time, until golden brown. Drain on kitchen paper.

**4** Put all the ingredients for the dip in a small pan and heat gently until the sugar has melted. Serve warm with the crab parcels.

# fish cakes

## ingredients

**SERVES 4**

450 g/1 lb skinned white fish
    fillets, cut into cubes
1 egg white
2 kaffir lime leaves,
    torn coarsely
1 tbsp Thai green curry paste
55 g/2 oz green beans,
    chopped finely
1 fresh red chilli, deseeded
    and chopped finely
bunch of fresh coriander,
    chopped
vegetable or peanut oil for
    cooking
1 fresh green chilli, deseeded
    and sliced, to serve

dipping sauce
115 g/4 oz caster sugar
50 ml/2 fl oz white wine
    vinegar
1 small carrot, cut into thin
    sticks
5-cm/2-inch piece cucumber,
    peeled, deseeded and cut
    into thin sticks

## method

**1** Put the fish into a food processor with the egg white, lime leaves and curry paste and process until smooth. Scrape the mixture into a bowl and stir in the green beans, red chilli and coriander. With dampened hands, shape the mixture into small patties, about 5 cm/2 inches across. Place them on a large plate in a single layer and chill for 30 minutes.

**2** Meanwhile, make the dipping sauce. Put the sugar in a saucepan with $1^{1/2}$ tablespoons water and the vinegar and heat gently, stirring until the sugar has dissolved. Add the carrot and cucumber, then remove from the heat and let cool.

**3** Heat the oil in a frying pan and cook the fish cakes, in batches, until golden brown on both sides. Drain on kitchen paper and keep warm while you cook the remaining batches. If desired, reheat the dipping sauce. Serve the fish cakes immediately with warm or cold dipping sauce, topped with the green chilli slices.

# wontons

## ingredients

SERVES 1

filling

2 tbsp vegetable or peanut oil

6 spring onions, chopped

125 g/4¹/₂ oz mushrooms,
    chopped

55 g/2 oz fine green beans,
    chopped

55 g/2 oz sweetcorn kernels,
    drained if canned

1 egg, beaten

3 tbsp Thai soy sauce

1 tbsp jaggery or soft light
    brown sugar

¹/₂ tsp salt

wontons

24 wonton skins

1 egg, beaten

vegetable or peanut oil,
    for deep-frying

plum or chilli sauce, to serve

## method

**1** To make the filling, heat the oil in a preheated wok and stir-fry the spring onions, mushrooms and beans for 1–2 minutes, until softened. Add the corn, stir well to mix, and then push the vegetables to the side. Pour in the egg. Stir until lightly set before incorporating the vegetables and adding the soy sauce, sugar and salt. Remove the wok from the heat.

**2** Place the wonton skins in a pile on a work surface. Put a teaspoonful of the filling in the centre of the top skin. Brush the edges with beaten egg and fold in half diagonally to make a small triangular package. Repeat with the remaining skins and filling.

**3** Heat the oil for deep-frying in a wok or large frying pan. Add the packages, in batches, and deep-fry for 3–4 minutes, until they are golden brown. Remove from the wok with a slotted spoon and drain on kitchen paper. Keep warm while you cook the remaining wontons. Serve hot with plum or chilli sauce.

# crispy crab wontons

## ingredients

**MAKES 24**

175 g/6 oz white crabmeat, drained if canned and thawed if frozen, flaked

50 g/1³/₄ oz canned water chestnuts, drained, rinsed and chopped

1 small fresh red chilli, chopped

1 spring onion, chopped

1 tbsp cornflour

1 tsp dry sherry

1 tsp light soy sauce

¹/₂ tsp lime juice

24 wonton skins

vegetable oil, for deep-frying

lime slices, to garnish

## method

**1** To make the filling, mix the crabmeat, water chestnuts, chilli, spring onion, cornflour, sherry, soy sauce and lime juice together in a bowl.

**2** Spread the wonton skins out on a work surface and spoon an equal portion of the filling into the centre of each wonton skin.

**3** Dampen the edges of the wonton skins with a little water and fold them in half to form triangles. Fold the pointed ends in towards the centre, moisten with a little water to secure, then pinch together to seal.

**4** Heat the oil in a wok, deep-fat fryer or large, heavy-based saucepan to 180–190°C/ 350–375°F, or until a cube of bread browns in 30 seconds. Deep-fry the wontons in batches for 2–3 minutes until golden brown and crisp (if you deep-fry too many at one time, the oil temperature will drop and they will be soggy).

**5** Remove the wontons with a slotted spoon, drain on kitchen paper and serve hot, garnished with lime slices.

# onion pancakes

## ingredients

**MAKES ABOUT 16**

4 tbsp oil

4 tbsp finely sliced spring
　　onions

2 eggs, plus 2 egg yolks

200 g/7 oz plain flour

1 tsp salt

400 ml/14 fl oz milk

225 ml/8 fl oz water

## method

**1** Heat 1 tablespoon of the oil in a frying pan and lightly cook the spring onions until beginning to soften. Remove and set aside.

**2** Lightly beat the eggs, together with the egg yolks, and set aside. Sift the flour and salt into a large bowl and lightly mix in the eggs.

**3** Slowly add the milk and water, beating by hand, until the batter is creamy. Stir in the remaining oil and continue to beat for a few more minutes. Finally, stir in the spring onions.

**4** Heat a non-stick frying pan, pour in 1 tablespoon of the batter and cook until set, but not brown. To serve, loosely roll the pancakes and cut each one into 3 pieces.

# tea-scented eggs

## ingredients

**SERVES 6**

6 eggs

water, about 100 ml/18 fl oz

2 tbsp black tea leaves

## method

**1** Bring to the boil a saucepan of water deep enough to cover the eggs. Lower the eggs into the saucepan and cook for 10 minutes. Remove the eggs from the saucepan and lightly crack the shells with the back of a spoon.

**2** Bring the water back to the boil, add the tea leaves and simmer for 5 minutes. Turn off the heat. Place the eggs in the tea and let stand until the tea has cooled.

**3** Serve the eggs whole for breakfast or as part of a meal, shelled or, more traditionally, unshelled.

# lettuce wraps

## ingredients

**MAKES 12**

100 g/3½ oz dried cellophane
    noodles

3 tbsp crunchy peanut butter

2 tbsp rice vinegar

1 tbsp oyster sauce

peanut or corn oil (optional)

soy sauce, to taste

4 red radishes, grated

2 carrots, peeled and roughly
    grated

1 courgette, roughly grated

115 g/4 oz canned sweetcorn
    kernels, drained

12 large lettuce leaves,
    such as iceberg, rinsed
    and dried

### dipping sauce

10 tbsp rice vinegar

4 tbsp clear honey

2 tbsp toasted sesame oil

1 tsp bottled chilli sauce

2.5-cm/1-inch piece fresh
    ginger, peeled and very
    finely chopped

## method

**1** Put the noodles in a bowl, pour over enough lukewarm water to cover and soak for 20 minutes, until soft. Alternatively, follow the packet instructions. Drain and rinse, then cut into 7.5-cm/3-inch lengths.

**2** Beat the peanut butter, vinegar and oyster sauce together in a large bowl, adding a little oil to lighten the mixture, if necessary. Toss with the noodles in the bowl to coat, then add soy sauce to taste. Cover and chill until 15 minutes before you plan to serve.

**3** Meanwhile, mix together the dipping sauce ingredients in a small bowl.

**4** When you are ready to serve, stir the radishes, carrots, courgette and sweetcorn into the noodles and transfer to a serving dish. To assemble the lettuce wraps, place some noodles in a lettuce leaf and roll up the leaf to enclose the filling.

# pickled baby cucumbers

## ingredients

**SERVES 4**

1 tbsp vegetable or peanut oil,
   for frying

400 g/14 oz baby cucumbers

500 ml/18 fl oz white rice
   vinegar

1 tbsp salt

3 tbsp sugar

3 red Thai chillies, deseeded
   and finely chopped

## method

**1** In a wok or deep saucepan, heat the oil and cook the cucumbers for 3–5 minutes, or until they are bright green. Drain and set aside. When cool, score the skin many times on all sides. Place in a large dish.

**2** Combine the vinegar, salt, sugar and chillies and pour over the cucumbers, immersing them in the liquid. Marinate for 24 hours, then serve cold in chunks.

# pickled cucumber

## ingredients

**SERVES 4**

1/2 cucumber

1 1/8 tsp salt

1 tbsp rice vinegar

1 tsp sugar

## method

**1** Slice the cucumber into thin rounds. Place the slices in a shallow bowl and sprinkle with 1 teaspoon of the salt. Set aside for 5 minutes.

**2** Rinse the cucumber slices under running water, then drain well.

**3** Place the remaining 1/8 teaspoon of salt, the rice vinegar and sugar in a bowl that is large enough to take the cucumber, and stir to mix. Add the cucumber slices and toss to coat. Refrigerate for 8 hours or overnight.

# corn fritters

## ingredients

**SERVES 4**

fritters

3 spring onions, chopped
  finely

325 g/11½ oz canned
  sweetcorn kernels, drained

1 red pepper, deseeded and
  finely chopped

small handful of fresh
  coriander, chopped

2 garlic cloves, crushed

2 eggs

2 tsp caster sugar

1 tbsp fish sauce

2 tbsp rice flour or cornflour

vegetable or peanut oil,
  for pan-frying

dip

2 red peppers, deseeded and
  halved

2 tomatoes, peeled, deseeded
  and chopped coarsely

1 tbsp vegetable or peanut oil,
  for pan-frying

1 onion, chopped

1 tbsp Thai red curry paste

3–4 sprigs fresh coriander,
  chopped

## method

**1** Combine all the ingredients for the fritters in a bowl. Heat the oil in a frying pan and cook spoonfuls of the mixture, in batches, until golden brown on the underside. Flip over with a spatula to cook the second side. Remove from the pan, drain on kitchen paper and keep warm.

**2** To make the dip, put the red peppers on a baking sheet and place, skin-side up, under a hot grill, until blackened. Using tongs, transfer to a plastic bag, tie the top and let cool slightly.

**3** When the peppers are cool enough to handle, peel off the skins and chop the flesh. Put into a blender or food processor with the tomatoes and process until smooth.

**4** Heat the oil in a heavy-based saucepan and cook the onion and curry paste for 3–4 minutes, until softened. Add the pepper and tomato purée and cook gently until tender and hot. Stir in the chopped coriander, cook for 1 minute and serve hot with the fritters.

# thai tofu cakes with chilli dip

## ingredients

**SERVES 8**

300 g/10$\frac{1}{2}$ oz firm tofu, drained weight, coarsely grated

1 lemon grass stalk, outer layer discarded, finely chopped

2 garlic cloves, chopped

2.5-cm/1-inch piece fresh ginger, grated

2 kaffir lime leaves, finely chopped (optional)

2 shallots, finely chopped

2 fresh red chillies, deseeded and finely chopped

4 tbsp chopped fresh coriander

90 g/3$\frac{1}{4}$ oz gluten-free plain flour, plus extra for flouring

$\frac{1}{2}$ tsp salt

corn oil, for cooking

### chilli dip

3 tbsp white distilled vinegar or rice wine vinegar

2 spring onions, finely sliced

1 tbsp caster sugar

2 fresh chillies, finely chopped

2 tbsp chopped fresh coriander

pinch of salt

## method

**1** To make the chilli dip, mix all the ingredients together in a small serving bowl and set aside.

**2** Mix the tofu with the lemon grass, garlic, ginger, lime leaves, if using, shallots, chillies and coriander in a mixing bowl. Stir in the flour and salt to make a coarse, sticky paste. Cover and chill in the refrigerator for 1 hour to let the mixture firm up slightly.

**3** Form the mixture into 8 large walnut-size balls and, using floured hands, flatten into circles. Heat enough oil to cover the bottom of a large, heavy-based frying pan over medium heat. Cook the cakes in 2 batches, turning halfway through, for 4–6 minutes, or until golden brown. Drain on kitchen paper and serve warm with the chilli dip.

# pickled daikon & carrot

## ingredients

**SERVES 4**

10-cm/4-inch daikon (long
    white radish), peeled

1 carrot, peeled

1/2 tsp salt

1 tbsp sugar

2 tbsp rice vinegar

1 tsp white sesame seeds,
    toasted

## method

**1** Use a mandolin or vegetable peeler to slice the daikon and carrot into long thin slivers. Sprinkle the slices with the salt, cover and set aside for 30 minutes. Place in a sieve and gently press to extract the water.

**2** Put the sugar and rice vinegar into a bowl that is large enough to take the daikon and carrot. Stir until the sugar has dissolved.

**3** Add the daikon and carrot, and toss to coat. Refrigerate for 8 hours or overnight. Sprinkle with the toasted sesame seeds before serving.

# home-made pickled ginger

## ingredients

**MAKES 115 G/1 CUP**

100 g/3$\frac{1}{2}$ oz fresh ginger

1 tsp salt

125 ml/4 fl oz rice vinegar

2 tbsp caster sugar

4 tbsp water

## method

**1** Peel the ginger. Use a mandolin or vegetable peeler to slice it into long thin slivers, cutting along the grain. Sprinkle the slices with the salt, cover and set aside for 30 minutes.

**2** Place the salted ginger in boiling water for 30 seconds to blanch. Drain well.

**3** Put the rice vinegar, sugar and water into a small bowl. Stir to dissolve the sugar.

**4** Place the ginger slices in a bowl, pour over the rice vinegar mixture and turn to coat. Cover and marinate for at least 24 hours in the refrigerator (it will turn slightly pink). Pickled ginger will keep for several weeks if stored in a sterile airtight container in the refrigerator.

# vegetable parcels

## ingredients

**SERVES 4**

2 tbsp vegetable or peanut oil

225 g/8 oz potatoes, diced
    and boiled for 5 minutes

2 garlic cloves, crushed

1 onion, chopped

2 tbsp Thai green curry paste

55 g/2 oz frozen peas, thawed

juice of 1 lime

1/2 tsp salt

16 x 10-cm/4-inch square egg
    roll skins

1 egg, beaten

vegetable or peanut oil,
    for deep-frying

sweet chilli sauce or Thai soy
    sauce, to serve

## method

**1** Heat the oil in a wok and stir-fry the potatoes, garlic, onion and curry paste until lightly browned. Stir in the peas, lime juice, and salt and stir-fry for 1–2 minutes. Remove from the heat.

**2** Brush 1 egg roll skin with egg. Put a small spoonful of the potato mixture in the centre and fold up the edges to enclose the filling and make a purse-shaped parcel. Press the skin tightly together to seal the parcel. Repeat with the remaining skins and filling to make 16 small parcels.

**3** Heat the oil for deep-frying in a wok. Add the vegetable parcels, in batches, and deep-fry for 3–4 minutes, until golden brown. Drain on kitchen paper and keep warm while you cook the remaining parcels.

**4** Serve hot with a bowl of chilli sauce or soy sauce for dipping.

# crispy seaweed

## ingredients

**SERVES 4**

1 kg/2 lb 4 oz pak choi
850 ml/1¹/₂ pints peanut oil
1 tsp salt
1 tbsp caster sugar
85 g/3 oz toasted pine nuts

## method

**1** Rinse the pak choi leaves under cold running water, then pat dry thoroughly with kitchen paper.

**2** Discarding any tough outer leaves, roll each pak choi leaf up, then slice thinly so that the leaves are finely shredded. Alternatively, use a food processor to shred the pak choi.

**3** Heat the peanut oil in a large preheated wok. Carefully add the shredded pak choi and cook for 30 seconds, or until it shrivels up and becomes crispy. (You will probably need to do this in several batches.) Remove from the wok with a slotted spoon and drain thoroughly on kitchen paper.

**4** Transfer to a large bowl, toss with the salt, sugar and toasted pine nuts, and serve.

# tempura

## ingredients

**SERVES 4**

150 g/5½ oz packet
   tempura mix
4 shiitake mushrooms
4 fresh asparagus spears
4 slices sweet potato
1 red pepper, deseeded and
   cut into strips
4 onion slices, cut widthways
   into rings
oil, for deep-frying

dipping sauce
2 tsp mirin
1 tbsp shoyu (Japanese
   soy sauce)
pinch of dashi granules,
   dissolved in 2 tbsp boiling
   water

## method

**1** To make the dipping sauce, mix the ingredients together in a small dipping dish.

**2** Mix the tempura with water according to the packet instructions. Don't try to make the batter smooth – it should be a little lumpy. Drop the vegetables into the batter.

**3** Preheat a wok, then fill two-thirds full with oil, or use a deep-fryer. Heat the oil to 180–190°C/350–375°F, or until a cube of bread browns in 30 seconds.

**4** Lift 2–3 pieces of tempura out of the batter, add to the oil and cook for 2–3 minutes, or until the batter is a light golden colour. Remove, drain on kitchen paper and keep hot while you cook the remaining tempura pieces.

**5** Serve with the dipping sauce.

# vegetable & tofu tempura

## ingredients

**SERVES 4**

150 g/5½ oz packet tempura mix

1 potato, peeled and cut into 1-cm/½-inch thick pieces

¼ butternut squash, peeled and cut into 1-cm/½-inch thick pieces

1 small sweet potato, peeled and cut into 1-cm/½-inch thick pieces

1 small aubergine, cut into 1-cm/½-inch thick pieces

6 green beans, trimmed

1 red pepper, deseeded and cut into thick strips

6 whole shiitake or white mushrooms, stalks removed

1 stalk broccoli, broken into florets

350 g/12 oz firm tofu, cubed

vegetable oil, for deep-frying

sweet chilli sauce or tempura dipping sauce, to serve

## method

**1** Blend the tempura mix with the amount of water indicated on the packet instructions until you have a lumpy batter full of air bubbles. Do not try to make the batter smooth or it will be too heavy.

**2** Coat all the prepared vegetables and cubed tofu in the batter.

**3** Add the oil to a deep-fryer and heat to 180–190°C/350–375°F, or until a cube of bread browns in 30 seconds.

**4** Put the battered vegetables and tofu into the oil 3 at a time. If you add too many pieces at one time the oil temperature will drop and the batter will be soggy. Cook for 2–3 minutes, until the batter turns a light golden colour. Remove and drain on kitchen paper to blot up the excess oil.

**5** Serve hot, with the sweet chilli sauce or tempura dipping sauce on the side.

# seafood tempura

## ingredients

**SERVES 4**

8 large raw prawns, peeled
    and deveined

8 squid rings

150 g/5$^1$/$_2$ oz packet tempura
    mix

4 scallops, without corals,
    cleaned

200 g/7 oz firm white fish
    fillets, cut into strips

vegetable oil, for deep-frying

Japanese soy sauce or
    tempura dipping sauce,
    to serve

## method

**1** Make little cuts on the underside of the prawns to keep them straight while they cook. Pull any membranes off the squid rings.

**2** Blend the tempura mix with the amount of water indicated on the packet instructions until you have a lumpy batter full of air bubbles. Do not try to make the batter smooth or it will be too heavy.

**3** Coat all the prepared seafood in the batter.

**4** Add the oil to a deep-fryer and heat to 180–190°C/350–375°F, or until a cube of bread browns in 30 seconds.

**5** Add the battered seafood pieces 3 at a time. If you add too many pieces at one time the oil temperature will drop and the batter will be soggy. Cook for 2–3 minutes, until the batter turns a light golden colour. Remove and drain on kitchen paper to blot up the excess oil.

**6** Serve hot, with the soy sauce or tempura dipping sauce on the side.

# classic tuna nori rolls

## ingredients

**MAKES 24 PIECES**

2 sheets of toasted nori

1/2 quantity freshly cooked
   sushi rice

wasabi paste

55 g/2 oz sashimi-grade tuna,
   cut into strips 5 mm/
   1/4 inch square

Japanese soy sauce and
   pickled ginger, to serve

## method

**1** Fold a nori sheet in half lengthways, press all along the fold and tear it into 2 equal pieces. Place a half-sheet smooth-side down on a sushi rolling mat so that one of the long edges is directly in front of you.

**2** Divide the rice into 4 equal portions. Wet your hands, then spread 1 portion of rice evenly over the nori, leaving a 1-cm/1/2-inch clear border along the furthest edge.

**3** Dab a thin line of wasabi paste across the rice at the end nearest you. Cover with a quarter of the tuna strips, arranged in a continuous line.

**4** Pick up the nearest edge of the rolling mat. Slowly roll the mat away from you to wrap the nori around the filling. Use gentle, even pressure and lift the mat out of the way as you go. Press the roll onto the uncovered border of the nori to seal it.

**5** Transfer the roll to a chopping board, seam-side down. Cut it in half and then cut each half into 3 equal pieces using a wet, very sharp knife. Wipe your knife between each cut. Repeat to make 3 more rolls. Serve with soy sauce, pickled ginger and extra wasabi.

# tuna sesame blocks

## ingredients

**MAKES 12 PIECES**

8 x 6-cm/3$^1$/$_4$ x 2$^1$/$_2$-inch
   piece of tuna fillet, about
   2 cm/$^3$/$_4$ inch thick

2 tsp sesame oil

2 tbsp white sesame seeds,
   toasted

3 sheets of toasted nori, each
   cut into 4 strips lengthways

2 tbsp vegetable oil

## method

**1** Cut the tuna into 12 cubes and roll the cubes first in the sesame oil and then in the toasted sesame seeds.

**2** Roll each sesame-covered cube in a strip of nori, trimming off any excess so that the nori goes round the tuna once with little overlap.

**3** Heat the vegetable oil in a frying pan and put the cubes into the pan, standing them up on one nori-free end. Cook for 2 minutes, then turn over to cook the other nori-free end. The sesame seeds should be a dark brown, but not burned, and the tuna should have cooked most of the way through, leaving a rare patch in the centre. If you prefer your tuna fully cooked, cook each end for a little longer.

# salmon & rocket rolls with pesto

## ingredients

**MAKES 24 PIECES**

2 sheets of toasted nori

$^{1}/_{2}$ quantity freshly cooked sushi rice

pesto

55 g/2 oz skinless sashimi-grade fillet of salmon, cut into strips 1 cm/$^{1}/_{2}$ inch wide

40 g/1$^{1}/_{2}$ oz rocket, stalks removed

Japanese soy sauce, pickled ginger and wasabi paste, to serve

## method

**1** Fold a nori sheet in half lengthways, press all along the fold and tear it into 2 equal pieces. Place a half-sheet smooth-side down on a sushi rolling mat so that one of the long edges is directly in front of you.

**2** Divide the rice into 4 equal portions. Using wet hands, spread 1 portion of the rice evenly over the nori, leaving a 1-cm/$^{1}/_{2}$-inch clear border along the furthest edge.

**3** Dab a thin line of pesto across the rice at the end nearest you. Cover with a quarter of the salmon strips, arranging them in a continuous line, and top with rocket.

**4** Pick up the nearest edge of the rolling mat. Slowly roll the mat away from you to wrap the nori around the filling. Use gentle, even pressure and lift the mat out of the way as you go. Press the roll onto the uncovered border of the nori to seal it.

**5** Transfer the roll to a chopping board, seam-side down. Cut it in half and then cut each half into 3 equal pieces using a wet, very sharp knife. Repeat to make 3 more rolls. Arrange on a plate, and serve with soy sauce, pickled ginger and wasabi paste.

# smoked salmon sushi balls

## ingredients

**MAKES 10 PIECES**

1–2 slices of smoked salmon

juice of 1/4 lemon

1/4 quantity freshly cooked
   sushi rice

wasabi paste

lemon zest, to garnish

Japanese soy sauce and
   pickled ginger, to serve

## method

**1** Cut the salmon into 10 small pieces about 2.5 cm/1 inch square, then squeeze the lemon juice over the top.

**2** Cut a square of clingfilm measuring 10 cm x 10 cm/4 inch x 4 inch. Place 1 piece of smoked salmon in the centre of the wrap.

**3** Take 11/2 teaspoons of sushi rice and gently roll it into a ball. Lay it on top of the salmon.

**4** Wrap the clingfilm around the rice and salmon, twisting the 4 corners together to form a tight packet so that the rice inside makes a smooth ball. Repeat to make 10 balls in total.

**5** Unwrap the balls just before serving. Put a dab of wasabi and a tiny strip of lemon zest on top of each ball to garnish. Serve with soy sauce, pickled ginger and wasabi paste.

# salmon, spinach & wasabi mash rolls

## ingredients

**MAKES 24 PIECES**

2 large floury potatoes, peeled
    and cut into quarters
salt
1 spring onion, finely chopped
wasabi paste
115 g/4 oz sashimi-grade
    salmon, or piece of salmon
    fillet, skin removed
1 tbsp vegetable oil (if using
    salmon fillet)
6 sheets of toasted nori
handful of baby spinach,
    stalks removed

## method

**1** Cook the potatoes in a pan of boiling salted water for 20–30 minutes, until tender. Mash, then mix with the spring onion and wasabi to taste. Season with salt. Allow to cool, then refrigerate for 30 minutes or until very firm.

**2** If using sashimi-grade salmon, cut into strips. If cooking the fish, use the fillet. Heat the oil in a frying pan, then cook the salmon fillet over medium heat for 4 minutes on each side, until cooked through. Allow to cool, then cut into strips.

**3** Place a sheet of nori smooth-side down on a rolling mat with one of the long ends in front of you. Spread a sixth of the mashed potatoes over the bottom third of the nori. Lay a sixth of the baby spinach on top, then add a layer of salmon strips.

**4** Pick up the nearest edge of the rolling mat. Slowly roll the mat away from you to wrap the nori around the filling, using gentle, even pressure. Press the roll onto the uncovered border of the nori to seal it.

**5** Transfer the roll to a chopping board, seam-side down. Cut into 4 even-sized pieces with a wet, very sharp knife. Repeat with the remaining ingredients.

# seven-spiced salmon rolls

## ingredients

**MAKES 24 PIECES**

150-g/5¹/₂-oz piece of salmon
    fillet, skin removed
sichimi togarashi (seven-spice
    powder)
red chilli flakes
1 tbsp vegetable oil
1 quantity freshly cooked
    sushi rice
6 sheets of toasted nori
2 tbsp Japanese mayonnaise
Japanese soy sauce, wasabi
    paste and pickled ginger,
    to serve

## method

**1** Remove any bones from the salmon fillet. Dust the surface heavily with sichimi togarashi and sprinkle over a few red chilli flakes. Heat the oil in a frying pan and cook the salmon over medium heat for 4 minutes on each side, or until cooked through. Allow to cool, then flake into large pieces.

**2** Divide the rice into 6 equal portions. Put a sheet of nori smooth-side down on a rolling mat with one of the long ends towards you. With wet hands, spread 1 portion of the rice evenly over the nori, leaving a 1-cm/¹/₂-inch clear border along the furthest edge.

**3** Spread 1 teaspoon of the mayonnaise across the rice at the end nearest you. Lay a sixth of the flaked salmon on top of the mayonnaise.

**4** Pick up the nearest edge of the rolling mat. Slowly roll the mat away from you to wrap the nori around the filling. Use gentle, even pressure and lift the mat out of the way as you go. Press the roll onto the uncovered border of the nori to seal it.

**5** Transfer the roll to a chopping board, seam-side down. Cut it into 4 equal pieces with a wet, very sharp knife. Repeat with the remaining ingredients. Serve with soy sauce, wasabi and pickled ginger.

# salmon, asparagus & mayonnaise rolls

## ingredients

**MAKES 24 PIECES**

6 thin asparagus spears

150 g/5½ oz sashimi-grade salmon, or piece of salmon fillet, skin and any bones removed

1 tbsp vegetable oil (if using salmon fillet)

6 sheets of toasted nori

1 quantity freshly cooked sushi rice

wasabi paste

1 tbsp Japanese mayonnaise

1 tbsp white sesame seeds, toasted

Japanese soy sauce and pickled ginger, to serve

## method

**1** Lay the asparagus spears flat in a frying pan filled with simmering water and cook for 3–4 minutes or until tender. Cut into 9-cm/3½-inch lengths and allow to cool.

**2** If using raw salmon, cut it into thin strips. If cooking the fish, heat the oil in a frying pan and cook over medium heat for 4 minutes on each side, or until cooked. Cool, then flake.

**3** Put a sheet of nori smooth-side down on a rolling mat so that one of the long ends is in front of you. With wet hands, spread a sixth of the rice over the nori, leaving a 1-cm/½-inch clear border along the furthest edge.

**4** Dab a line of wasabi across the rice at the end nearest you. Cover with ½ teaspoon of mayonnaise. Lay a cooked asparagus spear over the top and place a sixth of the salmon alongside. Sprinkle the filling with ½ teaspoon of the sesame seeds.

**5** Pick up the nearest edge of the mat. Roll it away from you to wrap the nori around the filling, using even pressure. Press the roll onto the clear border of nori to seal it, then transfer to a chopping board. Cut it into 4 even-sized pieces using a wet, very sharp knife. Repeat with the rest of the ingredients. Serve with soy sauce, pickled ginger and more wasabi.

# steamed prawn rolls with lime dipping sauce

## ingredients

**MAKES 24 PIECES**

400 g/14 oz peeled raw
  prawns, deveined
2 tbsp chopped fresh
  coriander
1 large kaffir lime leaf, finely
  shredded
1 tbsp freshly squeezed lime
  juice
2 tsp sweet chilli sauce
1$^1$/$_2$ tbsp fish sauce
2 tsp mirin
1 egg white
4 sheets of toasted nori
lime slices, to garnish


lime dipping sauce
4 tbsp sake
4 tbsp Japanese soy sauce
2 tsp mirin
1 tbsp freshly squeezed lime
  juice

## method

**1** Put the ingredients for the dipping sauce into a small bowl and stir to mix.

**2** Place the prawns in a blender with the chopped coriander, shredded lime leaf, lime juice, sweet chilli sauce, fish sauce and mirin. Blend until smooth, then add the egg white and blend briefly to mix.

**3** Lay a nori sheet smooth-side down on a rolling mat so that one of the short sides is in front of you. Spread a quarter of the prawn mixture over the nori, leaving a 1-cm/$^1$/$_2$-inch clear border along the furthest edge.

**4** Pick up the nearest edge of the mat. Roll the mat away from you to wrap the nori tightly around the filling, creating a pinwheel effect. Use gentle, even pressure, lifting the mat out of the way as you go. Press the roll onto the clear border to seal it. Repeat to make 3 more rolls. Place them in the refrigerator for 1 hour.

**5** Transfer each roll to a chopping board, seam-side down. Cut it in half and then cut each half into 3 equal pieces using a wet, very sharp knife. Place in a steamer and cook over boiling water for 5 minutes or until the prawn mixture is cooked. Arrange on serving plates, garnished with lime slices, with the lime dipping sauce alongside.

# pepper-wrapped prawn rolls

## ingredients

**MAKES 12 PIECES**

2 red peppers
1 small ripe avocado, stoned, peeled and cut into slices
8 large cooked peeled prawns
salt and black pepper

## method

**1** Preheat the oven to 200°C/400°F/Gas Mark 6. Put the peppers in a roasting tin and cook them for 30 minutes, or until the skins have browned and started to puff away from the flesh. Allow to cool, then pull off the skins. Cut each pepper in half and discard the stalk, seeds and membrane.

**2** Lay each pepper half on a chopping board and place a pile of avocado slices on one side. Top with 2 prawns and season well with salt and pepper. Roll up the peppers tightly, wrap each roll in clingfilm and chill for 30 minutes.

**3** Carefully unwrap the clingfilm from the peppers and trim each end to make it straight. Cut each roll into 3 pieces with a wet, very sharp knife. Turn the pieces on their ends and arrange them on a plate.

# crab, asparagus & shiitake rolls

## ingredients

**MAKES 24 PIECES**

6 thin asparagus spears

1 tbsp vegetable oil

6 fresh shiitake mushrooms, stalks discarded, then thinly sliced

6 sheets of toasted nori

1 quantity freshly cooked sushi rice

wasabi paste

6 crab sticks, split in half lengthways

ponzu dipping sauce, to serve

## method

**1** Lay the asparagus spears flat in a frying pan filled with simmering water and cook for 3 minutes or until tender. Cut the spears into 9-cm/$3^1/_2$-inch lengths and allow to cool.

**2** Heat the oil in a frying pan, add the mushrooms and cook over medium heat for 5 minutes, or until softened.

**3** Place a sheet of nori smooth-side down on a rolling mat so that one of the long ends is towards you. With wet hands, spread a sixth of the rice over the nori, leaving a 1-cm/$1/_2$-inch clear border along the furthest edge.

**4** Dab a line of wasabi across the rice at the end nearest to you. Lay some of the cooked asparagus lengths on top of the wasabi, then put 2 pieces of crab stick next to it. Add a line of sliced mushrooms.

**5** Pick up the nearest edge of the rolling mat. Roll the mat away from you to wrap the nori around the filling, using gentle, even pressure. Press the roll onto the clear border of nori to seal it. Remove the roll from the mat and cut it into 4 even-sized pieces with a wet, very sharp knife. Repeat with the remaining ingredients. Serve with the ponzu dipping sauce.

# scallop, potato & sesame rolls

## ingredients

**MAKES 24 PIECES**

2 large floury potatoes, peeled
    and cut into quarters
25 g/1 oz butter
salt and black pepper
1 tbsp olive oil
8 large scallops, without
    corals, cleaned
6 sheets of toasted nori
2 tbsp Japanese mayonnaise
2 tbsp white sesame seeds,
    toasted

## method

**1** Cook the potatoes in a pan of boiling salted water for 20–30 minutes, until tender. Mash with the butter and season with salt and pepper. Refrigerate for 30 minutes, until the mashed potatoes are very firm.

**2** Heat the oil in a frying pan and sauté the scallops for 2–3 minutes on each side, until cooked through. Slice them thinly into 3 coin-shaped pieces and season with salt to taste.

**3** Place a sheet of nori smooth-side down on a rolling mat so that one of the long ends is directly in front of you. Spread a sixth of the mashed potatoes over the bottom third of the nori. Spread 1 teaspoon of mayonnaise over the top, then sprinkle on 1 teaspoon of the toasted sesame seeds. Add a sixth of the scallop slices.

**4** Pick up the nearest edge of the rolling mat. Slowly roll the mat away from you to wrap the nori around the filling. Use gentle, even pressure until you have finished the roll, and lift the mat out of the way as you go.

**5** Transfer the roll seam-side down to a chopping board and cut it into 4 even-sized pieces using a wet, very sharp knife. Repeat with the remaining ingredients.

# prawn & avocado skewers

## ingredients

**MAKES 6 SKEWERS**

1 quantity freshly cooked
   sushi rice

6 sheets of toasted nori

1 tbsp Japanese mayonnaise

1 tsp lemon zest

12 cooked jumbo prawns,
   peeled and deveined

2 ripe avocados, stoned,
   peeled and cut into strips

2-inch/5-cm piece of
   cucumber, peeled and cut
   into thin sticks

pickled ginger and wasabi
   paste, to serve

## method

**1** Divide the rice into 6 equal portions. Put a sheet of nori smooth-side down on a rolling mat with one of the long ends towards you. Wet your hands, then spread 1 portion of the rice evenly over the nori, leaving a 1-cm/1/2-inch clear border along the furthest edge.

**2** Mix the mayonnaise with the lemon zest, and spread about 1/2 teaspoon of the mixture in a line across the rice at the end nearest to you. Lay 2 prawns end to end on top of the mayonnaise. Place a line of avocado next to the prawns and then add a line of cucumber sticks.

**3** Pick up the nearest edge of the rolling mat. Slowly roll the mat away from you to wrap the nori around the filling. Use gentle, even pressure and lift the mat out of the way as you go. Press the roll onto the uncovered border of the nori to seal it.

**4** Transfer the roll to a chopping board, seam-side down. Cut into 4 even-sized pieces with a wet, very sharp knife. Lay the pieces on their side and push a bamboo skewer through them. Repeat with the remaining ingredients to make 6 skewers in total. Serve with pickled ginger and wasabi paste.

# chicken teriyaki rolls

## ingredients

**MAKES 24 PIECES**

1 skinless, boneless chicken breast, weighing about 150 g/5$^{1}/_{2}$ oz, cut into strips

2 tbsp teriyaki sauce

1 tbsp vegetable oil

1 quantity freshly cooked sushi rice

6 sheets of toasted nori

5-cm/2-inch piece of cucumber, peeled and cut into thin sticks

Japanese soy sauce, wasabi paste and pickled ginger, to serve

## method

**1** Preheat the grill to its highest setting. Toss the chicken in the teriyaki sauce, then the oil, and lay out on a foil-lined grill pan. Grill the chicken strips for 4 minutes on each side, put into a bowl with any cooking juices and cool.

**2** Divide the rice into 6 equal portions. Place a sheet of nori smooth-side down on a rolling mat so that one of the long ends is directly in front of you. Wet your hands, then spread 1 portion of the rice evenly over the nori, leaving a 1-cm/$^{1}/_{2}$-inch clear border along the furthest edge.

**3** Lay some of the chicken strips across the rice at the end nearest to you. Place a line of thin cucumber sticks alongside.

**4** Pick up the nearest edge of the rolling mat. Slowly roll the mat away from you to wrap the nori around the filling. Use gentle, even pressure and lift the mat out of the way as you go. Press the roll onto the uncovered border of the nori to seal it.

**5** Transfer the roll to a chopping board and cut it into 4 even-sized pieces with a wet, very sharp knife. Repeat with the remaining ingredients. Serve with soy sauce, wasabi and pickled ginger.

# california rolls

## ingredients

**MAKES 24 PIECES**

1 quantity freshly cooked
    sushi rice
6 sheets of toasted nori
wasabi paste
$1/2$ ripe avocado, stoned,
    peeled and cut into thin
    strips
6 crab sticks, split in half
    lengthways
5-cm/2-inch piece of
    cucumber, peeled and cut
    into thin sticks
Japanese soy sauce and
    pickled ginger, to serve

## method

**1** Divide the rice into 6 equal portions. Place a sheet of nori smooth-side down on a rolling mat so that one of the long ends is directly in front of you. Wet your hands and then spread 1 portion of the rice evenly over the nori, leaving a 1-cm/$1/2$-inch clear border along the furthest edge.

**2** Dab a small amount of wasabi across the rice at the end nearest you. Lay a line of avocado strips on top of the wasabi, then put 2 pieces of crab stick next to them. Add a line of cucumber sticks.

**3** Pick up the nearest edge of the rolling mat. Slowly roll the mat away from you to wrap the nori around the filling. Use gentle, even pressure and lift the mat out of the way as you go. Press the roll onto the uncovered border of the nori to seal it.

**4** Transfer the roll to a chopping board, seam-side down. Cut it into 4 even-sized pieces using a wet, very sharp knife. Repeat with the remaining ingredients. Serve with soy sauce, pickled ginger and more wasabi.

# pork tonkatsu rolls

## ingredients

**MAKES 24 PIECES**

2 tbsp flour

1 egg, lightly beaten

4 tbsp tonkatsu crumbs or
dried white breadcrumbs

200 g/7 oz pork fillet, cut into
5-mm/$^1/_4$-inch thick slices

4 tbsp vegetable oil

1 quantity freshly cooked
sushi rice

6 sheets of toasted nori

2 tbsp Japanese mayonnaise

Japanese soy sauce, pickled
ginger and wasabi paste,
to serve

## method

**1** Put the flour, egg and crumbs into separate bowls. One by one, dust each piece of pork in the flour, dip it in the egg, then finally press it into the crumbs. Lay the breaded pork on a plate and refrigerate for 20 minutes.

**2** Heat the oil in a frying pan. Add the pork and cook over medium heat for 3 minutes on each side, or until the crumbs are golden brown and the pork is cooked through. Cut the cooked slices into thin strips.

**3** Divide the rice into 6 equal portions. Put a sheet of nori smooth-side down on a rolling mat so that one of the long ends is towards you. With wet hands, spread 1 portion of the rice evenly over the nori, leaving a 1-cm/$^1/_2$-inch clear border along the furthest edge.

**4** Spread 1 teaspoon of the mayonnaise across the rice at the end nearest to you. Lay a sixth of the pork strips on top.

**5** Pick up the nearest edge of the rolling mat. Roll the mat away from you to wrap the nori around the filling. Use gentle, even pressure and lift the mat out of the way as you go. Press the roll onto the clear border to seal it.

**6** Transfer the roll to a chopping board and cut it into 4 equal pieces with a wet, very sharp knife. Repeat with the remaining ingredients. Serve with soy sauce, pickled ginger and wasabi paste on the side.

# inside-out rolls with beef teriyaki

## ingredients

**MAKES 24 PIECES**

150 g/5¹/₂ oz tenderloin steak, trimmed

2 tbsp teriyaki sauce

1 tbsp vegetable oil

6 sheets of toasted nori

1 quantity freshly cooked sushi rice

2 spring onions, shredded

3 tbsp white sesame seeds, toasted

Japanese soy sauce, pickled ginger and wasabi paste, to serve

## method

**1** Beat the steak out flat using a meat mallet or rolling pin. Coat the steak in the teriyaki sauce and marinate for 1 hour. Heat the oil in a frying pan and cook the steak for 3 minutes on each side. Cut the cooked steak into strips.

**2** Place a sheet of nori smooth-side down on the mat with one of the long ends towards you. With wet hands, spread a sixth of the rice evenly over the nori. Lay a sheet of clingfilm on top and turn the whole thing over so that the clingfilm is under the rice and the nori side faces upward.

**3** Arrange a sixth of the beef teriyaki across the nori at the end nearest to you. Top with shredded spring onion and sprinkle with a few sesame seeds.

**4** Pick up the nearest edge of the rolling mat and slowly roll the mat away from you to wrap the rice-covered nori around the filling. Lift the mat and clingfilm out of the way as you go. Spread 2 tablespoons of the sesame seeds on a plate and roll the sushi in it to coat the rice.

**5** Transfer the roll to a chopping board, seam-side down. Cut it into 4 even-sized pieces with a wet, very sharp knife. Repeat with the remaining ingredients. Serve with soy sauce, pickled ginger and wasabi paste.

# steamed white rice

## ingredients

**SERVES 3–4**

225 g/8 oz rice

cold water

## method

**1** Wash the rice. Place in a saucepan with the same volume of water plus a little extra (the water should just cover the rice). Bring to the boil, then cover and simmer for about 15 minutes.

**2** Turn off the heat and let the rice continue to cook in its own steam for about 5 minutes. At this point, the grains should be cooked through but not sticking together.

# egg-fried rice

## ingredients

**SERVES 4**

2 tbsp vegetable or peanut oil

12 oz/350 g cooked rice,
   chilled

1 egg, well beaten

## method

**1** Heat the oil in a preheated wok or deep saucepan and stir-fry the rice for 1 minute, breaking it down as much as possible into individual grains.

**2** Quickly add the egg, stirring, so as to coat each piece of rice. Stir until the egg is cooked and the rice, as far as possible, is in single grains. Serve immediately.

# perfect sushi rice

## ingredients

**SERVES 4**

300 g/10 oz sushi rice

350 ml/12 fl oz water

5-cm/2-inch-square piece of
    kombu (sun-dried kelp,
    optional)

2 tbsp sushi rice seasoning
    (or 2 tbsp rice vinegar,
    1 tbsp sugar and 1/4 tsp
    salt combined)

## method

**1** Place the rice in a sieve and rinse under cold water until the water runs completely clear. Drain the rice, then place in a pan with the water.

**2** Cut a few slits in the kombu, if using, to help release the flavour, then add to the rice. Cover the pan with a tight-fitting lid and bring to the boil. Remove the kombu and quickly replace the lid. Reduce the heat and simmer for 10 minutes. Remove from the heat and let stand for 15 minutes. Do not lift the lid to take a look once you have removed the kombu.

**3** Turn the cooked rice into a large, flat-bottomed, non-metallic bowl. Pour the rice seasoning evenly over the surface of the rice, then use quick cutting strokes to mix it in with a spatula. Do not stir or you will break the rice grains. As you work, fan the rice with either a hand-held fan or an electric one set to the lowest setting.

**4** Keep slicing and fanning until the rice has reached room temperature and looks shiny. Cover with a damp cloth and use the same day; do not refrigerate.

# chinese fried rice

## ingredients

**SERVES 4**

700 ml/1¼ pints water

½ tsp salt

300 g/10½ oz long-grain rice

2 eggs

salt and pepper

4 tsp cold water

3 tbsp sunflower oil

4 spring onions, sliced
   diagonally

1 red, green or yellow pepper,
   cored, deseeded and thinly
   sliced

3–4 lean bacon slices, rinded
   and cut into strips

200 g/7 oz fresh beansprouts

125 g/4½ oz frozen peas,
   thawed

2 tbsp soy sauce (optional)

## method

**1** Pour the water into a saucepan with the salt and bring to the boil. Rinse the rice in a sieve under cold running water until the water runs clear, drain thoroughly, and add to the boiling water. Stir well, then cover tightly with a lid and simmer gently for 12–13 minutes. (Do not remove the lid during cooking or the steam will escape and the rice will not be cooked.)

**2** Remove the lid, give the rice a good stir, and spread out on a large plate or baking sheet to cool and dry.

**3** Meanwhile, beat each egg separately with salt and pepper and add 2 teaspoons of cold water. Heat 1 tablespoon of oil in a preheated wok or frying pan, pour in the first egg, swirl it around and cook undisturbed until set. Transfer to a cutting board and cook the second egg. Cut the omelettes into thin slices.

**4** Add the remaining oil to the wok or frying pan and when really hot stir-fry the spring onions and pepper for 1–2 minutes. Add the bacon and stir-fry for a further 2 minutes. Add the beansprouts and peas and toss together thoroughly. Stir in the soy sauce, if using.

**5** Add the rice and salt and pepper to taste and stir-fry for 1 minute, then add the strips of omelette and continue to stir-fry for 2 minutes, or until the rice is piping hot. Serve immediately.

# golden rice

## ingredients

**SERVES 4**

1 tsp saffron threads

2 tbsp hot water

2 tbsp ghee or vegetable oil

3 onions, chopped

3 tbsp butter

1 tsp ground cumin

1 tsp ground cinnamon

1 tsp salt

$^{1}/_{2}$ tsp pepper

$^{1}/_{2}$ tsp paprika

3 bay leaves

400 g/14 oz long-grain rice,
    rinsed and drained

about 850 ml/1$^{1}/_{2}$ pints
    vegetable stock or water

100 g/3$^{1}/_{2}$ oz cashew nut
    halves, toasted

## method

**1** Put the saffron threads and hot water into a small bowl and set aside to soak.

**2** Meanwhile, heat the ghee in a large saucepan over low heat, add the onions and cook, stirring frequently, for 5 minutes. Add the butter, cumin, cinnamon, salt, pepper, paprika and bay leaves and cook, stirring, for 2 minutes, then add the rice and cook, stirring, for 3 minutes. Add the saffron and its soaking liquid and pour in the stock.

**3** Bring to the boil, then reduce the heat, cover and simmer for 20–25 minutes or until all the liquid has been absorbed. If the rice grains have not cooked through, add a little more stock and cook until tender and all the liquid has been absorbed.

**4** Remove from the heat and remove and discard the bay leaves. Taste and adjust the seasoning, if necessary. Add the cashew nuts and stir well. Serve hot.

# crab fried rice

## ingredients

SERVES 4

150 g/5½ oz long-grain rice

salt

2 tbsp groundnut oil

125 g/4½ oz canned white
  crab meat, drained

1 leek, sliced

150 g/5½ oz beansprouts

2 eggs, beaten

1 tbsp light soy sauce

2 tsp lime juice

1 tsp sesame oil

sliced lime, to garnish

## method

1 Cook the rice in a saucepan of lightly salted boiling water for 15 minutes. Drain, rinse under cold running water, and drain again.

2 Heat the oil in a preheated wok or large, heavy-based frying pan until it is really hot. Add the crab meat, leek and beansprouts to the wok and stir-fry for 2–3 minutes. Remove the mixture with a slotted spoon and set aside.

3 Add the eggs to the wok and cook, stirring occasionally, for 2–3 minutes or until they begin to set. Stir the rice and crab meat mixture into the eggs in the wok.

4 Add the soy sauce and lime juice to the wok. Cook for 1 minute, stirring to combine. Sprinkle with the sesame oil and toss lightly to mix. Garnish with sliced lime and serve.

# sweet-&-sour vegetables with cashew nuts

## ingredients

**SERVES 4**

1 tbsp vegetable or peanut oil

1 tsp chilli oil

2 onions, sliced

2 carrots, thinly sliced

2 courgettes, thinly sliced

115 g/4 oz head of broccoli, cut into florets

115 g/4 oz white mushrooms, sliced

115 g/4 oz small pak choi, halved

2 tbsp brown sugar

2 tbsp Thai soy sauce

1 tbsp rice vinegar

55 g/2 oz cashew nuts

## method

**1** Heat both the oils in a preheated wok or frying pan, add the onions and stir-fry for 1–2 minutes until beginning to soften.

**2** Add the carrots, courgettes and broccoli and stir-fry for 2–3 minutes. Add the mushrooms, pak choi, sugar, soy sauce and vinegar and stir-fry for 1–2 minutes.

**3** Meanwhile, heat a dry, heavy-based frying pan over a high heat, add the cashew nuts and cook, shaking the frying pan frequently, until lightly toasted. Sprinkle the cashew nuts over the stir-fry and serve immediately.

# tuna rice

## ingredients

**SERVES 4**

3 tbsp peanut or corn oil

4 spring onions, chopped

2 garlic cloves, finely chopped

200 g/7 oz canned tuna in oil,
   drained and flaked

175 g/6 oz frozen or canned
   sweetcorn and peppers

750 g/1 lb 10 oz cold boiled
   rice

2 tbsp Thai fish sauce

1 tbsp light soy sauce

salt and pepper

2 tbsp chopped fresh
   coriander, to garnish

## method

**1** Heat the peanut oil in a preheated wok or large, heavy-based frying pan. Add the spring onions and stir-fry for 2 minutes, then add the garlic and stir-fry for a further 1 minute.

**2** Add the tuna and the sweetcorn and peppers and stir-fry for 2 minutes.

**3** Add the rice, fish sauce and soy sauce and stir-fry for 2 minutes. Season to taste with salt and pepper and serve immediately, garnished with chopped coriander.

# asian coconut rice

## ingredients

**SERVES 4**

2 tbsp vegetable oil

1 onion, chopped

400 g/14 oz long-grain rice,
    rinsed and drained

1 tbsp freshly chopped lemon
    grass

500 ml/18 fl oz coconut milk

400 ml/14 fl oz water

6 tbsp flaked coconut, toasted

## method

**1** Heat the oil in a large saucepan over low heat, add the onion and cook, stirring frequently, for 3 minutes. Add the rice and lemon grass and cook, stirring, for a further 2 minutes.

**2** Stir in the coconut milk and water and bring to the boil. Reduce the heat, cover and simmer for 20–25 minutes until all the liquid has been absorbed. If the rice grains have not cooked through, add a little more water and cook until tender and all the liquid has been absorbed.

**3** Remove from the heat and add half the flaked coconut. Stir gently. Sprinkle over the remaining coconut flakes and serve.

# jasmine rice with lemon & basil

## ingredients

SERVES 4

400 g/14 oz jasmine rice

725 ml/1¹/₄ pints water

finely grated rind of ¹/₂ lemon

2 tbsp shredded fresh basil,
   to serve

## method

1 Wash the rice in several changes of cold water until the water runs clear. Bring 725 ml/1¹/₄ pints of water to the boil in a large saucepan, then add the rice.

2 Return to a rolling boil. Turn the heat to a low simmer, then cover the pan and simmer for a further 12 minutes. Remove from the heat and stand, covered, for 10 minutes.

3 Fluff up the rice with a fork, then stir in the lemon rind. Serve sprinkled with shredded basil.

# ginger & sesame dipping sauce

## ingredients

MAKES 4 FL OZ/125 ML

4-cm/1$\frac{1}{2}$-inch piece very
    fresh ginger
4 tbsp Japanese soy sauce
2 tbsp mirin
2 tbsp sake
$\frac{1}{4}$ tsp sesame oil
1 tsp rice vinegar

## method

**1** Shred the ginger into a small bowl and then press the flesh with the back of a teaspoon. Pour off 1 teaspoon fresh ginger juice and discard the pulp.

**2** Place the ginger juice in a small bowl, add the soy sauce, mirin, sake, sesame oil and rice vinegar, and stir to combine. Serve straight away or keep in a sealed container in the refrigerator for up to a week.

# ponzu dipping sauce

## ingredients

**MAKES 4 FL OZ/125 ML**

2 tbsp mirin

1$\frac{1}{2}$ tbsp rice vinegar

2 tsp light soy sauce

1$\frac{1}{2}$ tbsp bonito flakes

3 tbsp fresh lemon juice

## method

**1** Place all the ingredients in a small pan and bring to the boil. Remove from the heat and cool before serving as a dipping sauce.

# teriyaki dipping sauce

## ingredients

**MAKES 4 FL OZ/125 ML**

4 tbsp Japanese soy sauce

2 tbsp mirin

2 tbsp sake

2 tsp caster sugar

1 tsp shredded fresh ginger
    (optional)

1 garlic clove, crushed
    (optional)

## method

**1** Place the soy sauce, mirin, sake and sugar in a small pan with the shredded ginger and crushed garlic, if using.

**2** Set over low heat and stir until the sugar has dissolved. Heat for 15 minutes or until the sauce has thickened. Cool before serving.

# meat & poultry

Nowhere is the diversity of Asian cooking more apparent than in meat dishes. This is partly because of topography and partly a cultural difference. In some countries, such as China, pork is a favourite meat not least because pigs are economical to rear and cooks can use just about every part of them. However, in places where there is a large Muslim population, such as Indonesia, lamb or beef is preferred. Chicken dishes are found throughout Asia, simply because it is such a versatile meat, while the Chinese have made a speciality of preparing and cooking duck.

South-east Asia is the natural habitat for many spices such as ginger and lemon grass, though, perhaps surprisingly, not chillies. Consequently, meat and poultry dishes are traditionally highly spiced – Thai curries and Indonesian satays are typical of the region. On the other hand, the Japanese, who were latecomers to cooking meat because of religious principles, have become masters of the subtle, aromatic marinade for pork, chicken and beef. Frying is the keynote, although braising in flavoured stock is also a favourite technique. Chinese meat and poultry dishes usually incorporate a wide range of other ingredients, including vegetables, seafood, noodles and flavourings such as hoisin and oyster sauce. Stir-frying is still the most

popular everyday cooking method with roasted and braised dishes reserved for special occasions. In short, you are sure to find dishes to suit all tastes and budgets in Asia's imaginative, varied and delicious ways of preparing and cooking meat and poultry.

# roast beef wraps with wasabi mayonnaise

## ingredients

**MAKES 6 PIECES**

55 g/2 oz fresh daikon (long white radish), peeled

3 sheets of toasted nori

1/4 quantity freshly cooked sushi rice

55 g/2 oz mizuna leaves

6 thin slices rare roast beef

wasabi mayonnaise

2 tbsp mayonnaise

1 tsp wasabi paste, or to taste

## method

**1** Shred the daikon using the finest setting on a mandolin. Alternatively, cut it into long thin slices and then cut each slice along its length as finely as possible. Rinse, drain and then place in the refrigerator until needed.

**2** Make the wasabi mayonnaise by combining the mayonnaise and wasabi paste in a bowl.

**3** Fold a nori sheet in half lengthways, press along the fold and then tear it into 2 pieces.

**4** Lay a half-sheet of nori smooth-side down on a work surface and place a heaped tablespoon of rice on the left-hand side. Spread 1 teaspoon of wasabi mayonnaise over the rice, then add a few mizuna leaves and a sixth of the chilled shredded daikon. Roll up 1 slice of beef into a cone shape and place it on top.

**5** Fold the bottom left-hand corner of the nori over the rice and filling, so that the folded edge forms a right angle with the bottom edge. Continue folding along that line to make a cone with a sharp point at the bottom. Place a drop of vinegared water on the underside of the join to seal it. Repeat with the rest of the ingredients to make 6 cones in total.

# marinated beef with vegetables

## ingredients

**SERVES 4**

500 g/1 lb 2 oz rump steak, cut into thin strips

3 tbsp sesame oil

1/2 tbsp cornflour

1/2 tbsp soy sauce

1 head of broccoli, cut into florets

2 carrots, cut into thin strips

125 g/4 oz mangetout

125 ml/4 fl oz beef stock

250 g/9 oz baby spinach, shredded

freshly cooked rice or noodles, to serve

marinade

1 tbsp dry sherry

1/2 tbsp soy sauce

1/2 tbsp cornflour

1/2 tsp caster sugar

2 garlic cloves, chopped finely

1 tbsp sesame oil

## method

**1** To make the marinade, mix the sherry, soy sauce, cornflour, sugar, garlic and sesame oil in a bowl. Add the beef to the mixture and cover with clingfilm. Set aside to marinate for 30 minutes, then remove the beef and discard the marinade.

**2** Heat 1 tablespoon of the sesame oil in a frying pan or wok. Stir-fry the beef for 2 minutes until medium-rare. Remove from the frying pan and set aside.

**3** Combine the cornflour and soy sauce in a bowl and set aside. Pour the remaining 2 tablespoons of sesame oil into the frying pan, add the broccoli, carrots and mangetout and stir-fry for 2 minutes.

**4** Add the stock, cover the frying pan and steam for one minute. Stir in the spinach, beef and the cornflour mixture. Cook until the juices boil and thicken. Serve on a bed of freshly cooked rice or noodles.

# beef chop suey

## ingredients

**SERVES 4**

450 g/1 lb ribeye or sirloin
steak, finely sliced

1 head of broccoli, cut into
small florets

2 tbsp vegetable or peanut oil

1 onion, finely sliced

2 celery sticks, finely sliced
diagonally

225 g/8 oz mangetout, sliced
in half lengthways

55 g/2 oz fresh or canned
bamboo shoots, rinsed and
julienned (if using fresh
shoots, boil in water first for
30 minutes)

8 water chestnuts, finely sliced

225 g/8 oz finely sliced
mushrooms

1 tbsp oyster sauce

1 tsp salt

marinade

1 tbsp Shaoxing rice wine

pinch of white pepper

pinch of salt

1 tbsp light soy sauce

1/2 tsp sesame oil

## method

**1** Combine all the marinade ingredients in a bowl and marinate the beef for at least 20 minutes. Blanch the broccoli florets in a large saucepan of boiling water for 30 seconds. Drain and set aside.

**2** In a preheated wok or deep saucepan, heat 1 tablespoon of the oil and stir-fry the beef until the colour has changed. Remove and set aside.

**3** In the clean wok or deep saucepan, heat the remaining oil and stir-fry the onion for 1 minute. Add the celery and broccoli and cook for 2 minutes. Add the mangetout, bamboo shoots, chestnuts and mushrooms and cook for 1 minute. Add the beef, then season with the oyster sauce and salt and serve immediately.

# hot sesame beef

## ingredients

**SERVES 4**

500 g/1 lb 2 oz beef fillet,
   cut into thin strips

1¹⁄₂ tbsp sesame seeds

125 ml/4 fl oz beef stock

2 tbsp soy sauce

2 tbsp grated fresh ginger

2 garlic cloves, finely chopped

1 tsp cornflour

¹⁄₂ tsp chilli flakes

3 tbsp sesame oil

1 large head of broccoli,
   cut into florets

1 orange pepper, thinly sliced

1 red chilli, seeded and finely
   sliced

1 tbsp chilli oil, to taste

1 tbsp chopped fresh
   coriander, to garnish

## method

**1** Mix the beef strips with 1 tablespoon of the sesame seeds in a small bowl. In a separate bowl, whisk together the beef stock, soy sauce, ginger, garlic, cornflour and chilli flakes.

**2** Heat 1 tablespoon of the sesame oil in a large frying pan or wok. Stir-fry the beef strips for 2–3 minutes. Remove and set aside.

**3** Discard any oil left in the pan, then wipe with kitchen paper to remove any stray sesame seeds. Heat the remaining oil, add the broccoli, orange pepper, chilli and chilli oil, if using, and stir-fry for 2–3 minutes. Stir in the beef stock mixture, cover and simmer for 2 minutes.

**4** Return the beef to the frying pan and simmer until the juices thicken, stirring occasionally. Cook for another 1–2 minutes.

**5** Sprinkle with the remaining sesame seeds. Serve garnished with chopped coriander.

# beef stir-fry

## ingredients

**SERVES 4**

2 tbsp vegetable or peanut oil

2 medium red onions, sliced
thinly

2 garlic cloves, chopped

2.5-cm/1-inch piece ginger,
cut into thin sticks

2 x 115-g/4-oz beef fillets,
sliced thinly

1 green pepper, deseeded
and sliced

150 g/5$^1$/$_2$ oz canned bamboo
shoots

115 g/4 oz beansprouts

2 tbsp Thai magic paste
(see below)

1 tbsp Thai red curry paste

handful of fresh coriander,
chopped

few sprigs Thai basil

boiled rice, to serve


thai magic paste

whole bulb of garlic, peeled

bunch of fresh coriander
leaves and roots,
roughly chopped

55 g/2 oz white peppercorns

## method

**1** To make the Thai magic paste, pulse all the ingredients briefly in a blender or food processor to form a thick paste, or pound with a pestle until well mixed. Store in the refrigerator for 3–4 days or freeze in small amounts.

**2** Heat the oil in a wok and stir-fry the onions, garlic and root ginger for 1 minute.

**3** Add the beef strips and stir-fry over high heat until browned all over.

**4** Add the vegetables and the magic and curry pastes and cook for 2–3 minutes until blended and cooked.

**5** Stir in the coriander and basil and serve immediately with rice.

# stir-fried beef with broccoli & ginger

## ingredients

SERVES 4–6

350 g/12 oz fillet steak,
  cut into thin strips
175 g/6 oz head of broccoli,
  cut into florets
2 tbsp vegetable or peanut oil
1 garlic clove, finely chopped
1 tsp finely chopped fresh
  ginger
1 small onion, finely sliced
1 tsp salt
1 tsp light soy sauce

marinade
1 tbsp light soy sauce
1 tsp sesame oil
1 tsp Shaoxing rice wine
1 tsp sugar
pinch of white pepper

## method

**1** Combine the marinade ingredients in a bowl, then mix in the beef. Cover and set aside for 1 hour, basting occasionally. Blanch the broccoli in a large saucepan of boiling water for 30 seconds. Drain and set aside.

**2** In a preheated wok or deep saucepan, heat 1 tablespoon of the oil and stir-fry the garlic, ginger and onion for 1 minute. Add the broccoli and stir-fry for a further minute. Remove from the wok and set aside.

**3** In the clean preheated wok or deep saucepan, heat the remaining oil and stir-fry the beef until it has changed colour. Return the broccoli mixture to the saucepan with the salt and light soy sauce and stir until cooked through. Serve immediately.

# stir-fried beef with beansprouts

## ingredients

**SERVES 4**

1 bunch of spring onions

2 tbsp corn oil

1 garlic clove, crushed

1 tsp finely chopped fresh root
    ginger

500 g/1 lb 2 oz lean beef fillet,
    cut into thin strips

1 large red pepper, deseeded
    and sliced

1 small fresh red chilli,
    deseeded and chopped

225 g/8 oz fresh beansprouts

1 small lemon grass stem,
    finely chopped

2 tbsp smooth peanut butter

4 tbsp coconut milk

1 tbsp rice vinegar or white
    wine vinegar

1 tbsp soy sauce

1 tsp brown sugar

250 g/9 oz medium egg
    noodles

salt and pepper

## method

**1** Thinly slice the spring onions, reserving some slices to use as a garnish.

**2** Heat the oil in a frying pan or preheated wok over high heat. Add the spring onions, garlic and ginger and stir-fry for 2–3 minutes to soften. Add the beef and continue stir-frying for 4–5 minutes, or until evenly browned.

**3** Add the pepper and stir-fry for a further 3–4 minutes. Add the chilli and beansprouts and stir-fry for 2 minutes. Mix the lemon grass, peanut butter, coconut milk, vinegar, soy sauce and sugar together in a bowl, then stir into the pan.

**4** Meanwhile, cook the egg noodles in boiling salted water for 4 minutes, or according to the packet directions. Drain and stir into the pan, tossing to mix evenly. Season to taste with salt and pepper. Sprinkle with the reserved spring onions and serve hot.

# ginger beef with yellow peppers

## ingredients

**SERVES 4**

500 g/1 lb 2 oz beef fillet,
    cut into 2.5-cm/1-inch
    cubes
2 tsp peanut oil
2 garlic cloves, crushed
2 tbsp grated fresh ginger
pinch of chilli flakes
2 yellow peppers, thinly sliced
125 g/4$^1$/$_2$ oz baby corn
175 g/6 oz mangetout
hot noodles drizzled with
    sesame oil, to serve

marinade
2 tbsp soy sauce
2 tsp peanut oil
1$^1$/$_2$ tsp caster sugar
1 tsp cornflour

## method

**1** To make the marinade, mix the soy sauce, peanut oil, sugar and cornflour in a bowl. Stir in the beef cubes, then cover with clingfilm and set aside to marinate for 30 minutes.

**2** Heat the peanut oil in a frying pan or wok over a medium heat. Add the garlic, ginger and chilli flakes and cook for 30 seconds. Stir in the yellow peppers and baby corn, and stir-fry for 2 minutes. Add the mangetout and cook for another minute.

**3** Remove the vegetables from the frying pan. Put the beef cubes and marinade into the frying pan and stir-fry for 3–4 minutes or until cooked to taste. Return the vegetables to the frying pan, mix well and cook until all the ingredients are heated through. Remove from the heat and serve over noodles.

# beef with onions & broccoli

## ingredients

**SERVES 4**

2 tbsp vegetable or peanut oil

2 tbsp Thai green curry paste

2 x 175-g/6-oz sirloin steaks,
   sliced thinly

2 onions, sliced

6 spring onions, chopped

2 shallots, chopped finely

225 g/8 oz head of broccoli,
   cut into florets

400 ml/14 fl oz coconut milk

3 kaffir lime leaves, chopped
   roughly

4 tbsp chopped fresh
   coriander

few Thai basil leaves

## method

**1** Heat the oil in a wok and stir-fry the curry paste for 1–2 minutes. Add the meat, in batches if necessary, and stir-fry until starting to brown.

**2** Add the onions, spring onions and shallots, and stir-fry for 2–3 minutes. Add the broccoli and stir-fry for 2–3 minutes.

**3** Pour in the coconut milk, add the lime leaves and bring to the boil. Simmer gently for 8–10 minutes, until the meat is tender. Stir in the coriander and basil and serve immediately.

# mussaman curry

## ingredients

**SERVES 4**

1 tbsp vegetable or peanut oil

450 g/1 lb beef topside,
    cut into cubes

2 tbsp Mussaman curry paste

2 large onions, cut into
    wedges

2 large potatoes, cut into
    chunks

400 ml/14 fl oz coconut milk

150 ml/5 fl oz water

2 cardamom pods

2 tbsp tamarind paste

2 tsp jaggery or soft light
    brown sugar

75 g/2¾ oz unsalted peanuts,
    toasted or dry-fried

1 fresh red chilli, sliced thinly

boiled rice, to serve

## method

**1** Heat the oil in a wok and cook the meat, in batches, until browned all over. Remove with a slotted spoon and set aside.

**2** Add the curry paste to the wok and stir-fry for 1–2 minutes. Add the onions and potatoes and stir-fry for 4–5 minutes, until golden brown. Remove with a slotted spoon and set aside.

**3** Pour the coconut milk into the wok with the measured water and bring to the boil. Reduce the heat and simmer for 8–10 minutes.

**4** Return the meat and cooked vegetables to the wok. Add the cardamom, tamarind paste and sugar and simmer for 15–20 minutes, until the meat is tender. Stir in the peanuts and chilli and serve with rice.

# spicy beef with potato

## ingredients

**SERVES 4**

450 g/1 lb beef fillet

2 tbsp Thai soy sauce

2 tbsp fish sauce

2 tbsp vegetable or peanut oil

3–4 coriander roots, chopped

1 tbsp crushed black
    peppercorns

2 garlic cloves, chopped

1 tbsp jaggery or soft light
    brown sugar

350 g/12 oz potatoes, diced

150 ml/5 fl oz water

bunch of spring onions,
    chopped

225 g/8 oz baby spinach
    leaves

cooked rice or noodles,
    to serve

## method

**1** Cut the beef into thick slices and place in a shallow dish. Put the soy sauce, fish sauce, 1 tablespoon of the oil, the coriander roots, peppercorns, garlic and sugar in a food processor and process to a thick paste. Scrape the paste into the dish and toss the beef to coat. Cover with clingfilm and set aside to marinate in the refrigerator for at least 3 hours, and preferably overnight.

**2** Heat the remaining oil in a wok. Lift the beef out of the marinade, reserving the marinade, and cook for 3–4 minutes on each side, until browned. Add the reserved marinade and the potatoes with the measured water and gradually bring to the boil. Simmer for 6–8 minutes, or until the potatoes are tender.

**3** Add the spring onions and spinach. Cook gently until the greens have wilted. Serve immediately with rice or noodles.

# ma po doufu

## ingredients

**SERVES 4**

450 g/1 lb tofu

2 tbsp vegetable or peanut oil

1 tsp Szechuan peppers

100 g/3$^1$/$_2$ oz minced beef

2 tbsp chilli bean sauce

1 tsp fermented black beans, rinsed and lightly mashed

100 ml/3$^1$/$_2$ fl oz hot chicken stock

pinch of sugar

1 tsp light soy sauce

pinch of salt

2 tbsp thinly sliced spring onion, cut on the diagonal

## method

**1** Cut the tofu into 2-cm/$^3$/$_4$-inch cubes and arrange in a large pan. Pour over enough boiling water to cover and set aside.

**2** In a preheated wok, heat the oil until almost smoking. Throw in the Szechuan peppers and stir until fragrant. Add the beef and stir-fry until brown and crispy.

**3** Lower the heat and add the chilli bean sauce and black beans and stir for about 30 seconds, or until the oil is richly red.

**4** Pour in the hot chicken stock and gently add the drained tofu. Season with the sugar, light soy sauce and salt. Simmer for about 5 minutes.

**5** Finally, toss in the spring onion. Transfer into 1 large or 4 individual bowls and serve.

# beef noodles with oyster sauce

## ingredients

SERVES 4

300 g/10¹/₂ oz boneless sirloin steak, thinly sliced

250 g/9 oz dried thick Chinese egg noodles

2 tbsp peanut or corn oil

225 g/8 oz fresh asparagus spears, woody ends cut off, chopped

2 large garlic cloves, finely chopped

1-cm/¹/₂-inch piece fresh ginger, peeled and finely chopped

¹/₂ red onion, thinly sliced

4 tbsp beef or vegetable stock

1¹/₂ tbsp rice wine

2–3 tbsp bottled oyster sauce

toasted sesame seeds, to garnish

marinade
1 tbsp light soy sauce
1 tsp toasted sesame oil
2 tsp rice wine

## method

1 To make the marinade, stir the ingredients together in a non-metallic bowl. Stir in the steak so all the slices are coated, then set aside to marinate for at least 15 minutes.

2 Meanwhile, boil the noodles in a saucepan of boiling water for 4 minutes, or according to the packet instructions, until soft. Drain, rinse and drain again, then set aside.

3 When you are ready to stir-fry, heat a wok or large frying pan over a high heat. Add 1 tablespoon of the oil and heat. Add the asparagus and stir-fry for 1 minute. Tip the beef and marinade into the wok, standing back because it will splutter, and continue stir-frying until the beef is cooked to your taste, about 1¹/₂ minutes for medium. Remove the beef and asparagus from the wok and set aside.

4 Heat the remaining oil and stir-fry the garlic, ginger and onion for about 1 minute, until the onion is soft. Add the stock, rice wine and oyster sauce and bring to the boil, stirring. Return the beef and asparagus to the wok, along with the noodles. Use 2 forks to mix all the ingredients together and stir around until the noodles are hot. Sprinkle with toasted sesame seeds.

# beef chow mein

## ingredients

**SERVES 4**

280 g/10 oz tenderloin steak,
  cut into slivers
225 g/8 oz dried egg noodles
2 tbsp vegetable or peanut oil
1 onion, finely sliced
1 green pepper, finely sliced
140 g/5 oz beansprouts,
  trimmed
1 tsp salt
pinch of sugar
2 tsp Shaoxing rice wine
2 tbsp light soy sauce
1 tbsp dark soy sauce
1 tbsp finely shredded spring
  onion

marinade
1 tsp light soy sauce
dash of sesame oil
$1/2$ tsp Shaoxing rice wine
pinch of white pepper

## method

**1** Combine all the marinade ingredients in a bowl and marinate the beef for at least 20 minutes.

**2** Cook the noodles according to the directions on the packet. When cooked, rinse under cold water and set aside.

**3** In a preheated wok, heat the oil and stir-fry the beef for about 1 minute, or until the meat has changed colour, then add the onion and cook for 1 minute, followed by the pepper and beansprouts. Evaporate off any water from the vegetables. Add the salt, sugar, Shaoxing and soy sauces. Stir in the noodles and toss for 1 minute. Finally, stir in the spring onion and serve.

# rice sticks with beef in black bean sauce

## ingredients

**SERVES 4–6**

225 g/8 oz rump steak, finely
   sliced
225 g/8 oz rice sticks
2–3 tbsp vegetable or
   peanut oil
1 small onion, finely sliced
1 green pepper, finely sliced
1 red pepper, finely sliced
2 tbsp black bean sauce
2–3 tbsp light soy sauce

marinade
1 tbsp dark soy sauce
1 tsp Shaoxing rice wine
$^1/_2$ tsp sugar
$^1/_2$ tsp white pepper

## method

**1** Combine all the marinade ingredients in a bowl, add the beef and marinate for at least 20 minutes.

**2** Cook the rice sticks according to the directions on the packet. When cooked, drain and set aside.

**3** In a preheated wok or deep saucepan, heat the oil and stir-fry the beef for 1 minute, or until the meat has changed colour. Drain the meat and set aside.

**4** Pour off any excess oil from the wok and stir-fry the onion and peppers for 1 minute. Add the black bean sauce and stir well, then pour in the light soy sauce. Toss the rice sticks in the vegetables and when fully incorporated, add the beef and stir until warmed through. Serve immediately.

# red-hot beef with cashew nuts

## ingredients

**SERVES 4**

500 g/1 lb 2 oz lean boneless
   beef sirloin
1 tsp vegetable oil

marinade

1 tbsp sesame seeds
1 garlic clove, chopped
1 tbsp finely chopped fresh
   root ginger
1 fresh red Thai chilli,
   chopped
2 tbsp dark soy sauce
1 tsp Thai red curry paste

to finish

1 tsp sesame oil
4 tbsp unsalted cashew nuts
1 spring onion, thickly sliced
   diagonally
cucumber slices, to garnish

## method

**1** Using a sharp knife, cut the beef into 1-cm/ 1/2-inch wide strips. Place them in a large, non-metallic bowl.

**2** To make the marinade, toast the sesame seeds in a heavy-based frying pan over medium heat for 2–3 minutes, or until golden brown, shaking the pan occasionally.

**3** Place the seeds in a mortar with the garlic, ginger and chilli and, using a pestle, grind to a smooth paste. Add the soy sauce and curry paste and mix well.

**4** Spoon the paste over the beef strips and toss to coat the meat evenly. Cover and marinate in the refrigerator for at least 2–3 hours or overnight.

**5** Heat a heavy-based frying pan or ridged griddle pan until very hot and brush with vegetable oil. Place the beef strips in the pan and cook quickly, turning frequently, until lightly browned. Remove the pan from the heat and spoon the beef into a pile on a hot serving dish.

**6** Heat the sesame oil in a small frying pan. Add the cashew nuts and quickly cook until golden. Add the spring onion and stir-fry for 30 seconds. Sprinkle the mixture on top of the beef strips, then garnish with cucumber slices and serve immediately.

# hot beef & coconut curry

## ingredients

**SERVES 4**

400 ml/14 fl oz coconut milk

2 tbsp Thai red curry paste

2 garlic cloves, crushed

500 g/1 lb 2 oz braising steak

2 fresh kaffir lime leaves,
  shredded

3 tbsp lime juice

2 tbsp Thai fish sauce

1 large fresh red chilli,
  deseeded and sliced

$1/2$ tsp ground turmeric

salt and pepper

2 tbsp chopped fresh basil
  leaves

2 tbsp chopped coriander
  leaves

shredded coconut, to garnish

freshly cooked rice, to serve

## method

**1** Place the coconut milk in a large saucepan and bring to the boil. Reduce the heat and simmer gently for 10 minutes, or until it has thickened. Stir in the curry paste and garlic and simmer for a further 5 minutes.

**2** Cut the beef into 2-cm/$3/4$-inch chunks. Add to the pan and bring to the boil, stirring constantly. Reduce the heat and add the kaffir lime leaves, lime juice, fish sauce, sliced chilli, turmeric and $1/2$ teaspoon of salt.

**3** Cover the pan and continue simmering for 20–25 minutes, or until the meat is tender, adding a little water if the sauce looks too dry.

**4** Stir in the basil and coriander and season to taste with salt and pepper. Sprinkle with shredded coconut and serve with freshly cooked rice.

# egg-fried rice with seven-spice beef

## ingredients

**SERVES 4**

225 g/8 oz long-grain white
   rice
600 ml/1 pint water
350 g/12 oz beef tenderloin
2 tbsp dark soy sauce
2 tbsp tomato ketchup
1 tbsp seven-spice seasoning
2 tbsp peanut oil
1 onion, diced
3 small carrots, diced
100 g/3$\frac{1}{2}$ oz frozen peas
2 eggs, beaten
2 tbsp cold water

## method

**1** Rinse the rice under cold running water, then drain thoroughly. Place the rice in a saucepan with the water, bring to the boil, cover and simmer for 12 minutes. Turn the cooked rice out onto a baking sheet and set aside to cool.

**2** Using a sharp knife, thinly slice the beef tenderloin and place in a large, shallow dish. Mix the soy sauce, tomato ketchup and seven-spice seasoning. Spoon over the beef and toss well to coat.

**3** Heat the peanut oil in a preheated wok. Add the beef and stir-fry for 3–4 minutes. Add the onion, carrots and peas and stir-fry for a further 2–3 minutes. Add the cooked rice to the wok and mix together.

**4** Beat the eggs with 2 tablespoons of cold water. Drizzle the egg mixture over the rice and stir-fry for 3–4 minutes or until the rice is heated through and the egg has set. Transfer the rice and beef to a warm serving bowl and serve immediately.

# singapore noodles

## ingredients

**SERVES 4**

200 g/7 oz dried rice vermicelli
    noodles
1 tbsp mild, medium or hot
    curry paste, to taste
1 tsp ground turmeric
6 tbsp water
2 tbsp peanut or corn oil
1/2 onion, very thinly sliced
2 large garlic cloves, thinly
    sliced
85 g/3 oz head of broccoli,
    cut into very small florets
85 g/3 oz green beans,
    trimmed, and cut into
    2.5-cm/1-inch pieces
85 g/3 oz pork fillet, cut in
    half lengthways, and then
    into thin strips, or skinless,
    boneless chicken breast,
    thinly sliced
85 g/3 oz small cooked peeled
    prawns, thawed if frozen
55 g/2 oz Chinese cabbage
    or romaine lettuce, thinly
    shredded
1/4 Thai chilli, or to taste,
    deseeded and thinly sliced
2 spring onions, light green
    parts only, thinly shredded
fresh coriander, to garnish

## method

**1** Soak the noodles in enough lukewarm water to cover for 20 minutes, or according to the packet instructions, until soft. Drain and set aside until required. While the noodles are soaking, put the curry paste and turmeric in a small bowl and stir in 4 tablespoons of the water, then set aside.

**2** Heat a wok or large frying pan over a high heat. Add the oil and heat until it shimmers. Add the onion and garlic and stir-fry for 1 minute, or until the onion softens. Add the broccoli florets and beans to the wok with the remaining 2 tablespoons of water and continue stir-frying for 2 minutes. Add the pork and stir-fry for 1 more minute. Add the prawns, cabbage and chilli to the wok and continue stir-frying for a further 2 minutes, until the meat is cooked through and the vegetables are tender, but still with a little bite. Scoop out of the wok and keep warm.

**3** Add the spring onions, noodles and curry paste mixture to the wok. Use 2 forks to mix the noodles and onions together, and continue stir-frying for about 2 minutes, until the noodles are hot and have picked up a dark golden colour from the turmeric. Return the other ingredients to the wok and continue stir-frying and mixing for 1 minute. Garnish with fresh coriander.

# pork lo mein

## ingredients

**SERVES 4–6**

175 g/6 oz boneless lean pork, shredded

225 g/8 oz egg noodles

1¹/₂ tbsp vegetable or peanut oil

2 tsp finely chopped garlic

1 tsp finely chopped fresh ginger

1 carrot, julienned

225 g/8 oz finely sliced mushrooms

1 green pepper, thinly sliced

1 tsp salt

125 ml/4 fl oz hot chicken stock

200 g/7 oz beansprouts, trimmed

2 tbsp finely chopped spring onions

### marinade

1 tsp light soy sauce

dash of sesame oil

pinch of white pepper

## method

**1** Combine all the marinade ingredients in a bowl, add the pork and marinate for at least 20 minutes.

**2** Cook the noodles according to the packet instructions. When cooked, drain and set aside.

**3** In a preheated wok or deep saucepan, heat 1 teaspoon of the oil and stir-fry the pork until it has changed colour. Remove and set aside.

**4** In the clean wok or saucepan, heat the remaining oil and stir-fry the garlic and ginger until fragrant. Add the carrot and cook for 1 minute, then add the mushrooms and cook for a further 1 minute. Toss in the pepper and cook for 1 minute more. Add the pork, salt and stock and heat through. Finally, toss in the noodles, followed by the beansprouts, and stir well. Sprinkle with the spring onions and serve.

# chirashi sushi with soy-glazed steak

## ingredients

**SERVES 4**

8 dried shiitake mushrooms

5-cm/2-inch piece of daikon (long white radish), peeled

5-cm/2-inch piece of carrot, peeled

1 tbsp soy sauce

1 tsp mirin

1 tsp brown sugar

200 g/7 oz tenderloin steak, trimmed

1 quantity freshly cooked sushi rice

2 tsp wasabi paste

1 sheet of toasted nori, cut into strips

pickled ginger, to serve

## method

**1** Cover the mushrooms with boiling water and allow to soak for 20 minutes, then simmer them in the same liquid for 3 minutes. Lift them out and squeeze them dry. Chop 4 mushrooms finely and halve the rest.

**2** Shred the daikon and carrot using the finest setting on a mandolin or a very sharp knife. If you are using a knife, then cut the daikon and carrot into long, thin slices and cut each slice along its length as finely as you can. Rinse, drain and refrigerate.

**3** Preheat the grill to its highest setting. Mix together the soy sauce, mirin and brown sugar, then brush the mixture all over the steak. Grill the coated steak for 3 minutes on each side. Let it rest for a minute, then cut into strips.

**4** Mix the sushi rice with the chopped shiitake mushrooms. Divide the mushroom rice between 4 serving bowls and arrange the grilled steak and halved mushrooms on top. Add a neat pile of shredded daikon and carrot to each bowl, together with 1/2 teaspoon of the wasabi. Garnish each bowl with nori strips and serve with pickled ginger on the side.

# spicy szechuan pork

## ingredients

**SERVES 4**

280 g/10 oz pork belly, thinly
    sliced
1 tbsp vegetable or peanut oil
1 tbsp chilli bean sauce
1 tbsp fermented black beans,
    rinsed and lightly mashed
1 tsp sweet red bean paste
    (optional)
1 green pepper, finely sliced
1 red pepper, finely sliced
1 tsp sugar
1 tsp dark soy sauce
pinch of white pepper

## method

**1** Bring a saucepan of water to the boil and place the pork slices in the pan, then cover and simmer for about 20 minutes, skimming occasionally. Let the pork cool and rest before slicing thinly.

**2** In a preheated wok or deep saucepan, heat the oil and stir-fry the pork slices until they begin to shrink. Stir in the chilli bean sauce, then add the black beans and the red bean paste, if using. Finally, toss in the peppers and the remaining ingredients and stir-fry for a couple of minutes.

# szechuan-style pork & pepper

## ingredients

**SERVES 4**

500 g/1 lb 2 oz pork fillet, cubed

2 tbsp cornflour

3 tbsp soy sauce

1 tbsp white wine vinegar

250 ml/9 fl oz water

2 tbsp peanut oil

2 leeks, thinly sliced

1 red pepper, cut into thin strips

1 courgette, cut into thin strips

1 carrot, cut into thin strips

pinch of salt

freshly cooked white and wild rice, to serve

marinade

1 tbsp soy sauce

pinch of chilli flakes

## method

**1** To make the marinade, mix the soy sauce and chilli flakes in a bowl. Add the pork cubes and toss to coat. Cover with clingfilm and set aside for 30 minutes.

**2** Combine the cornflour, soy sauce and white wine vinegar in a small bowl. Stir in the water gradually, then set aside.

**3** Heat 1 tablespoon of the oil in a wok or frying pan. Add the pork and marinade mixture and stir-fry for 2–3 minutes. Remove the pork from the frying pan with a slotted spoon and set aside.

**4** Heat the remaining oil in the frying pan, add the leeks and red pepper and stir-fry for 2 minutes. Then add the courgette, carrot and salt and stir-fry for a further 2 minutes.

**5** Stir in the pork and the cornflour mixture and bring to the boil, stirring constantly until the sauce thickens. Remove from the heat and serve immediately with freshly cooked white and wild rice.

# ants climbing a tree

## ingredients

**SERVES 4**

250 g/9 oz dried thick rice
noodles

1 tbsp cornflour

3 tbsp soy sauce

1½ tbsp rice wine

1½ tsp sugar

1½ tsp toasted sesame oil

350 g/12 oz lean fresh
pork mince

1½ tbsp peanut or toasted
sesame oil

2 large garlic cloves, finely
chopped

1 large fresh red chilli,
or to taste, deseeded
and thinly sliced

3 spring onions, finely
chopped

finely chopped fresh coriander
or parsley, to garnish

## method

**1** Soak the rice noodles in enough lukewarm water to cover for 20 minutes, until soft, or cook according to the packet instructions. Drain well and set aside.

**2** Meanwhile, put the cornflour in another large bowl, then stir in the soy sauce, rice wine, sugar and sesame oil, stirring so that no lumps form. Add the pork mince and use your hands to toss the ingredients together without squeezing the pork; set aside to marinate for 10 minutes.

**3** Heat a wok or large frying pan over a high heat. Add the oil and heat until it shimmers. Add the garlic, chilli and spring onions and stir around for about 30 seconds. Tip in the pork mince together with any marinade left in the bowl and stir-fry for about 5 minutes, or until the pork is no longer pink. Add the noodles and use 2 forks to mix together. Sprinkle with the chopped herbs and serve.

# sour-&-spicy pork

## ingredients

**SERVES 4**

55 g/2 oz dried Chinese
   cloud ear mushrooms,
   soaked in boiling water
   for 20 minutes
100 g/3$^{1}/_{2}$ oz baby corn,
   halved lengthways
2 tbsp honey
1 tbsp tamarind paste
4 tbsp boiling water
2 tbsp dark soy sauce
1 tbsp rice vinegar
2 tbsp peanut or corn oil
1 large garlic clove, very finely
   chopped
1-cm/ $^{1}/_{2}$-inch piece fresh
   ginger, peeled and very
   finely chopped
$^{1}/_{2}$ tsp dried red pepper flakes,
   or to taste
350 g/12 oz pork fillet, thinly
   sliced
4 spring onions, thickly sliced
   diagonally
1 green pepper, cored,
   deseeded and sliced
250 g/9 oz fresh Hokkien
   noodles
chopped fresh coriander,
   to garnish

## method

**1** Drain the mushrooms well, then cut off and discard any thick stems, and slice the cups if they are large. Meanwhile, bring a large saucepan of lightly salted water to the boil, add the baby corn and blanch for 3 minutes. Drain the corn and run them under cold running water to stop the cooking, then set aside.

**2** Put the honey and tamarind paste in a small bowl and stir in the water, stirring until the paste dissolves. Then stir in the soy sauce and rice vinegar and set aside.

**3** Heat a wok or large frying pan over a high heat. Add 1 tablespoon of the oil and heat until it shimmers. Add the garlic, ginger and red pepper flakes and stir-fry for about 30 seconds. Add the pork and continue stir-frying for 2 minutes.

**4** Add the remaining oil to the wok and heat. Add the spring onions, pepper, mushrooms and baby corn, along with the tamarind mixture, and stir-fry for a further 2–3 minutes, until the pork is cooked through and the vegetables are tender, but still firm to the bite. Add the noodles and use 2 forks to mix all the ingredients together. When the noodles and sauce are hot, sprinkle with coriander.

# hoisin pork with garlic noodles

## ingredients

**SERVES 4**

250 g/9 oz dried thick Chinese egg noodles, or Chinese wholemeal egg noodles

450 g/1 lb pork fillet, thinly sliced

1 tsp sugar

1 tbsp peanut or corn oil

4 tbsp rice vinegar

4 tbsp white wine vinegar

4 tbsp bottled hoisin sauce

2 spring onions, sliced diagonally

about 2 tbsp garlic-flavoured corn oil

2 large garlic cloves, thinly sliced

## method

**1** Cook the noodles in a saucepan of boiling water for 3 minutes, or according to the packet instructions, until soft. Drain well, rinse under cold water to stop the cooking and drain again, then set aside.

**2** Sprinkle the pork slices with the sugar and use your hands to toss together. Heat a wok or large frying pan over a high heat. Add the oil and heat until it shimmers. Add the pork and stir-fry for about 3 minutes, until the pork is cooked through and is no longer pink. Use a slotted spoon to remove the pork from the wok and keep warm. Add both vinegars to the wok and boil until they are reduced to about 5 tablespoons. Pour in the hoisin sauce with the spring onions and let bubble until reduced by half. Add to the pork and stir together. Remove and set aside.

**3** Quickly wipe out the wok and reheat. Add the garlic-flavoured oil and heat until it shimmers. Add the garlic slices and stir around for about 30 seconds, until they are golden and crisp, then use a slotted spoon to scoop them out of the wok and set aside.

**4** Add the noodles to the wok and stir to warm through. Divide the noodles between 4 plates, top with the pork and onion mixture and sprinkle with cooked garlic slices.

# katsudon

## ingredients

**SERVES 4**

4 tbsp plain flour

1 egg, lightly beaten

115 g/4 oz Tonkatsu (panko) breadcrumbs

4 pork chops, about 150 g/ 5$^{1}$/$_{2}$ oz each, bones removed

oil, for pan-frying

600 ml/1 pint dashi stock

4 tbsp shoyu (Japanese soy sauce)

2 tbsp mirin

1 onion, sliced

4 eggs

600 g/1 lb 5 oz cooked Japanese short-grain rice

## method

**1** Put the flour, egg and breadcrumbs separately into 3 shallow bowls large enough to fit a pork chop. Roll a rolling pin over each chop to thin it a little.

**2** Dip each chop first in the flour, then in the egg and finally in the breadcrumbs to coat. Cover with clingfilm and chill in the refrigerator for 10 minutes, then dip again in the egg and the breadcrumbs.

**3** Preheat a wok over high heat. Add oil to a depth of about 2 cm/3/4 inch and heat until very hot. Add the chops, one at a time, reduce the heat to medium and cook for 4 minutes on each side, or until the pork is cooked through and the breadcrumbs are golden. Remove and slice.

**4** Meanwhile, put the stock, soy sauce and mirin in a pan and bring to a simmer. Add the onion and simmer for 5 minutes. Beat the eggs in a bowl, then pour over the onions in the stock. Cover and cook for 1 minute.

**5** Divide the rice between 4 bowls. Lay the pork slices on top, then ladle some of the egg, onion and stock over the pork and rice. Serve immediately.

# fried rice with pork & prawns

## ingredients

**SERVES 4**

3 tsp vegetable or peanut oil

1 egg, lightly beaten

100 g/3$^1$/$_2$ oz raw prawns, peeled, deveined and cut into 2 pieces

100 g/3$^1$/$_2$ oz cha siu (roast honeyed pork), finely chopped

2 tbsp finely chopped spring onions

200 g/7 oz cooked rice, chilled

1 tsp salt

## method

**1** In a preheated wok or deep saucepan, heat 1 teaspoon of the oil and pour in the egg. Cook until scrambled. Remove and set aside.

**2** Add the remaining oil and stir-fry the prawns, cha siu and spring onions for about 2 minutes. Add the rice and salt, breaking up the rice into grains, and cook for a further 2 minutes. Finally, stir in the cooked egg. Serve immediately.

# red curry pork with peppers

## ingredients

**SERVES 4**

2 tbsp vegetable or peanut oil

1 onion, coarsely chopped

2 garlic cloves, chopped

450 g/1 lb pork fillet, sliced
thickly

1 red pepper, deseeded and
cut into squares

175 g/6 oz mushrooms,
quartered

2 tbsp Thai red curry paste

115 g/4 oz block creamed
coconut, chopped

300 ml/10 fl oz pork or
vegetable stock

2 tbsp Thai soy sauce

4 tomatoes, peeled, deseeded
and chopped

handful of fresh coriander,
chopped

boiled noodles or rice, to serve

## method

**1** Heat the oil in a wok or large frying pan and sauté the onion and garlic for 1–2 minutes, until they are softened but not browned.

**2** Add the pork slices and stir-fry for 2–3 minutes until browned all over. Add the pepper, mushrooms and curry paste.

**3** Dissolve the coconut in the hot stock and add to the wok with the soy sauce. Bring to the boil and simmer for 4–5 minutes until the liquid has reduced and thickened.

**4** Add the tomatoes and coriander and cook for 1–2 minutes before serving with noodles or rice.

# pad thai

## ingredients

**SERVES 4**

225 g/8 oz thick rice-stick
noodles

2 tbsp vegetable or peanut oil

2 garlic cloves, chopped

2 fresh red chillies, deseeded
and chopped

175 g/6 oz pork fillet, sliced
thinly

115 g/4 oz uncooked prawns,
shelled and chopped

8 fresh Chinese chives,
chopped

2 tbsp fish sauce

juice of 1 lime

2 tsp jaggery or soft light
brown sugar

2 eggs, beaten

115 g/4 oz beansprouts

4 tbsp chopped fresh
coriander

115 g/4 oz unsalted peanuts,
chopped, plus extra
to serve

crispy fried onions, to serve

## method

**1** Soak the noodles in warm water for
10 minutes, drain well and set aside.

**2** Heat the oil in a wok and stir-fry the garlic,
chillies and pork for 2–3 minutes. Add the
prawns and stir-fry for a further 2–3 minutes.

**3** Add the chives and noodles, then cover and
cook for 1–2 minutes. Add the fish sauce, lime
juice, sugar and eggs. Cook, stirring and tossing
constantly to mix in the eggs.

**4** Stir in the beansprouts, coriander and
peanuts and serve with small dishes of crispy
fried onions and extra chopped peanuts.

# pork with vegetables

## ingredients

**SERVES 4**

8 tbsp vegetable or peanut oil

115 g/4 oz rice vermicelli
noodles

4 belly pork strips, sliced
thickly

1 red onion, sliced

2 garlic cloves, chopped

2.5-cm/1-inch piece fresh root
ginger, sliced thinly

1 large fresh red chilli,
deseeded and chopped

115 g/4 oz baby corn,
halved lengthways

1 red pepper, deseeded and
sliced

175 g/6 oz head of broccoli,
cut into florets

150 g/5$^1$/$_2$ oz jar black bean
sauce

115 g/4 oz beansprouts

## method

**1** Heat the oil in a wok and cook the rice noodles, in batches, for 15–20 seconds, until they puff up. Remove with a slotted spoon, drain on kitchen paper and set aside.

**2** Pour off all but 2 tablespoons of the oil and stir-fry the pork, onion, garlic, ginger and chilli for 4–5 minutes, or until the meat has browned.

**3** Add the corn, red pepper and broccoli and stir-fry for 3–4 minutes, until the vegetables are just tender. Stir in the black bean sauce and beansprouts, then cook for a further 2–3 minutes. Serve immediately, topped with the crispy noodles.

# pork with peppers

## ingredients

**SERVES 4**

1 tbsp vegetable or peanut oil

1 tbsp chilli oil

450 g/1 lb pork fillet, sliced
    thinly

2 tbsp green chilli sauce

6 spring onions, sliced

2.5-cm/1-inch piece fresh
    ginger, sliced thinly

1 red pepper, deseeded and
    sliced

1 yellow pepper, deseeded
    and sliced

1 orange pepper, deseeded
    and sliced

1 tbsp fish sauce

2 tbsp Thai soy sauce

juice of $1/2$ lime

4 tbsp chopped fresh parsley

cooked flat rice noodles,
    to serve

## method

**1** Heat both the oils in a wok. Add the pork, in batches, and stir-fry until browned all over. Remove with a slotted spoon and set aside.

**2** Add the chilli sauce, spring onions and ginger to the wok and stir-fry for 1–2 minutes. Add the peppers and stir-fry for 2–3 minutes.

**3** Return the meat to the wok, stir well and add the fish sauce, soy sauce and lime juice. Cook for a further 1–2 minutes, then stir in the parsley and serve with flat rice noodles.

# spicy fried minced pork

## ingredients

**SERVES 4**

2 tbsp corn oil

2 garlic cloves, finely chopped

3 shallots, finely chopped

2.5-cm/1-inch piece fresh
    ginger, finely chopped

500 g/1 lb 2 oz minced
    lean pork

2 tbsp Thai fish sauce

1 tbsp dark soy sauce

1 tbsp Thai red curry paste

4 dried kaffir lime leaves,
    crumbled

4 plum tomatoes, chopped

3 tbsp chopped coriander

salt and pepper

freshly cooked fine egg
    noodles, to serve

coriander sprigs and spring
    onion tassels, to garnish

## method

**1** Heat the oil in a large frying pan or preheated wok over medium heat. Add the garlic, shallots and ginger and stir-fry for 2 minutes. Stir in the pork and continue stir-frying until golden brown.

**2** Stir in the fish sauce, soy sauce, curry paste and lime leaves and stir-fry for a further 1–2 minutes over high heat.

**3** Add the chopped tomatoes and cook for a further 5–6 minutes, stirring occasionally. Stir in the chopped coriander and season to taste with salt and pepper.

**4** Serve hot, spooned onto freshly cooked fine egg noodles, garnished with coriander sprigs and spring onion tassels.

# five-spice crispy pork with egg-fried rice

## ingredients

**SERVES 4**

275 g/9¹/₂ oz long-grain
　　white rice
600 ml/1 pint cold water
salt and pepper
350 g/12 oz pork tenderloin
2 tsp Chinese five-spice
　　powder
4 tbsp cornflour
3 extra-large eggs
2 tbsp raw brown sugar
2 tbsp corn oil
1 onion, chopped
2 garlic cloves, crushed
1 large carrot, diced
1 red pepper, deseeded and
　　diced
100 g/3¹/₂ oz peas
1 tbsp butter

## method

**1** Rinse the rice in a sieve under cold running water. Place in a large saucepan, then add the cold water and a pinch of salt. Bring to the boil, cover, then reduce the heat and simmer for about 9 minutes or until all of the liquid has been absorbed and the rice is tender.

**2** Meanwhile, slice the pork into very thin, even-sized pieces, using a sharp knife or meat cleaver. Set aside.

**3** Stir together the Chinese five-spice powder, cornflour, 1 egg and the raw brown sugar. Toss the pork in the mixture until coated.

**4** Heat the oil in a preheated wok or frying pan. Add the pork and cook over high heat until the pork is cooked through and crispy. Remove the pork from the wok or frying pan with a slotted spoon and keep warm.

**5** Add the onion, garlic, carrot, pepper and peas to the wok or frying pan and stir-fry for 5 minutes. Return the pork to the wok, together with the cooked rice, and stir-fry for 5 minutes.

**6** Heat the butter in a frying pan. Beat the remaining eggs, add to the frying pan, and cook until set. Turn out onto a clean board and slice thinly. Toss the strips of egg into the rice mixture and serve immediately.

# spareribs in a sweet-&-sour sauce

## ingredients

**SERVES 4**

450 g/1 lb spareribs, cut into
    bite-size pieces (you or
    your butcher can cut ribs
    into pieces with a cleaver)
vegetable or peanut oil,
    for deep-frying

**marinade**

2 tsp light soy sauce
$1/2$ tsp salt
pinch of white pepper

**sauce**

3 tbsp white rice vinegar
2 tbsp sugar
1 tbsp light soy sauce
1 tbsp tomato ketchup
$1^1/2$ tbsp vegetable or
    peanut oil
1 green pepper, roughly
    chopped
1 small onion, roughly
    chopped
1 small carrot, finely sliced
$1/2$ tsp finely chopped garlic
$1/2$ tsp finely chopped ginger
100 g/$3^1/2$ oz pineapple
    chunks

## method

**1** Combine the marinade ingredients in a bowl with the pork and marinate for at least 20 minutes.

**2** Heat enough oil for deep-frying in a wok or deep-fat fryer until it reaches 180–190°C/ 350–375°F, or until a cube of bread browns in 30 seconds. Deep-fry the spareribs for 8 minutes. Drain and set aside.

**3** To prepare the sauce, first mix together the vinegar, sugar, light soy sauce and ketchup. Set aside.

**4** In a preheated wok, heat 1 tablespoon of the oil and stir-fry the pepper, onion and carrot for 2 minutes. Remove and set aside.

**5** In the clean preheated wok, heat the remaining oil and stir-fry the garlic and ginger until fragrant. Add the vinegar mixture. Bring back to the boil and add the pineapple chunks. Finally add the spareribs and the pepper, onion and carrot. Stir until warmed through and serve immediately.

# xinjiang rice pot with lamb

## ingredients

**SERVES 6–8**

2 tbsp vegetable or peanut oil

300 g/10$^1$/$_2$ oz lamb or
   mutton, cut into bite-sized
   cubes

2 carrots, roughly chopped

2 onions, roughly chopped

1 tsp salt

1 tsp ground ginger

1 tsp Szechuan peppers,
   lightly roasted and lightly
   crushed

450 g/1 lb short- or medium-
   grain rice

850 ml/1$^1$/$_2$ pints water

## method

**1** In a large casserole, heat the oil and stir-fry the meat for 1–2 minutes, or until the pieces are sealed on all sides. Add the carrots and onions and stir-fry until the vegetables are beginning to soften. Add the salt, ginger and Szechuan peppers and mix well.

**2** Finally, add the rice and water and bring to the boil. Cover the pan and cook over a low heat for 30 minutes, or until the rice has absorbed all the water. Serve alone or as part of a meal.

# xinjiang lamb casserole

## ingredients

**SERVES 5–6**

1–2 tbsp vegetable or
    peanut oil
400 g/14 oz lamb or mutton,
    cut into bite-sized cubes
1 onion, roughly chopped
1 green pepper, roughly
    chopped
1 carrot, roughly chopped
1 turnip, roughly chopped
2 tomatoes, roughly chopped
2.5-cm/1-inch piece of fresh
    ginger, finely sliced
300 ml/10 fl oz water
1 tsp salt

## method

**1** In a preheated wok or deep saucepan, heat the oil and stir-fry the lamb for 1–2 minutes, or until the meat is sealed on all sides.

**2** Transfer the meat to a large casserole and add all the other ingredients. Bring to the boil, then cover and simmer over a low heat for 35 minutes.

# red lamb curry

## ingredients

**SERVES 4**

2 tbsp vegetable oil

1 large onion, sliced

2 garlic cloves, crushed

500 g/1 lb 2 oz lean boneless
    leg of lamb, cut into 3-cm/
    1¼ -inch cubes

2 tbsp Thai red curry paste

150 ml/5 fl oz coconut milk

1 tbsp brown sugar

1 large red pepper, deseeded
    and thickly sliced

150 ml/5 fl oz lamb or beef
    stock

1 tbsp Thai fish sauce

2 tbsp lime juice

225 g/8 oz canned water
    chestnuts, drained

2 tbsp chopped coriander

2 tbsp chopped fresh basil

salt and pepper

fresh basil leaves, to garnish

freshly cooked jasmine rice,
    to serve

## method

**1** Heat the oil in a large frying pan or preheated wok over high heat. Add the onion and garlic and stir-fry for 2–3 minutes to soften. Add the meat and stir-fry the mixture quickly until lightly browned.

**2** Stir in the curry paste and cook for a few seconds, then add the coconut milk and sugar and bring to the boil. Reduce the heat and simmer for 15 minutes, stirring occasionally.

**3** Stir in the pepper, stock, fish sauce and lime juice, then cover and simmer for a further 15 minutes, or until the meat is tender.

**4** Add the water chestnuts, coriander and basil and season to taste with salt and pepper. Transfer to serving plates, then garnish with basil leaves and serve with jasmine rice.

# lamb with lime leaves

## ingredients

**SERVES 4**

2 fresh red Thai chillies

2 tbsp peanut oil

2 garlic cloves, crushed

4 shallots, chopped

2 lemon grass stems, sliced

6 fresh kaffir lime leaves

1 tbsp tamarind paste

2 tbsp palm sugar

450 g/1 lb lean boneless lamb
(leg or loin fillet)

300 ml/10 fl oz coconut milk

175 g/6 oz cherry tomatoes,
halved

1 tbsp chopped coriander

freshly cooked Thai fragrant
rice, to serve

## method

**1** Using a sharp knife, deseed and very finely chop the chillies. Reserve until required.

**2** Heat the oil in a large, preheated wok. Add the garlic, shallots, lemon grass, lime leaves, tamarind paste, sugar and chillies to the wok and stir-fry for 2 minutes.

**3** Using a sharp knife, cut the lamb into thin strips or cubes.

**4** Add the lamb to the wok and stir-fry for 5 minutes, tossing well so that the lamb is evenly coated in the spice mixture.

**5** Pour the coconut milk into the wok and bring to the boil. Reduce the heat and simmer for 20 minutes.

**6** Add the cherry tomatoes and chopped coriander to the wok and simmer for 5 minutes. Transfer to serving plates and serve hot with fragrant rice.

# stir-fried lamb with mint

## ingredients

**SERVES 4**

2 tbsp vegetable oil

2 garlic cloves, finely sliced

2 fresh red chillies, deseeded
and cut into thin strips

1 onion, thinly sliced

1 1/2 tbsp Madras curry paste

500 g/1 lb 2 oz lamb fillet,
cut into thin strips

225 g/8 oz canned baby corn
cobs, drained

4 spring onions, finely
chopped

55 g/2 oz fresh mint leaves,
coarsely shredded

1 tbsp Thai fish sauce

freshly cooked rice, to serve

## method

**1** Heat half the oil in a preheated wok or large frying pan. Add the garlic and chillies and cook until soft. Remove and reserve. Add the onion and cook for 5 minutes, or until soft. Remove and reserve.

**2** Heat the remaining oil in the wok. Add the curry paste and cook for 1 minute. Add the lamb, in batches if necessary, and cook for 5–8 minutes, or until cooked through and tender.

**3** Return the onion to the wok with the baby corn cobs, spring onions, mint and fish sauce. Cook until heated through. Sprinkle the garlic and chillies over and serve with rice.

# shredded chilli chicken pouches

## ingredients

**MAKES 8 PIECES**

4 sheets of abura-age
   (deep-fried tofu)
175 ml/6 fl oz dashi stock
3 tbsp Japanese soy sauce
2 tbsp caster sugar
1 tbsp sake
1 skinless, boneless chicken
   breast, about 150 g/5½ oz
1 tbsp vegetable oil
1 tsp red chilli flakes
2 tbsp pine nuts, toasted
1 tbsp chopped flat-leaf
   parsley
¼ quantity freshly cooked
   sushi rice

## method

**1** Put the tofu in a bowl and pour boiling water over it to remove any excess oil, then drain and cool. Cut each piece in half and gently open out each half into a bag.

**2** Place the dashi stock, soy sauce, sugar and sake in a pan, stir and bring to the boil. Add the tofu bags and simmer for 10–15 minutes, until almost all the liquid has been absorbed. Remove from the heat, drain and cool. Press any remaining liquid out of the bags with a clean tea towel (the bags should be moist but not wet).

**3** While the bags are simmering, cut the chicken into thin strips. Heat the oil in a wok or large frying pan, then add the chilli flakes. Heat for a few seconds, then add the chicken strips. Cook for 3–4 minutes, until the chicken is cooked through. Drain on kitchen paper and then chop very finely. Allow to cool.

**4** Gently stir the chilli chicken, toasted pine nuts and parsley into the sushi rice. Fill the seasoned tofu bags with the rice mixture and fold over the tops to enclose them. Serve them at room temperature.

# thai-style chicken chunks

## ingredients

**SERVES 4**

4 skinless, boneless chicken
    breasts, cut into small
    chunks
freshly cooked jasmine rice,
    to serve
chopped fresh coriander,
    to garnish

marinade

1 red chilli and 1 green chilli,
    deseeded and finely
    chopped
2 garlic cloves, chopped
50 g/1$^3$/4 oz chopped fresh
    coriander
1 tbsp finely chopped fresh
    lemon grass
$^1$/2 tsp ground turmeric
$^1$/2 tsp garam masala
2 tsp brown sugar
2 tbsp Thai fish sauce
1 tbsp lime juice
salt and pepper

## method

**1** To make the marinade, put the red and green chillies, garlic, coriander and lemon grass into a food processor and process until coarsely chopped. Add the turmeric, garam masala, sugar, fish sauce and lime juice, season to taste with salt and pepper and blend until smooth.

**2** Put the chicken chunks into a non-metallic (glass or ceramic) bowl, which will not react with acid. Pour over enough marinade to cover the chicken, then cover with clingfilm and chill for at least 2$^1$/2 hours. Cover the remaining marinade with clingfilm and chill until the chicken is ready.

**3** When the chicken chunks are thoroughly marinated, lift them out and barbecue them over hot coals for 20 minutes, or until cooked right through, turning them frequently and basting with the remaining marinade. Arrange the chicken on serving plates with some freshly cooked jasmine rice. Garnish with chopped fresh coriander and serve.

# gingered chicken kebabs

## ingredients

**SERVES 4**

3 skinless, boneless chicken
   breasts, cut into cubes

juice of 1 lime

2.5-cm/1-inch piece fresh
   ginger, peeled and
   chopped

1 fresh red chilli, deseeded
   and sliced

2 tbsp vegetable or peanut oil

1 onion, sliced

2 garlic cloves, chopped

1 aubergine, cut into chunks

2 courgettes, cut into thick
   slices

1 red pepper, deseeded and
   cut into squares

2 tbsp Thai red curry paste

2 tbsp Thai soy sauce

1 tsp jaggery or soft light
   brown sugar

boiled rice, with chopped fresh
   coriander, to serve

## method

**1** Put the chicken cubes in a shallow, non-metallic dish. Mix the lime, ginger and chilli together and pour over the chicken pieces. Stir gently to coat. Cover and chill for at least 3 hours to marinate.

**2** Thread the chicken pieces onto soaked wooden skewers and cook under a hot grill for 3–4 minutes, turning often, until cooked through.

**3** Meanwhile, heat the oil in a wok or large frying pan and sauté the onion and garlic for 1–2 minutes, until softened but not browned. Add the aubergine, courgettes and pepper and cook for 3–4 minutes, until cooked but still firm. Add the curry paste, soy sauce and sugar and cook for 1 minute.

**4** Serve the vegetables and kebabs hot with boiled rice, stirred through with chopped coriander.

# minced chicken skewers

## ingredients

### SERVES 4

450 g/1 lb minced chicken

1 onion, chopped finely

1 fresh red chilli, deseeded
and chopped

2 tbsp Thai red curry paste

1 tsp jaggery or soft light
brown sugar

1 tsp ground coriander

1 tsp ground cumin

1 egg white

8 lemon grass stalks

boiled rice with chopped
spring onion, to serve

## method

**1** Combine the chicken, onion, chilli, curry paste and sugar in a bowl and stir well to make a thick paste. Stir in the ground coriander, cumin and egg white and mix again.

**2** Divide the mixture into 8 equal portions and squeeze them around each of the lemon grass stalks. Arrange on a griddle pan and cook under high heat, turning frequently, until browned and cooked through. Serve hot with the rice with the spring onion stirred through it.

374 meat & poultry

# chirashi sushi with teriyaki chicken

## ingredients

**SERVES 4**

4 skinless, boneless chicken
    breasts, weighing about
    150 g/5$^1$/$_2$ oz each
1 tbsp vegetable oil
1 quantity freshly cooked
    sushi rice
finely chopped spring onion,
    green parts only, and sticks
    of cucumber, to garnish
sweet chilli sauce, to serve

teriyaki marinade
4 tbsp Japanese soy sauce
2 tbsp mirin
2 tbsp sake
2 tsp caster sugar
1 tsp shredded fresh ginger
    (optional)
1 garlic clove, crushed
    (optional)

## method

**1** Combine all the ingredients for the marinade in a bowl that is large enough to take the chicken as well. Add the chicken and turn to coat. Cover and marinate in the refrigerator for 30 minutes.

**2** Heat the oil in a frying pan. Remove the chicken from the marinade, add to the frying pan and cook for 4 minutes. Turn over, brush with marinade and cook for another 4–6 minutes, or until the chicken is tender and the juices run clear when a skewer is inserted into the thickest part of the meat. Once you have brushed on the marinade, do not add any more during the cooking process.

**3** Transfer the cooked chicken to a chopping board and cut into thin diagonal slices, holding your knife at a 45° angle to the board.

**4** Divide the rice between 4 serving bowls. Top with the sliced chicken and garnish with chopped spring onion and cucumber sticks. Serve with the sweet chilli sauce.

# chicken fried rice

## ingredients

**SERVES 4**

$^1/_2$ tbsp sesame oil

6 shallots, peeled and cut
    into quarters

450 g/1 lb cooked, cubed
    chicken meat

3 tbsp soy sauce

2 carrots, diced

1 celery stick, diced

1 red pepper, diced

175 g/6 oz fresh peas

100 g/3$^1/_2$ oz canned
    sweetcorn

275 g/9$^3/_4$ oz cooked
    long-grain rice

2 large eggs, scrambled

## method

**1** Heat the oil in a large frying pan over a medium heat. Add the shallots and fry until soft, then add the chicken and 2 tablespoons of the soy sauce and stir-fry for 5–6 minutes.

**2** Stir in the carrots, celery, red pepper, peas and sweetcorn and stir-fry for a further 5 minutes. Add the rice and stir thoroughly.

**3** Finally, stir in the scrambled eggs and the remaining tablespoon of soy sauce. Serve immediately.

# sweet-&-sour chicken

## ingredients

**SERVES 4–6**

450 g/1 lb lean chicken meat, cubed

5 tbsp vegetable or peanut oil

1/2 tsp minced garlic

1/2 tsp finely chopped fresh ginger

1 green pepper, roughly chopped

1 onion, roughly chopped

1 carrot, finely sliced

1 tsp sesame oil

1 tbsp finely chopped spring onions

m a r i n a d e

2 tsp light soy sauce

1 tsp Shaoxing rice wine

pinch of white pepper

1/2 tsp salt

dash of sesame oil

s a u c e

8 tbsp rice vinegar

4 tbsp sugar

2 tsp light soy sauce

6 tbsp tomato ketchup

## method

**1** Place all the marinade ingredients in a bowl and marinate the chicken cubes for at least 20 minutes.

**2** To prepare the sauce, heat the vinegar in a saucepan and add the sugar, light soy sauce and tomato ketchup. Stir to dissolve the sugar, then set aside.

**3** In a preheated wok or deep saucepan, heat 3 tablespoons of the oil and stir-fry the chicken until it starts to turn golden brown. Remove and set aside.

**4** In the clean wok or deep saucepan, heat the remaining oil and cook the garlic and ginger until fragrant. Add the vegetables and cook for 2 minutes. Add the chicken and cook for 1 minute or until the chicken is thoroughly cooked. Finally add the sauce and sesame oil, then stir in the spring onions and serve.

# gong bao chicken

## ingredients

**SERVES 4**

2 boneless chicken breasts,
   with or without skin,
   cut into 1-cm/1/2-inch
   cubes
1 tbsp vegetable or peanut oil
10 dried red chillies or more,
   to taste, snipped into
   2–3 pieces
1 tsp Szechuan peppers
3 garlic cloves, finely sliced
2.5-cm/1-inch piece of fresh
   ginger, finely sliced
1 tbsp roughly chopped spring
   onions, white part only
85 g/3 oz peanuts, roasted

marinade
2 tsp light soy sauce
1 tsp Shaoxing rice wine
1/2 tsp sugar

sauce
1 tsp light soy sauce
1 tsp dark soy sauce
1 tsp black Chinese
   rice vinegar
a few drops of sesame oil
2 tbsp chicken stock
1 tsp sugar

## method

**1** Combine all the ingredients for the marinade in a bowl and marinate the chicken, covered, for at least 20 minutes. Combine all the ingredients for the sauce and set aside.

**2** In a preheated wok or deep saucepan, heat the oil and stir-fry the chillies and peppers until crisp and fragrant. Toss in the chicken pieces. When they begin to turn white, add the garlic, ginger and spring onions. Stir-fry for about 5 minutes, or until the chicken is cooked.

**3** Pour in the sauce, and when everything is well mixed, stir in the peanuts. Serve immediately.

# bang bang chicken

## ingredients

**SERVES 4**

350 g/12 oz boneless, skinless
   chicken meat
few drops of sesame oil
2 tbsp sesame paste
1 tbsp light soy sauce
1 tbsp chicken stock
1/2 tsp salt
pinch of sugar
8 tbsp shredded lettuce leaves
   and 1 tbsp sesame seeds,
   roasted, to serve

## method

**1** Place the chicken in a saucepan of cold water, then bring to the boil and simmer for 8–10 minutes. Drain and cool a little, then cut or tear the chicken into bite-sized pieces.

**2** Mix together the sesame oil, sesame paste, light soy sauce, chicken stock, salt and sugar and whisk until the sauce is thick and smooth. Toss in the chicken.

**3** To serve, put the shredded lettuce on a large plate and spoon the chicken and sauce on top. Sprinkle with the sesame seeds and serve at room temperature.

# chicken with cashew nuts

## ingredients

**SERVES 4–6**

450 g/1 lb boneless chicken
   meat, cut into bite-sized
   pieces
3 dried Chinese mushrooms,
   soaked in warm water for
   20 minutes
2 tbsp vegetable or peanut oil
4 slices of fresh ginger
1 tsp finely chopped garlic
1 red pepper, cut into
   2.5-cm/1-inch squares
1 tbsp light soy sauce
85 g/3 oz cashew nuts,
   roasted

marinade
3 tbsp light soy sauce
1 tsp Shaoxing rice wine
pinch of sugar
1/2 tsp salt

## method

**1** Combine all the ingredients for the marinade in a bowl and marinate the chicken, covered, for at least 20 minutes.

**2** Squeeze any excess water from the mushrooms and finely slice, discarding any tough stems. Reserve the soaking water.

**3** In a preheated wok or deep saucepan, heat 1 tablespoon of the oil. Add the ginger and stir-fry until fragrant. Stir in the chicken and cook for 2 minutes, or until it begins to turn brown. Before the chicken is cooked through, remove and set aside.

**4** In the clean wok or deep saucepan, heat the remaining oil and stir-fry the garlic until fragrant. Add the mushrooms and red pepper and stir-fry for 1 minute. Add about 2 tablespoons of the mushroom soaking water and cook for about 2 minutes, or until the water has evaporated. Return the chicken to the wok, then add the light soy sauce and cashew nuts and stir-fry for 2 minutes, or until the chicken is thoroughly cooked through.

# ginger chicken with toasted sesame seeds

## ingredients

**SERVES 4**

500 g/1 lb 2 oz chicken
   breasts, skinned,
   cut into strips
2 tbsp peanut oil
1 leek, thinly sliced
1 head of broccoli, cut into
   small florets
2 carrots, thinly sliced
1/2 cauliflower, cut into small
   florets
1 tsp grated fresh ginger
5 tbsp white wine
2 tbsp sesame seeds
1 tbsp cornflour
1 tbsp water
freshly cooked rice, to serve

marinade
4 tbsp soy sauce
4 tbsp water

## method

**1** In a medium dish, combine the soy sauce with 4 tablespoons of water. Toss and coat the chicken strips in the sauce. Cover the dish with clingfilm and chill in the refrigerator for 1 hour.

**2** Remove the chicken from the marinade with a slotted spoon. Heat the oil in a frying pan or wok and stir-fry the chicken and leek until the chicken is browned and the leek is beginning to soften. Stir in the vegetables, ginger and wine. Reduce the heat, cover and simmer for 5 minutes.

**3** Place the sesame seeds on a baking sheet under a hot grill. Stir them once to make sure they toast evenly. Set aside to cool.

**4** In a small bowl, combine the cornflour with 1 tablespoon of water and whisk until smooth. Gradually add the liquid to the frying pan, stirring constantly until thickened.

**5** Pile onto a bed of freshly cooked rice, top with the sesame seeds and serve.

# sweet-&-sour noodles with chicken

## ingredients

**SERVES 4**

250 g/9 oz dried medium
   Chinese egg noodles
2 tbsp peanut or corn oil
1 onion, thinly sliced
4 boneless chicken thighs,
   skinned and cut into thin
   strips
1 carrot, peeled and cut into
   thin half-moon slices
1 red pepper, cored, deseeded
   and finely chopped
100 g/3½ oz canned bamboo
   shoots, drained weight
55 g/2 oz cashew nuts

sweet-&-sour sauce
125 ml/4 fl oz water
1½ teaspoons arrowroot
4 tbsp rice vinegar
3 tbsp brown sugar
2 tsp dark soy sauce
2 tsp tomato purée
2 large garlic cloves,
   very finely chopped
1-cm/½-inch piece fresh
   ginger, peeled and very
   finely chopped
pinch of salt

## method

**1** Cook the noodles in a large saucepan of boiling water for 3 minutes, or according to the packet instructions, until soft. Drain, rinse and drain again, then set aside.

**2** Meanwhile, to make the sauce, stir half the water into the arrowroot and set aside. Stir the remaining sauce ingredients and the remaining water together in a small saucepan and bring to the boil. Stir in the arrowroot mixture and continue boiling until the sauce becomes clear, glossy and thick. Remove from the heat and set aside.

**3** Heat a wok or large frying pan over a high heat. Add the oil and heat it until it shimmers. Add the onion and stir-fry for 1 minute. Stir in the chicken, carrot and pepper and continue stir-frying for about 3 minutes, or until the chicken is cooked through. Add the bamboo shoots and cashew nuts and stir them around to brown the nuts lightly. Stir the sauce into the wok and heat until it starts to bubble. Add the noodles and use 2 forks to mix them with the chicken and vegetables.

# chicken chow mein

## ingredients

**SERVES 4**

250 g/9 oz dried medium
   Chinese egg noodles
2 tbsp sunflower oil
280 g/10 oz cooked chicken
   breasts, shredded
1 garlic clove, finely chopped
1 red pepper, deseeded and
   thinly sliced
100 g/3$^{1}$/$_{2}$ oz shiitake
   mushrooms, sliced
6 spring onions, sliced
100 g/3$^{1}$/$_{2}$ oz beansprouts
3 tbsp soy sauce
1 tbsp sesame oil

## method

**1** Place the noodles in a large bowl or dish and break them up slightly. Pour enough boiling water over the noodles to cover and set aside while preparing the other ingredients.

**2** Preheat a wok over a medium heat. Add the sunflower oil and swirl it around to coat the sides of the wok. When the oil is hot, add the shredded chicken, garlic, pepper, mushrooms, spring onions and beansprouts to the wok and stir-fry for about 5 minutes.

**3** Drain the noodles thoroughly then add them to the wok, toss well and stir-fry for a further 5 minutes. Drizzle over the soy sauce and sesame oil and toss until thoroughly combined.

**4** Transfer to warmed serving bowls and serve immediately.

# chicken chow mein baskets

## ingredients

**SERVES 4**

250 g/9 oz fresh thin or
    medium Chinese egg
    noodles

3 tbsp peanut or corn oil,
    plus extra for deep-frying

6 tbsp water

3 tbsp soy sauce

1 tbsp cornflour

4 boneless chicken thighs,
    skinned and chopped

2.5-cm/1-inch piece fresh
    ginger, peeled and finely
    chopped

2 large garlic cloves, crushed

2 celery sticks, thinly sliced

100 g/3$^{1}/_{2}$ oz white
    mushrooms, wiped and
    thinly sliced

## method

**1** Dip a large wire sieve in oil, then line it completely and evenly with one quarter of the tangled noodles. Dip a smaller wire sieve in oil, then position it inside the larger sieve. Heat 10 cm/4 inches of oil in a wok to 180– 190°C/ 350–375°F, or until a cube of bread browns in 30 seconds. Lower the sieves into the oil and deep-fry the noodles for 2–3 minutes, until golden brown. Remove from the oil and drain on kitchen paper. Carefully remove the small sieve and remove the noodle basket. Repeat to make 3 more baskets. Let cool.

**2** Stir the water and soy sauce into the cornflour in a small bowl and set aside.

**3** Heat a wok or large frying pan over a high heat. Add 2 tablespoons of the oil and heat until it shimmers. Add the chicken and stir-fry for about 3 minutes, or until it is cooked through. Remove the chicken from the wok.

**4** Add the remaining oil, then add the ginger, garlic and celery and stir-fry for 2 minutes. Add the mushrooms and continue stir-frying for 2 minutes. Remove the vegetables and add them to the chicken.

**5** Pour the cornflour mixture into the wok and bring to the boil, stirring until it thickens. Return the chicken and vegetables to the wok and reheat in the sauce. Divide the chicken mixture between the noodle baskets to serve.

# cross the bridge noodles

## ingredients

**SERVES 4**

300 g/10$\frac{1}{2}$ oz thin Chinese
   egg noodles or rice sticks
200 g/7 oz choi sum or similar
   green vegetable
2 litres/3$\frac{1}{2}$ pints chicken
   stock
1-cm/$\frac{1}{2}$-inch piece fresh
   ginger, peeled
1–2 tsp salt
1 tsp sugar
1 boneless, skinless chicken
   breast, finely sliced
   diagonally
200 g/7 oz white fish fillet,
   finely sliced diagonally
1 tbsp light soy sauce

## method

**1** Cook the noodles according to the directions on the packet. When cooked, rinse under cold water and set aside. Blanch the choi sum in a large saucepan of boiling water for 30 seconds. Rinse under cold water and set aside.

**2** In a large saucepan, bring the chicken stock to the boil, then add the ginger, 1 teaspoon of the salt and the sugar and skim the surface. Add the chicken and cook for about 4 minutes, then add the fish slices and simmer for a further 4 minutes, or until the fish and chicken are cooked through.

**3** Add the noodles and choi sum with the light soy sauce and bring back to the boil. Taste and adjust the seasoning if necessary. Serve immediately in large individual noodle bowls.

# chicken & peanut curry

## ingredients

**SERVES 4**

1 tbsp vegetable or peanut oil

2 red onions, sliced

2 tbsp Penang curry paste

400 ml/14 fl oz coconut milk

150 ml/5 fl oz chicken stock

4 kaffir lime leaves,
    torn coarsely

1 lemon grass stalk, chopped
    finely

6 skinless, boneless chicken
    thighs, chopped

1 tbsp fish sauce

2 tbsp Thai soy sauce

1 tsp jaggery or soft,
    light brown sugar

50 g/1¾ oz unsalted peanuts,
    roasted and chopped, plus
    extra to garnish

175 g/6 oz fresh pineapple,
    chopped coarsely

15-cm/6-inch piece
    cucumber, peeled,
    deseeded and sliced
    thickly, plus extra
    to garnish

## method

**1** Heat the oil in a wok and stir-fry the onions for 1 minute. Add the curry paste and stir-fry for 1–2 minutes.

**2** Pour in the coconut milk and stock. Add the lime leaves and lemon grass and simmer for 1 minute. Add the chicken and gradually bring to the boil. Simmer for 8–10 minutes, until the chicken is tender.

**3** Stir in the fish sauce, soy sauce and sugar and simmer for 1–2 minutes. Stir in the peanuts, pineapple and cucumber and cook for 30 seconds. Serve immediately, sprinkled with extra nuts and cucumber.

# green chicken curry

## ingredients

SERVES 4

1 tbsp vegetable or peanut oil

1 onion, sliced

1 garlic clove, chopped finely

2–3 tbsp Thai green curry
   paste

400 ml/14 fl oz coconut milk

150 ml/5 fl oz chicken stock

4 kaffir lime leaves

4 skinless, boneless chicken
   breasts, cut into cubes

1 tbsp fish sauce

2 tbsp Thai soy sauce

grated rind and juice of
   $1/2$ lime

1 tsp jaggery or soft light
   brown sugar

4 tbsp chopped fresh
   coriander, to garnish

## method

**1** Heat the oil in a wok or large frying pan and stir-fry the onion and garlic for 1–2 minutes, until starting to soften. Add the curry paste and stir-fry for 1–2 minutes.

**2** Add the coconut milk, stock and lime leaves, bring to the boil and add the chicken. Reduce the heat and simmer gently for 15–20 minutes, until the chicken is tender.

**3** Add the fish sauce, soy sauce, lime rind and juice and sugar. Cook for 2–3 minutes, until the sugar has dissolved. Serve immediately, garnished with chopped coriander.

# thai red chicken curry

## ingredients

**SERVES 4**

6 garlic cloves, chopped

2 fresh red chillies, chopped

2 tbsp chopped fresh lemon grass

1 tsp finely grated lime rind

1 tbsp chopped fresh kaffir lime leaves

1 tbsp Thai red curry paste

1 tbsp coriander seeds, toasted and crushed

1 tbsp chilli oil

4 skinless, boneless chicken breasts, sliced

300 ml/10 fl oz coconut milk

300 ml/10 fl oz chicken stock

1 tbsp soy sauce

55 g/2 oz shelled unsalted peanuts, toasted and ground

3 spring onions, diagonally sliced

1 red pepper, deseeded and sliced

3 Thai aubergines, sliced

2 tbsp chopped fresh Thai basil or fresh coriander

fresh coriander, to garnish

freshly cooked jasmine rice, to serve

## method

**1** Place the garlic, chillies, lemon grass, lime rind, lime leaves, curry paste and coriander seeds in a food processor and process until the mixture is smooth.

**2** Heat the oil in a preheated wok or large frying pan over high heat. Add the chicken and the garlic mixture and stir-fry for 5 minutes. Add the coconut milk, stock and soy sauce and bring to the boil. Reduce the heat and cook, stirring, for a further 3 minutes. Stir in the ground peanuts and simmer for 20 minutes.

**3** Add the spring onions, pepper and aubergines and simmer, stirring occasionally, for a further 10 minutes. Remove from the heat, stir in the basil and garnish with coriander. Serve immediately with freshly cooked jasmine rice.

# chicken with yellow curry sauce

## ingredients

**SERVES 4**

spice paste

6 tbsp Thai yellow curry paste
150 ml/5 fl oz plain yogurt
400 ml/14 fl oz water
handful of fresh coriander,
    chopped
handful of fresh Thai basil
    leaves, shredded

stir-fry

2 tbsp vegetable or peanut oil
2 onions, cut into thin wedges
2 garlic cloves, chopped finely
2 skinless, boneless chicken
    breasts, cut into strips
175 g/6 oz baby corn, halved
    lengthways

to garnish

chopped fresh coriander
shredded fresh basil

## method

**1** To make the spice paste, stir-fry the yellow curry paste in a wok for 2–3 minutes, then stir in the yogurt, water and herbs. Bring to the boil, then simmer for 2–3 minutes.

**2** Meanwhile, heat the oil in a wok and stir-fry the onions and garlic for 2–3 minutes. Add the chicken and corn and stir-fry for 3–4 minutes, until the meat and corn are tender.

**3** Stir in the spice paste and bring to the boil. Simmer for 2–3 minutes, until heated through. Serve immediately, garnished with extra herbs.

# spiced coriander chicken

## ingredients

**SERVES 4**

4 skinless, boneless chicken
   breasts
2 garlic cloves
1 fresh green chilli, deseeded
2-cm/³/₄-inch piece fresh
   ginger
4 tbsp chopped coriander
finely grated rind of 1 lime
3 tbsp lime juice
2 tbsp light soy sauce
1 tbsp caster sugar
170 ml/6 fl oz coconut milk

to garnish
finely chopped coriander
cucumber slices
radish slices
¹/₂ fresh red chilli, deseeded
   and sliced into rings
freshly cooked rice, to serve

## method

**1** Using a sharp knife, cut 3 deep slashes into the skinned side of each chicken breast. Place the breasts in a single layer in a non-metallic dish.

**2** Place the garlic, chilli, ginger, coriander, lime rind and juice, soy sauce, sugar and coconut milk in a food processor and process to a smooth paste.

**3** Spread the paste over both sides of the chicken breasts, coating them evenly. Cover with clingfilm and marinate in the refrigerator for 1 hour.

**4** Preheat the grill to medium. Lift the chicken from the marinade, then drain off the excess and place on a grill pan. Cook under the hot grill for 12–15 minutes, or until thoroughly and evenly cooked.

**5** Meanwhile, place the remaining marinade in a saucepan and bring to the boil. Reduce the heat and simmer for several minutes. Transfer the chicken breasts to serving plates. Garnish with chopped coriander, cucumber slices, radish slices and chilli rings and serve with rice.

# chicken with vegetables & coriander rice

## ingredients

**SERVES 4**

3 tbsp vegetable or peanut oil
2 red onions, 1 chopped and
   1 sliced
2 garlic cloves, chopped
2.5-cm/1-inch piece fresh
   root ginger, peeled and
   chopped
2 skinless, boneless chicken
   breasts, cut into strips
115 g/4 oz white mushrooms
400 ml/14 oz canned coconut
   milk
55 g/2 oz sugar snap peas
3 tbsp Thai soy sauce
1 tbsp fish sauce
350 g/12 oz rice, cooked and
   cooled
8 oz/250 g pak choi, torn into
   large pieces
handful of fresh coriander,
   chopped

## method

**1** Heat 2 tablespoons of the oil in a wok or large frying pan and sauté the chopped onion, garlic and ginger together for 1–2 minutes.

**2** Add the chicken and mushrooms and cook over high heat until browned. Add the coconut milk, sugar snap peas, 2 tablespoons of the soy sauce and the fish sauce and bring to the boil. Simmer gently for 4–5 minutes until tender.

**3** Meanwhile, heat the remaining oil in a separate wok or large frying pan and cook the sliced onion until softened but not browned.

**4** Add the cooked rice, pak choi and fresh coriander and heat through gently until the leaves have wilted and the rice is hot. Sprinkle over the remaining soy sauce and serve immediately with the chicken.

# chicken steamed with rice in lotus leaves

## ingredients

SERVES 4–8

450 g/1 lb glutinous rice,
   soaked in cold water for
   2 hours
450 ml/16 fl oz cold water
1 tsp salt
1 tsp vegetable or peanut oil
4 dried lotus leaves, soaked in
   hot water for 1 hour

### filling

100 g/3½ oz raw small
   prawns, shelled and
   deveined
2-inch/5-cm piece of very
   fresh ginger
200 g/7 oz lean chicken meat,
   cut into bite-size strips
2 tsp light soy sauce
55 g/2 oz dried Chinese
   mushrooms, soaked in
   warm water for 20 minutes
1 tbsp vegetable or peanut oil,
   for frying
200 g/7 oz cha siu or pork loin
1 tbsp Shaoxing rice wine
1 tsp dark soy sauce
½ tsp white pepper
1 tsp sugar

## method

**1** For the filling, steam the prawns for 5 minutes and set aside. Finely grate the ginger, discarding the fibrous parts on the grater and reserving the liquid that drips through. Marinate the chicken in the light soy sauce and ginger juices for at least 20 minutes. Steam for a few minutes in the marinade. Set aside.

**2** Drain the rice and place in a saucepan with the water. Bring to the boil, then add the salt and oil. Cover and cook over very low heat for 15 minutes. Divide into 8 portions and set aside.

**3** Squeeze out any excess water from the mushrooms, then finely slice, discarding any tough stems. Reserve the soaking water.

**4** In a preheated wok or deep saucepan, heat the oil and stir-fry the pork, prawns and mushrooms for 2 minutes. Stir in the Shaoxing, dark soy sauce, pepper and sugar. Add the reserved mushroom soaking water, if necessary.

**5** Rinse and dry the lotus leaves. Place a portion of rice in the centre of each and flatten out to form a 10-cm/4-inch square. Top with the pork mixture and some pieces of chicken. Top with another portion of rice, then fold the lotus leaf to form a tight package. Steam for about 15 minutes. Let rest for 5 minutes, then serve.

# hainan chicken rice

## ingredients

**SERVES 4–6**

1 chicken, weighing
    1.5 kg/3 lb 5 oz
55 g/2 oz fresh young ginger,
    smashed
2 garlic cloves, smashed
1 spring onion, tied in a knot
1 tsp salt
2 tbsp vegetable or peanut oil
chilli or soy dipping sauce,
    to serve

### rice

2 tbsp vegetable or peanut oil
5 garlic cloves, finely chopped
5 shallots, finely chopped
350 g/12 oz long-grain rice
950 ml/30 fl oz chicken stock
1 tsp salt

## method

**1** Wash the chicken and dry thoroughly. Stuff the body cavity with the ginger, garlic, spring onion and salt.

**2** In a large saucepan, bring enough water to the boil to submerge the chicken. Place the chicken in the pan, breast-side down. Bring the water back to the boil, then turn down the heat and simmer, covered, for 30–40 minutes. Turn the chicken over once.

**3** Remove the chicken and wash in running cold water for 2 minutes to stop the cooking. Drain, then rub the oil into the skin. Set aside.

**4** To prepare the rice, heat the oil in a preheated wok. Stir-fry the garlic and shallots until fragrant. Add the rice and cook for 3 minutes, stirring rapidly. Transfer to a large saucepan and add the chicken stock and salt. Bring to the boil, then turn down the heat and simmer, covered, for 20 minutes. Turn off the heat and steam for a further 5–10 minutes, or until the rice is perfectly cooked.

**5** To serve, chop the chicken horizontally through the bone and skin into chunky wedges. Serve with the rice and a chilli or soy dipping sauce.

# egg-fried rice with chicken

## ingredients

**SERVES 4**

225 g/8 oz jasmine rice

3 skinless, boneless chicken
   breasts, cut into cubes

400 ml/14 fl oz canned
   coconut milk

50 g/1³/4 oz block creamed
   coconut, chopped

2–3 coriander roots, chopped

thinly pared rind of 1 lemon

1 fresh green chilli, deseeded
   and chopped

3 fresh Thai basil leaves

1 tbsp fish sauce

1 tbsp oil

3 eggs, beaten

fresh chives and fresh
   coriander sprigs, to garnish

## method

**1** Cook the rice in boiling water for
12–15 minutes, drain well, then let cool and
chill overnight.

**2** Put the chicken into a saucepan and cover
with the coconut milk. Add the creamed
coconut, coriander roots, lemon rind and chilli
and bring to the boil. Simmer for 8–10 minutes,
until the chicken is tender. Remove from the
heat. Stir in the basil and fish sauce.

**3** Meanwhile, heat the oil in a wok and stir-fry
the rice for 2–3 minutes. Pour in the eggs and
stir until they have cooked and mixed with the
rice. Line 4 small ovenproof bowls or ramekins
with clingfilm and pack with the rice. Turn out
carefully onto serving plates and remove the
clingfilm. Garnish with long chives and sprigs of
coriander. Serve with the chicken.

# ginger chicken with noodles

## ingredients

SERVES 4

2 tbsp vegetable or peanut oil

1 onion, sliced

2 garlic cloves, chopped finely

5-cm/2-inch piece fresh
    ginger, sliced thinly

2 carrots, sliced thinly

4 skinless, boneless chicken
    breasts, cut into cubes

300 ml/10 fl oz chicken stock

4 tbsp Thai soy sauce

225 g/8 oz canned bamboo
    shoots, drained and rinsed

75 g/2³/₄ oz flat rice noodles

4 spring onions, chopped,
    and 4 tbsp chopped fresh
    coriander, to garnish

## method

1 Heat the oil in a wok and stir-fry the onion, garlic, ginger and carrots for 1–2 minutes, until softened. Add the chicken and stir-fry for 3–4 minutes, until the chicken is cooked through and lightly browned.

2 Add the stock, soy sauce and bamboo shoots and gradually bring to the boil. Simmer for 2–3 minutes. Meanwhile, soak the noodles in boiling water for 6–8 minutes. Drain well, then garnish with the spring onions and coriander and serve immediately, with the chicken stir-fry.

# chinese chicken rice

## ingredients

### SERVES 4

350 g/12 oz long-grain white
   rice
1 tsp ground turmeric
salt
2 tbsp corn oil
350 g/12 oz skinless, boneless
   chicken thighs, sliced
1 red pepper, deseeded and
   sliced
1 green pepper, deseeded and
   sliced
1 fresh green chilli, deseeded
   and finely chopped
1 carrot, grated coarsely
150 g/5½ oz beansprouts
6 spring onions, sliced, plus
   extra to garnish
2 tbsp light soy sauce

## method

**1** Place the rice and turmeric in a large saucepan of lightly salted water and cook until the grains of rice are just tender, about 10 minutes. Drain the rice thoroughly and press out any excess water with kitchen paper.

**2** Heat the corn oil in a large preheated frying pan. Add the strips of chicken and stir-fry over high heat until just starting to turn a golden colour. Add the sliced peppers and green chilli to the wok and stir-fry for 2–3 minutes.

**3** Add the cooked rice to the wok, a little at a time, tossing well after each addition until well mixed and the grains of rice are separated. Add the carrot, beansprouts and spring onions to the wok and stir-fry for a further 2 minutes. Drizzle with the soy sauce and toss to mix.

**4** Transfer the Chinese chicken rice to a warmed serving dish, garnish with extra spring onions, if you like, and serve immediately.

# yaki soba

## ingredients

**SERVES 2**

400 g/14 oz ramen noodles

1 onion, finely sliced

200 g/7 oz beansprouts

1 red pepper, deseeded and
    finely shredded

1 boneless, skin-on cooked
    chicken breast, about
    150 g/5$^{1}/_{2}$ oz, cooked
    and sliced

12 cooked peeled prawns

1 tbsp oil

2 tbsp shoyu (Japanese
    soy sauce)

$^{1}/_{2}$ tbsp mirin

1 tsp sesame oil

1 tsp roasted sesame seeds

2 spring onions, finely sliced

## method

**1** Cook the noodles according to the packet instructions, drain well, and tip into a bowl.

**2** Mix the onion, beansprouts, red pepper, chicken and prawns together in a separate bowl. Stir through the noodles.

**3** Preheat a wok over high heat. Add the oil and heat until very hot. Add the noodle mixture and stir-fry for 4 minutes, or until golden, then add the shoyu, mirin and sesame oil and toss together.

**4** Divide the mixture between 2 bowls, sprinkle with the sesame seeds and spring onions and serve at once.

# teriyaki chicken with sesame noodles

## ingredients

**SERVES 4**

4 boneless chicken breasts,
    about 175 g/6 oz each,
    with or without skin,
    as you wish
about 4 tbsp bottled teriyaki
    sauce, or homemade
    teriyaki sauce
peanut or corn oil

sesame noodles
250 g/9 oz dried thin
    buckwheat noodles
1 tbsp toasted sesame oil
2 tbsp toasted sesame seeds
2 tbsp finely chopped fresh
    parsley
salt and pepper

## method

**1** Using a sharp knife, score each chicken breast diagonally across 3 times and rub all over with teriyaki sauce. Set aside to marinate for at least 10 minutes, or cover and chill all day.

**2** When you are ready to cook the chicken, preheat the grill to high. Bring a saucepan of water to the boil, add the buckwheat noodles and boil for 3 minutes, until soft. Alternatively, cook according to the packet instructions. Drain and rinse well in cold water to stop the cooking and remove excess starch, then drain again.

**3** Lightly brush the grill rack with oil. Add the chicken breasts, skin side up, and brush again with a little extra teriyaki sauce. Grill the chicken breasts about 10 cm/4 inches from the heat, brushing occasionally with extra teriyaki sauce, for 15 minutes, or until cooked through and the juices run clear.

**4** Meanwhile, heat a wok over high heat. Add the sesame oil and heat until it shimmers. Add the noodles and stir round to heat through, then stir in the sesame seeds and parsley. Finally, add salt and pepper to taste.

**5** Transfer the chicken breasts to plates and add a portion of noodles to each.

# noodle baskets with chicken lime salad

## ingredients

**SERVES 4**

peanut or corn oil,
    for deep-frying
250 g/9 oz fresh thin or
    medium Chinese egg
    noodles

chicken lime salad

6 tbsp sour cream
6 tbsp mayonnaise
2.5-cm/1-inch piece fresh
    ginger, peeled and grated
grated rind and juice of 1 lime
4 skinless, boneless chicken
    thighs, poached and
    cooled, then cut into thin
    strips
1 carrot, peeled and grated
1 cucumber, cut in half
    lengthways, seeds removed
    and sliced
salt and pepper
1 tbsp finely chopped fresh
    coriander
1 tbsp finely chopped fresh
    mint
1 tbsp finely chopped fresh
    parsley
several fresh basil leaves, torn

## method

**1** To shape noodle baskets, you will need a special set of 2 long-handled wire baskets that clip inside each other, available from gourmet kitchen stores. Dip the larger wire basket in oil, then line it completely and evenly with one quarter of the tangled noodles. Dip the smaller wire basket in oil, then position it inside the larger basket and clip it into position.

**2** Heat 10 cm/4 inches of oil in a wok or deep-fat fryer to 180–190°C/350–375°F, or until a cube of bread browns in 30 seconds. Lower the baskets into the oil and deep-fry for 2–3 minutes, or until the noodles are golden brown. Remove the baskets from the oil and drain on kitchen paper. Unclip the 2 wire baskets and carefully remove the small one. Use a round-bladed knife, if necessary, to prise the noodle basket from the wire frame. Repeat to make 3 more baskets. Set aside to cool.

**3** To make the salad, combine the sour cream, mayonnaise, ginger and lime rind. Gradually add the lime juice until you get the flavour you like. Stir in the chicken, carrot, cucumber and seasoning to taste. Cover and chill. Just before serving, stir in the herbs and spoon the salad into the noodle baskets.

# chicken with plum sauce

## ingredients

**SERVES 4–6**

1 tbsp vegetable or
groundnut oil

100 g/3¹/₂ oz chicken, finely
chopped

25 g/1 oz water chestnuts,
finely chopped

1 tsp finely chopped Chinese
chives

25 g/1 oz pine nuts, lightly
toasted

1 tsp salt

¹/₂ tsp white pepper

6 salad leaves, washed

3 tsp plum sauce, to serve

## method

**1** In a preheated wok or deep saucepan, heat the oil and stir-fry the chicken for 1 minute. Add the water chestnuts and chives and cook for 2 minutes. Add the pine nuts and cook for 1 minute. Add the salt and pepper and stir.

**2** To serve, place a spoonful in the centre of each salad leaf, top with the plum sauce and fold the lettuce leaf to make a small roll.

# turkey with bamboo shoots & water chestnuts

## ingredients

**SERVES 4**

marinade

4 tbsp sweet sherry

1 tbsp lemon juice

1 tbsp soy sauce

2 tsp grated fresh ginger

1 clove garlic, crushed

stir-fry

1 tbsp sesame oil

2 tbsp vegetable oil

450 g/1 lb turkey breast, cubed

125 g/4½ oz small mushrooms, cut into halves

1 green pepper, cut into strips

1 courgette, sliced thinly

4 spring onions, cut into quarters

115 g/4 oz canned bamboo shoots, drained

115 g/4 oz canned sliced water chestnuts, drained

cooked noodles or rice, to serve

## method

**1** Blend the sherry, lemon juice, soy sauce, ginger and garlic in a bowl, then add the turkey and stir. Cover the dish with clingfilm and refrigerate to marinate for 3–4 hours.

**2** In a wok, add the sesame oil and vegetable oil and heat slowly. Remove the turkey from the marinade with a slotted spoon (reserving the marinade) and stir-fry a few pieces at a time until browned. Remove the turkey from the wok and set aside.

**3** Add the mushrooms, green pepper and courgette to the wok and stir-fry for 3 minutes. Add the spring onions and stir-fry for 1 minute more. Add the bamboo shoots and water chestnuts to the wok, then the turkey along with half of the reserved marinade. Stir over a medium-high heat for another 2–3 minutes, or until the ingredients are evenly coated and the marinade has reduced.

**4** Serve immediately over noodles or rice.

# duck & hoisin hand rolls

## ingredients

**MAKES 6 PIECES**

1/4 prepared barbecued or
    Peking duck

4 tbsp hoisin or plum sauce

3 sheets of toasted nori

1/4 quantity freshly cooked
    sushi rice

3 spring onions, halved
    lengthways and shredded,
    plus extra to garnish

## method

**1** Pull the flesh and skin off the duck and slice into strips. If you have lots of skin, just keep the crispiest bits. Discard any excess fat.

**2** Put half the hoisin or plum sauce into a large bowl, add the duck strips and toss to coat.

**3** Fold a nori sheet in half lengthways, press along the fold and then tear it into 2 pieces. Lay a half-sheet smooth-side down on a work surface and place a heaped tablespoon of rice on the left-hand side. Lay a sixth of the duck and duck skin on the rice, scatter with some of the shredded spring onion, then drizzle over 1 teaspoon of the remaining hoisin or plum sauce.

**4** Fold the bottom left-hand corner of the nori over the rice and filling, so that the folded edge forms a right angle with the bottom edge. Continue folding along that line to make a cone with a sharp point at the bottom. Place a drop of vinegared water on the underside of the join to seal it.

**5** Repeat with the rest of the ingredients to make 6 cones in total, transfer to a serving plate and garnish with the remaining shredded spring onions.

# duck with mixed peppers

## ingredients

**SERVES 4**

1 tbsp vegetable or peanut oil

2 duck breasts, skin on

1 onion, sliced

2 garlic cloves, chopped

1 red pepper, deseeded and
  chopped

1 green pepper, deseeded and
  chopped

1 yellow pepper, deseeded
  and chopped

4 tomatoes, peeled, deseeded
  and chopped

150 ml/5 fl oz stock

3 tbsp Thai soy sauce

boiled noodles, garnished with
  chopped onion, to serve

## method

**1** Heat the oil in a wok and cook the duck breasts over high heat until crisp and brown. Turn over and cook until cooked through. Lift out and keep warm.

**2** Pour off any excess fat and stir-fry the onion and garlic for 2–3 minutes, until softened and lightly browned.

**3** Add the peppers and stir-fry for 2–3 minutes, until tender. Add the tomatoes, stock and soy sauce, and simmer for 1–2 minutes. Transfer to a serving plate. Slice the duck thickly and arrange on top, spooning any sauce over it. Serve with noodles.

# chinese crispy duck

## ingredients

**SERVES 4**

3 tbsp soy sauce

1/4 tsp Chinese five-spice
powder

1/4 tsp pepper and pinch
of salt

4 duck legs or breasts,
cut into pieces

3 tbsp vegetable oil

1 tsp dark sesame oil

1 tsp finely chopped fresh
ginger

1 large garlic clove, finely
chopped

4 spring onions, white part
thickly sliced, green part
shredded

2 tbsp rice wine or dry sherry

1 tbsp oyster sauce

3 whole star anise

2 tsp black peppercorns

450–600 ml/16 fl oz–1 pint
chicken stock or water

6 dried shiitake mushrooms,
soaked in warm water for
20 minutes

225 g/8 oz canned water
chestnuts, drained

2 tbsp cornflour

## method

**1** Combine 1 tablespoon of the soy sauce, the five-spice powder, pepper and salt and rub over the duck pieces. Place 2 1/2 tablespoons of vegetable oil in a flameproof casserole, add the duck pieces and cook until browned, then transfer to a plate and set aside.

**2** Drain the fat from the casserole and wipe out. Add the sesame oil and remaining vegetable oil and heat. Add the ginger and garlic and cook for a few seconds. Add the sliced white spring onions and cook for a few more seconds. Return the duck to the casserole. Add the rice wine, oyster sauce, star anise, peppercorns and remaining soy sauce. Pour in enough stock to just cover the duck. Bring to the boil, cover and simmer gently for 1 1/2 hours, adding more stock if necessary.

**3** Drain the mushrooms and squeeze dry. Slice the caps, add to the duck with the water chestnuts, and simmer for a further 20 minutes.

**4** Mix the cornflour with 2 tablespoons of the cooking liquid to form a smooth paste. Add to the remaining liquid, stirring, until thickened. To serve, garnish with shredded green spring onions.

# peking duck

## ingredients

**SERVES 6–10**

1 duck, weighing 2 kg/
    4 lb 8 oz
1.7 litres/3 pints boiling water
1 tbsp honey
1 tbsp Shaoxing rice wine
1 tsp white rice vinegar
1 cucumber, peeled,
    deseeded and julienned
10 spring onions, white part
    only, shredded
30 Peking duck pancakes
plum or hoisin sauce, or both

## method

**1** To prepare the duck, massage the skin to separate it from the meat.

**2** Pour the boiling water into a large saucepan, then add the honey, Shaoxing and vinegar and lower in the duck. Baste for about 1 minute. Remove the duck and hang it to dry for a few hours or overnight.

**3** Preheat the oven to 200°C/400°F/Gas Mark 5. Place the duck on a rack above a roasting tin and roast for at least 1 hour, or until the skin is very crispy and the duck cooked through.

**4** To serve, bring the duck to the table, together with the cucumber, spring onions and pancakes, and carve off the skin first. On a pancake, arrange a little skin with some cucumber and spring onion pieces. Top with a little plum or hoisin sauce, or both. Roll up and eat. Repeat the process with the lean meat.

# duck breasts with chilli & lime

## ingredients

**SERVES 4**

4 boneless duck breasts

2 garlic cloves, crushed

4 tsp brown sugar

3 tbsp lime juice

1 tbsp soy sauce

1 tsp chilli sauce

1 tsp vegetable oil

2 tbsp plum jam

150 ml/5 fl oz chicken stock

salt and pepper

freshly cooked rice and crisp
    salad leaves, to serve

## method

**1** Using a small, sharp knife, cut deep slashes in the skin of the duck to make a diamond pattern. Place the duck breasts in a wide, non-metallic dish.

**2** Mix the garlic, sugar, lime juice, soy sauce and chilli sauce together in a bowl, then spoon over the duck breasts, turning well to coat evenly. Cover and marinate in the refrigerator for at least 3 hours or overnight.

**3** Drain the duck, reserving the marinade. Heat a large, heavy-based frying pan until very hot and brush with the oil. Add the duck breasts, skin-side down, and cook for 5 minutes, or until the skin is browned and crisp. Tip away the excess fat. Turn the duck breasts over.

**4** Continue cooking on the other side for 2–3 minutes to brown. Add the reserved marinade, plum jam and stock and simmer for 2 minutes. Season to taste with salt and pepper. Transfer to individual serving plates, then spoon over the pan juices and serve hot with freshly cooked rice and crisp salad leaves.

# fish & seafood

When it comes to fish and seafood, finding authentic ingredients may be difficult for the Western cook. Fortunately, many types are as popular and easily available in the West as in the East – tuna, prawns, crab, squid and scallops, for example. It is sometimes possible to find more exotic species in Asian grocers and speciality shops, usually deep-frozen, but it's rarely necessary as the recipes work well with a wide variety of more easily available fish.

Of all the countries of Asia, Japan must take the crown for its fish dishes. Not only is the country made up of a group of islands, but for many years the government prohibited the population from eating meat, so fish and seafood occupied the central place in the Japanese diet. No one will repeat the mistake of thinking that fish is only ever eaten raw in Japan after tasting any of the fabulous traditional ways in which it is cooked.

Many other Asian countries are also made up of islands – Indonesia comprises nearly 14,000 of them – and China's coastline is immensely long, so fish and seafood are important ingredients in all Asian kitchens. As fish can easily dry out during cooking, it is especially well suited to the speedy method of stir-frying or the moist techniques of

steaming or braising. Wrapping whole fish in a banana leaf parcel before cooking it is a popular South-east Asian method of retaining its delicate texture. Westerners may have to rely on the more prosaic wrappings of greaseproof paper or foil.

# mixed sashimi

## ingredients

**SERVES 2**

1 fresh mackerel, cleaned and
  filleted
100 ml/3$^{1}$/$_{2}$ oz rice vinegar
3 raw scallops, in their shells
150 g/5$^{1}$/$_{2}$ oz sashimi-grade
  tuna, trimmed
150 g/5$^{1}$/$_{2}$ oz sashimi-grade
  salmon, trimmed
55 g/2 oz daikon (long white
  radish), shredded
whole trimmed chives to
  garnish
wasabi paste, Japanese
soy sauce and pickled ginger,
  to serve

## method

**1** Place the mackerel fillets in a shallow, non-metallic dish, pour over the rice vinegar and cover with clingfilm. Marinate in the refrigerator for 1 hour.

**2** Remove the mackerel from the marinade, pat dry with kitchen paper and take off the skin. Holding a wet, very sharp knife at a 45° angle to the chopping board, cut the fish into 8-mm/$^{1}$/$_{3}$-inch thick, diagonal slices.

**3** To prepare the scallops, insert a short, strong knife between the shells and twist to prise apart. Separate the scallops from their shells. Remove and discard any corals and black matter, the white frills and membranes. Slice the scallops in half horizontally.

**4** Put the halved scallops into a heatproof dish and cover with boiling water. Remove with a slotted spoon straight away. Pat the scallops dry with kitchen paper.

**5** Slice the tuna and salmon into 8-mm/$^{1}$/$_{3}$-inch thick rectangles, using a wet, very sharp knife and cutting across the grain. Wipe your knife on a damp cloth between each cut.

**6** Place the shredded daikon on a serving platter, place the scallops on top and arrange the sliced fish around it. Garnish with fresh chives. Add a mound of wasabi paste and serve with soy sauce and pickled ginger.

# clams in black bean sauce

## ingredients

**SERVES 4**

900 g/2 lb small clams
   (discard any clams that
   remain closed after
   cooking)
1 tbsp vegetable or peanut oil
1 tsp finely chopped fresh
   ginger
1 tsp finely chopped garlic
1 tbsp fermented black
   beans, rinsed and roughly
   chopped
2 tsp Shaoxing rice wine
1 tbsp finely chopped spring
   onions
1 tsp salt (optional)

## method

**1** Start by washing the clams thoroughly, then soak them in clean water until needed.

**2** In a preheated wok or deep saucepan, heat the oil and stir-fry the ginger and garlic until fragrant. Add the black beans and cook for 1 minute.

**3** Over a high heat, add the drained clams and Shaoxing and stir-fry for 2 minutes to mix everything together. Cover and cook for about 3 minutes. Add the spring onions and salt, if necessary, and serve immediately.

# chillies stuffed with fish paste

## ingredients

**SERVES 4–6**

225 g/8 oz white fish, minced

2 tbsp lightly beaten egg

4–6 mild red and green
   chillies

vegetable or peanut oil,
   for shallow-frying

2 garlic cloves, finely chopped

1/2 tsp fermented black beans,
   rinsed and lightly mashed

1 tbsp light soy sauce

pinch of sugar

1 tbsp water

marinade

1 tsp finely chopped fresh
   ginger

pinch of salt

pinch of white pepper

1/2 tsp vegetable or peanut oil

## method

**1** Combine all the ingredients for the marinade in a bowl and marinate the fish for 20 minutes. Add the egg and mix by hand to create a smooth paste.

**2** To prepare the chillies, cut in half lengthways and scoop out the seeds and loose flesh. Cut into bite-sized pieces. Spread each piece of chilli with about 1/2 teaspoon of the fish paste.

**3** In a preheated wok or deep saucepan, heat plenty of the oil and cook the chilli pieces on both sides until beginning to turn golden brown. Drain and set aside.

**4** Heat 1 tablespoon of the oil in a wok or deep saucepan and stir-fry the garlic until aromatic. Stir in the black beans and mix well. Add the light soy sauce and sugar and stir, then add the chilli pieces. Add the water, then cover and simmer over a low heat for 5 minutes. Serve immediately.

# stir-fried scallops with asparagus

## ingredients

**SERVES 4**

225 g/8 oz scallops

2 tsp salt

225 g/8 oz asparagus

3 tbsp vegetable or peanut oil

55 g/2 oz fresh or canned
    bamboo shoots, rinsed and
    thinly sliced (if using fresh
    shoots, boil in water first for
    30 minutes)

1 small carrot, finely sliced

4 thin slices of fresh ginger

pinch of white pepper

2 tbsp Shaoxing rice wine

2 tbsp chicken stock

1 tsp sesame oil

## method

**1** Sprinkle the scallops with 1 teaspoon of the salt and set aside for 20 minutes.

**2** Trim the asparagus, discarding the tough ends. Cut into 5-cm/2-inch pieces and blanch in a large saucepan of boiling water for 30 seconds. Drain and set aside.

**3** In a preheated wok, heat 1 tablespoon of the oil and cook the scallops for 30 seconds. Drain and set aside.

**4** In the clean wok, heat another tablespoon of the oil and stir-fry the asparagus, bamboo shoots and carrot for 2 minutes. Season with the remaining salt. Drain and set aside.

**5** In the clean wok, heat the remaining oil, then add the ginger and stir-fry until fragrant. Return the scallops and vegetables to the wok and sprinkle with the pepper, Shaoxing and stock. Cover and continue cooking for 2 minutes, then toss through the sesame oil and serve.

# spicy scallops with lime & chilli

## ingredients

**SERVES 4**

16 large scallops, shelled
1 tbsp butter
1 tbsp vegetable oil
1 tsp crushed garlic
1 tsp grated fresh ginger
1 bunch of spring onions,
    finely sliced
finely grated rind of 1 lime
1 small fresh red chilli,
    deseeded and very finely
    chopped
3 tbsp lime juice
lime wedges, to garnish
freshly cooked rice, to serve

## method

**1** Using a sharp knife, trim the scallops to remove any black intestine, then wash and pat dry with kitchen paper. Separate the corals from the white parts, then slice each white part in half horizontally, making 2 circles.

**2** Heat the butter and oil in a frying pan or preheated wok.

**3** Add the garlic and ginger and stir-fry for 1 minute without browning. Add the spring onions and stir-fry for a further 1 minute.

**4** Add the scallops and continue stir-frying over high heat for 4–5 minutes. Stir in the lime rind, chilli and lime juice and cook for a further 1 minute.

**5** Transfer the scallops to serving plates, then spoon over the pan juices and garnish with lime wedges. Serve hot with freshly cooked rice.

# prawn tempura & lettuce wraps

## ingredients

**MAKES 6 PIECES**

6 large raw prawns, peeled
and deveined

1/4 x 150-g/51/2-oz packet
tempura mix

vegetable oil, for deep-frying

3 sheets of toasted nori

1/4 quantity freshly cooked
sushi rice

handful of iceberg lettuce
leaves, shredded

1 red and 1 green chilli,
deseeded and cut into very
fine strips (optional)

tempura dipping sauce,
to serve

## method

**1** Cut a few slits on the underside of the prawns to keep them straight as they cook.

**2** Blend the tempura mix with water according to the packet instructions. The batter should be lumpy with plenty of air bubbles. Heat the vegetable oil in a deep-fryer to 180–190°C/ 350–375°F, or until a cube of bread browns in 30 seconds.

**3** Dip the prepared prawns in the batter mix, then drop them into the oil 3 at a time. Cook for 2–3 minutes, until golden and cooked. Remove from the oil, drain on kitchen paper and cool.

**4** Halve the nori sheets. Lay a half-sheet of nori smooth-side down on a work surface and place a heaped tablespoon of rice on the left-hand side. Top with shredded lettuce and 1 tempura prawn, then add a strip of red and a strip of green chilli, if using.

**5** Fold the bottom left-hand corner of the nori over the rice and filling, so that the folded edge forms a right angle with the bottom edge. Continue folding along that line to make a cone with a sharp point at the bottom. Place a drop of vinegared water on the underside of the join to seal it. Repeat with the rest of the ingredients to make 6 cones in total. Serve with the tempura dipping sauce.

# chirashi sushi with prawn, crab & avocado

## ingredients

### SERVES 4

1 tbsp vegetable oil

6 large raw prawns, peeled and deveined

1 cooked prepared crab

1 quantity freshly cooked sushi rice

juice and zest of 1 lemon

1 ripe avocado, stoned, peeled and cut into strips

1/2 cucumber, peeled and cut into slices

Japanese soy sauce, pickled ginger and wasabi paste, to serve

## method

1 Heat the oil in a frying pan, then cook the prawns by sautéing for 2 minutes on each side. Once they are cooked through, cool, then cut in half lengthways. Lift the crabmeat out of the shell.

2 Mix the sushi rice with the lemon juice and lemon zest, then divide between 4 serving bowls. Arrange the cooked prawns, crabmeat, and avocado and cucumber slices on top of the rice. Serve with soy sauce, pickled ginger and wasabi paste.

# ginger prawns with oyster mushrooms

## ingredients

**SERVES 4**

about 3 tbsp vegetable oil
3 carrots, thinly sliced
350 g/12 oz oyster
    mushrooms, thinly sliced
1 large red pepper, thinly
    sliced
450 g/1 lb large prawns,
    peeled
2 garlic cloves, crushed
fresh coriander leaves,
    to garnish

sauce

150 ml/5 fl oz chicken stock
2 tsp sesame seeds
3 tsp grated fresh ginger
1 tbsp soy sauce
1/4 tsp hot pepper sauce
1 tsp cornflour

## method

**1** In a small bowl, stir together the chicken stock, sesame seeds, ginger, soy sauce, hot pepper sauce and cornflour until well blended. Set aside.

**2** In a large frying pan or wok, heat 2 tablespoons of the oil. Stir-fry the carrots for 3 minutes, then remove from the pan and set aside.

**3** Add another 1 tablespoon of the oil to the frying pan and fry the mushrooms for 2 minutes. Remove from the pan and set aside.

**4** Add more oil if needed and stir-fry the pepper with the prawns and garlic for 3 minutes, until the prawns turn pink and opaque.

**5** Stir the sauce again and pour it into the frying pan. Cook until the mixture bubbles, then return the carrots and mushrooms to the pan. Cover and cook for a further 2 minutes, until heated through. Serve garnished with coriander.

# prawns, mangetout & cashew nuts

## ingredients

**SERVES 4**

85 g/3 oz cashew nuts

3 tbsp peanut oil

4 spring onions, slivered

2 celery sticks, thinly sliced

3 carrots, finely sliced

100 g/3$^1$/$_2$ oz baby corn, halved

175 g/6 oz mushrooms, finely sliced

1 clove of garlic, roughly chopped

450 g/1 lb raw prawns, peeled

1 tsp cornflour

2 tbsp soy sauce

50 ml/2 fl oz chicken stock

225 g/8 oz Savoy cabbage, shredded

175 g/6 oz mangetout

freshly cooked rice, to serve

## method

**1** Put a frying pan or wok over a medium heat, add the cashew nuts and toast them until they begin to brown. Remove with a slotted spoon and set aside.

**2** Add the oil to the frying pan and heat. Add the spring onions, celery, carrots and baby corn and cook, stirring occasionally, over a medium–high heat for 3–4 minutes.

**3** Add the mushrooms and cook until they become brown. Mix in the garlic and prawns, stirring until the prawns turn pink.

**4** Mix the cornflour with the soy sauce and chicken stock until smooth. Add the liquid to the prawn mixture and stir. Then add the Savoy cabbage, mangetout and all but a few of the cashew nuts and cook for 2 minutes.

**5** Serve on a bed of rice, garnished with the reserved cashew nuts.

# curried noodles with prawns & straw mushrooms

## ingredients

**SERVES 4**

1 tbsp vegetable or peanut oil

3 shallots, chopped

1 fresh red chilli, deseeded
    and chopped

1 tbsp Thai red curry paste

1 lemon grass stalk (white
    part only), chopped finely

225 g/8 oz cooked shelled
    prawns

400 g/14 oz canned straw
    mushrooms, drained

2 tbsp fish sauce

2 tbsp Thai soy sauce

225 g/8 oz fresh egg noodles

fresh coriander, chopped,
    to garnish

## method

**1** Heat the oil in a wok and stir-fry the shallots and chilli for 2–3 minutes. Add the curry paste and lemon grass and stir-fry for 2–3 minutes.

**2** Add the prawns, mushrooms, fish sauce and soy sauce and stir well to mix.

**3** Meanwhile, cook the noodles in boiling water for 3–4 minutes, drain and transfer to warmed plates.

**4** Top with the prawn curry, sprinkle the coriander over and serve immediately.

# prawn & pineapple curry

## ingredients

**SERVES 4**

$1/2$ fresh pineapple

400 ml/14 fl oz coconut cream

2 tbsp Thai red curry paste

2 tbsp fish sauce

2 tsp sugar

350 g/12 oz raw jumbo
    prawns

2 tbsp chopped coriander

steamed jasmine rice, to serve

## method

**1** Peel the pineapple and chop the flesh. Heat the coconut cream, pineapple, curry paste, fish sauce and sugar in a wok or saucepan until almost boiling.

**2** Shell and devein the prawns. Add the prawns and chopped coriander to the wok and simmer for 3 minutes, or until the prawns are cooked – they are cooked when they have turned a bright pink colour.

**3** Serve the prawns with steamed jasmine rice.

# noodles with prawns & green peppers

## ingredients

**SERVES 4**

250 g/9 oz rice noodles

1 tbsp vegetable oil

2 garlic cloves, crushed

1 fresh red chilli, deseeded
  and thinly sliced

1 green pepper, deseeded and
  thinly sliced

6 spring onions, coarsely
  chopped

2 tsp cornflour

2 tbsp oyster sauce

1 tbsp Thai fish sauce

1 tsp sugar

300 ml/10 fl oz chicken stock

250 g/9 oz small cooked
  prawns, shelled

## method

**1** Prepare the noodles according to the packet directions. Drain, then rinse under cold water and drain again.

**2** Heat the oil in a preheated wok. Add the garlic, chilli, pepper and spring onions. Cook for 1 minute, then transfer to a plate and reserve.

**3** Blend the cornflour with a little water and add to the wok with the oyster sauce, fish sauce, sugar and stock. Stir over medium heat until the mixture boils and thickens.

**4** Return the pepper and spring onion mixture to the wok with the prawns and noodles. Cook, stirring, for 2 minutes, or until heated through. Transfer to a heated serving bowl and serve immediately.

# prawns with noodles

## ingredients

**SERVES 4**

450 g/1 lb uncooked jumbo
   prawns
1 tbsp vegetable or peanut oil
3 shallots, chopped finely
2 garlic cloves, chopped finely
2.5-cm/1-inch piece fresh
   ginger, sliced thinly
400 ml/14 fl oz canned
   coconut milk
1 tbsp Thai green curry paste
3–4 fresh Thai basil leaves
1 tsp jaggery or soft light
   brown sugar
225 g/8 oz flat rice noodles
2 tsp sesame oil
2 tbsp sesame seeds, toasted
sprigs fresh Thai basil,
   to garnish

## method

**1** Remove and discard the heads and shell the prawns. Cut a slit along the back of each and remove and discard the dark vein.

**2** Heat the oil in a wok and stir-fry the shallots, garlic and ginger for 2–3 minutes. Add the coconut milk and curry paste and simmer for 2–3 minutes.

**3** Add the prawns, basil leaves and sugar and cook until the prawns turn pink.

**4** Meanwhile, cook the noodles in boiling water according to the packet instructions, then drain well. Stir in the sesame oil and seeds, garnish with the sprigs of basil and serve immediately with the prawns.

# prawns with coconut rice

## ingredients

**SERVES 4**

115 g/4 oz dried Chinese
   mushrooms
2 tbsp vegetable or peanut oil
6 spring onions, chopped
55 g/2 oz dry unsweetened
   coconut
1 fresh green chilli, deseeded
   and chopped
225 g/8 oz jasmine rice
150 ml/5 fl oz fish stock
400 ml/14 fl oz coconut milk
350 g/12 oz cooked shelled
   prawns
6 sprigs fresh Thai basil

## method

**1** Place the mushrooms in a small bowl, cover with hot water and set aside to soak for 30 minutes. Drain, then cut off and discard the stalks and slice the caps.

**2** Heat 1 tablespoon of the oil in a wok and stir-fry the spring onions, coconut and chilli for 2–3 minutes, until lightly browned. Add the mushrooms and stir-fry for 3–4 minutes.

**3** Add the rice and stir-fry for 2–3 minutes, then add the stock and bring to the boil. Reduce the heat and add the coconut milk. Simmer for 10–15 minutes, until the rice is tender. Stir in the prawns and basil, heat through and serve.

# prawns with spring onions & straw mushrooms

## ingredients

**SERVES 4**

2 tbsp vegetable or peanut oil
bunch of spring onions,
    chopped
2 garlic cloves, chopped finely
175 g/6 oz block creamed
    coconut, chopped coarsely
2 tbsp Thai red curry paste
450 ml/15 fl oz fish stock
2 tbsp fish sauce
2 tbsp Thai soy sauce
6 sprigs fresh Thai basil
400 g/14 oz canned straw
    mushrooms, drained
350 g/12 oz large cooked
    shelled prawns
boiled jasmine rice, to serve

## method

**1** Heat the oil in a wok and stir-fry the spring onions and garlic for 2–3 minutes. Add the creamed coconut, red curry paste and fish stock and heat gently until the coconut has dissolved.

**2** Stir in the fish sauce and soy sauce, then add the basil, mushrooms and prawns. Gradually bring to the boil and serve immediately with jasmine rice.

# malaysian-style coconut noodles with prawns

## ingredients

**SERVES 4**

2 tbsp vegetable oil

1 small red pepper, deseeded and diced

200 g/7 oz pak choi, stalks thinly sliced and leaves chopped

2 large garlic cloves, chopped

1 tsp ground turmeric

2 tsp garam masala

1 tsp chilli powder (optional)

125 ml/4 fl oz hot vegetable stock

2 heaped tbsp smooth peanut butter

350 ml/12 fl oz coconut milk

1 tbsp soy sauce

250 g/9 oz thick rice noodles

280 g/10 oz cooked peeled jumbo prawns

2 spring onions, finely shredded and 1 tbsp sesame seeds, to garnish

## method

**1** Heat the oil in a preheated wok or large, heavy-based frying pan over a high heat. Add the red pepper, pak choi stalks and garlic and stir-fry for 3 minutes. Add the turmeric, garam masala, chilli powder, if using, and pak choi leaves and stir-fry for 1 minute.

**2** Mix the hot stock and peanut butter together in a heatproof bowl until the peanut butter has dissolved, then add to the stir-fry with the coconut milk and soy sauce. Cook for 5 minutes over a medium heat, or until reduced and thickened.

**3** Meanwhile, immerse the noodles in a bowl of just boiled water. Let stand for 4 minutes, then drain and refresh the noodles under cold running water. Add the cooked noodles and prawns to the coconut curry and cook for a further 2–3 minutes, stirring frequently, until heated through.

**4** Serve the noodle dish sprinkled with spring onions and sesame seeds.

# prawn laksa

## ingredients

**SERVES 4**

20–24 large raw unpeeled
    prawns
450 ml/16 fl oz fish stock
pinch of salt
1 tsp peanut oil
450 ml/16 fl oz coconut milk
2 tsp nam pla (Thai fish sauce)
1/2 tablespoon lime juice
115 g/4 oz dried medium
    rice-flour noodles
115 g/4 oz beansprouts
fresh coriander, chopped,
    to garnish

laksa paste

6 fresh coriander stalks with
    leaves
3 large garlic cloves, crushed
1 fresh red chilli, deseeded
    and chopped
1 lemon grass stalk, centre
    part only, chopped
2.5-cm/1-inch piece fresh
    ginger, peeled and
    chopped
1 1/2 tbsp shrimp paste
1/2 tsp ground turmeric
2 tbsp peanut oil

## method

**1** Remove the heads and shells from the prawns, leaving the tails intact, and devein. Reserve the heads and shells. Put the fish stock, salt and the prawn heads and shells in a saucepan over a high heat and slowly bring to the boil. Lower the heat and simmer for 10 minutes.

**2** Meanwhile, make the laksa paste. Put all the ingredients, except the oil, in a food processor and blend. With the motor running, slowly add up to 2 tablespoons of peanut oil just until a paste forms. (If your food processor is too large to work efficiently with this small quantity, use a mortar and pestle.)

**3** Heat the 1 teaspoon of peanut oil in a large saucepan over a high heat. Add the paste and stir-fry until it is fragrant. Strain the fish stock through a sieve lined with muslin. Stir the stock into the laksa paste, along with the coconut milk, nam pla and lime juice. Bring to the boil, then cover and simmer for 30 minutes.

**4** Meanwhile, soak the noodles in a large bowl with enough lukewarm water to cover for 20 minutes, until soft. Drain and set aside.

**5** Add the prawns and beansprouts to the soup and continue simmering just until the prawns turn opaque and curl. Divide the noodles between 4 bowls and ladle the soup over. Serve garnished with chopped coriander.

# thai fisherman's catch

## ingredients

**SERVES 4**

20 cooked jumbo prawns

20 cooked mussels in their
shells (discard any mussels
that remain closed after
cooking)

55 g/2 oz oyster mushrooms,
wiped

2 spring onions, finely sliced

3 kaffir lime leaves, thinly
sliced

1 lemon grass stalk, centre
part only, finely chopped

1/2 red onion, very thinly sliced

100 g/3 1/2 oz dried medium
rice noodles


thai coconut
dressing

125 ml/4 fl oz creamed
coconut

3 tbsp lime juice

1 1/2 tbsp nam pla (Thai
fish sauce)

1 1/2 tbsp brown sugar

1–2 fresh red chillies, to taste,
deseeded and thinly sliced

1 small garlic clove, crushed

## method

**1** To make the dressing, stir all the ingredients together in a large bowl until the sugar dissolves. Add the prawns, mussels, mushrooms, spring onions, lime leaves, lemon grass and red onion, then cover and chill until required.

**2** Meanwhile, soak the noodles in a bowl with enough lukewarm water to cover for 20 minutes, until soft, or cook according to the packet instructions. Drain well.

**3** To serve, divide the noodles between 4 bowls. Spoon the seafood salad over them, adding any extra dressing.

# prawns fu yung

## ingredients

### SERVES 4–6

1 tbsp vegetable or peanut oil

115 g/4 oz raw prawns, peeled and deveined

4 eggs, lightly beaten

1 tsp salt

pinch of white pepper

2 tbsp finely chopped Chinese chives

## method

**1** In a preheated wok, heat the oil and stir-fry the prawns until they begin to turn pink.

**2** Season the beaten eggs with the salt and pepper and pour over the prawns. Stir-fry for 1 minute, then add the chives.

**3** Cook for a further 4 minutes, stirring all the time, until the eggs are cooked through but still soft in texture, and serve immediately.

# wok-fried jumbo prawns in spicy sauce

## ingredients

**SERVES 4**

3 tbsp vegetable or peanut oil

450 g/1 lb raw king prawns,
    deveined but unpeeled

2 tsp finely chopped fresh
    ginger

1 tsp finely chopped garlic

1 tbsp chopped spring onion

2 tbsp chilli bean sauce

1 tsp Shaoxing rice wine

1 tsp sugar

$^1/_2$ tsp light soy sauce

1–2 tbsp chicken stock

## method

**1** In a preheated wok, heat the oil, then toss in the prawns and stir-fry over high heat for about 4 minutes. Arrange the prawns on the sides of the wok out of the oil, then throw in the ginger and garlic and stir until fragrant. Add the spring onion and chilli bean sauce. Stir the prawns into this mixture.

**2** Lower the heat slightly and add the Shaoxing, sugar, light soy sauce and a little chicken stock. Cover and cook for a further minute. Serve immediately.

# somen noodles with prawns

## ingredients

**SERVES 2**

1 tbsp oil

16 raw prawns, peeled and
    deveined

3 shiitake mushrooms, finely
    sliced

1/4 white or green cabbage,
    shredded

1 carrot, shredded

2 bundles of somen noodles

6 shiso leaves, shredded

dressing

3 tbsp oil

1 tbsp sesame seeds, toasted

125 ml/4 fl oz Japanese rice
    vinegar

1 tbsp sugar

1 tbsp usukuchi shoyu
    (Japanese light soy sauce)

salt

## method

**1** To make the dressing, mix all the dressing ingredients together, with salt to taste, in a non-metallic bowl.

**2** Preheat a wok over high heat. Add the oil and heat until very hot. Add the prawns and cook, tossing occasionally, until they have turned pink.

**3** Add the mushrooms to the wok and stir-fry for 1 minute, then add the cabbage and carrot and toss together. Remove from the heat and set aside to cool.

**4** Cook the noodles according to the packet instructions, then drain. Put in a large bowl with the prawn mixture. Add the dressing and toss well. Sprinkle with the shiso leaves and serve.

# thai-style chirashi sushi with crabmeat

## ingredients

### SERVES 4

175 g/6 oz cooked crabmeat

juice of 2 limes, plus 4 thin slices of lime to garnish

2 large red chillies, deseeded and finely chopped

115 g/4 oz shelled fresh peas

salt

1 quantity freshly cooked sushi rice

2 tbsp chopped fresh coriander

1 sheet of toasted nori, cut into thin strips

## method

**1** Put the crabmeat in a bowl and squeeze over the lime juice. Stir in the chopped chilli.

**2** Place the peas in a pan of boiling salted water for 2 minutes or until just tender, then plunge into ice-cold water to stop the cooking. Drain well.

**3** Add the peas to the sushi rice, turning the rice to mix evenly. Divide the mixture between 4 serving bowls.

**4** Top each bowl with a quarter of the crab mixture and sprinkle with 1/2 tablespoon of the chopped coriander. Add a quarter of the nori strips and garnish with a slice of lime.

# fried fish with pine kernels

## ingredients

**SERVES 4–6**

1/2 tsp salt

450 g/1 lb thick white fish
    fillets, cut into 2.5-cm/
    1-inch cubes

2 dried Chinese mushrooms,
    soaked in warm water
    for 20 minutes

3 tbsp vegetable or peanut oil

2.5-cm/1-inch piece of fresh
    ginger, finely shredded

1 tbsp chopped spring onions

1 red pepper, cut into
    2.5-cm/1-inch squares

1 green pepper, cut into
    2.5-cm/1-inch squares

25 g/1 oz fresh or canned
    bamboo shoots, rinsed
    and cut into small cubes
    (if using fresh shoots,
    boil in water first for
    30 minutes)

2 tsp Shaoxing rice wine

2 tbsp pine kernels, toasted

## method

**1** Sprinkle the salt over the fish and set aside for 20 minutes. Squeeze out any excess water from the mushrooms and finely slice, discarding any tough stems.

**2** In a preheated wok, heat 2 tablespoons of the oil and fry the fish for 3 minutes. Drain and set aside.

**3** In a clean, preheated wok, heat the remaining oil and toss in the ginger. Stir until fragrant, then add the spring onions, peppers, bamboo shoots, mushrooms and Shaoxing and cook for 1–2 minutes.

**4** Finally add the fish and stir to warm through. Sprinkle with the pine kernels and serve.

# whole deep-fried fish with soy & ginger

## ingredients

**SERVES 4–6**

6 dried Chinese mushrooms, soaked in warm water for 20 minutes

3 tbsp rice vinegar

2 tbsp brown sugar

3 tbsp dark soy sauce

7.5-cm/3-inch piece fresh ginger, finely chopped

4 spring onions, sliced diagonally

2 tsp cornflour

2 tbsp lime juice

1 sea bass, cleaned and scaled, about 1 kg/ 2 lb 4 oz

4 tbsp plain flour

sunflower oil, for deep-frying

salt and pepper

shredded Napa cabbage and radish slices, to serve

1 radish, sliced but left whole, to garnish

## method

**1** Drain the mushrooms, reserving 100 ml/ 3¹/₂ fl oz of the liquid. Cut the mushrooms into thin slices. Mix the reserved mushroom liquid with the vinegar, sugar and soy sauce. Put in a saucepan with the mushrooms and bring to the boil. Reduce the heat and simmer for 3–4 minutes. Add the ginger and spring onions and simmer for 1 minute.

**2** Blend the cornflour and lime juice, stir into the pan, and cook, stirring, for 1–2 minutes until the sauce thickens and clears. Set aside.

**3** Season the fish inside and out with salt and pepper, then dust lightly with flour.

**4** Heat 2.5 cm/1 inch of oil in a wide, heavy-based saucepan to 180–190°C/350–375°F, or until a cube of bread browns in 30 seconds. Lower the fish carefully into the oil and deep-fry on one side for 3–4 minutes until golden brown. Use 2 metal spatulas to turn the fish carefully and deep-fry on the other side for a further 3–4 minutes, until golden brown.

**5** Remove the fish, drain off the excess oil and put on a serving plate. Reheat the sauce until boiling, then spoon it over the fish. Serve immediately with shredded Napa cabbage and sliced radishes, garnished with the radish.

# five-willow fish

## ingredients

**SERVES 4–6**

1 whole sea bass or similar,
   weighing 450–650 g/
   1 lb–1 lb 7 oz, gutted
2 tsp salt
6 tbsp vegetable or peanut oil
2 slices fresh ginger
2 garlic cloves, finely sliced
2 spring onions, roughly
   chopped
1 green pepper, thinly sliced
1 red pepper, thinly sliced
1 carrot, finely sliced
55 g/2 oz fresh or canned
   bamboo shoots, rinsed and
   thinly sliced (if using fresh
   shoots, boil in water first for
   30 minutes)
2 tomatoes, peeled, deseeded
   and thinly sliced
1 tbsp Shaoxing rice wine
2 tbsp white rice vinegar
1 tbsp light soy sauce
1 tbsp sugar

## method

**1** To prepare the fish, clean and dry it thoroughly. Score the fish on both sides with deep, diagonal cuts. Press 1/2 teaspoon of the salt into the skin.

**2** In a preheated wok or deep saucepan, heat 4 tablespoons of the oil and cook the fish for about 4 minutes on each side, or until the flesh is soft. Drain, then set aside and keep warm.

**3** In a preheated wok or deep saucepan, heat the remaining oil and stir-fry the ginger, garlic and spring onions until fragrant. Toss in the vegetables with the remaining salt and stir rapidly for 2–3 minutes. Add the remaining ingredients and cook, mixing well, for 2–3 minutes. Pour the sauce over the fish and serve immediately.

# steamed sole with black bean sauce

## ingredients

**SERVES 3-4**

1 sole, gutted

1/2 tsp salt

2 tsp fermented black beans, rinsed and chopped

2 tsp finely chopped garlic

1 tsp finely shredded fresh ginger

1 tbsp shredded spring onions

1 tbsp light soy sauce

1 tsp Shaoxing rice wine

1 tsp vegetable or peanut oil

dash of sesame oil

1/2 tsp sugar

pinch of white pepper

## method

**1** Place the fish on a plate or create a small dish with foil.

**2** Arrange all the other ingredients on top of the fish. Place in a steamer for about 10–12 minutes, or until the fish is cooked through.

# deep-fried river fish with chilli bean sauce

## ingredients

**SERVES 4–6**

1 whole freshwater fish, such
    as trout or carp, weighing
    400 g/14 oz, gutted
1 heaped tbsp plain flour
pinch of salt
100 ml/3½ fl oz water
vegetable or peanut oil,
    for deep-frying

s a u c e

1 tsp dried chilli flakes
100 ml/3½ fl oz vegetable or
    peanut oil
1 garlic clove, finely chopped
1 tsp finely chopped fresh
    ginger
1 tbsp chilli bean sauce
½ tsp white pepper
2 tsp sugar
1 tbsp white rice vinegar
1 tsp finely chopped spring
    onions

## method

**1** To prepare the fish, clean and dry thoroughly. Mix together the flour, salt and water to create a light batter. Coat the fish.

**2** Heat enough oil for deep-frying in a wok, deep-fat fryer, or large heavy-based saucepan to 180–190°C/350–375°F, or until a cube of bread browns in 30 seconds. Deep-fry the fish until the skin is crisp and golden brown. Drain, then set aside and keep warm.

**3** To make the sauce, put the dried chilli flakes in a heatproof dish. Heat all but 1 tablespoon of the oil in a small saucepan and, when smoking, pour over the dried chilli flakes. Set aside.

**4** In a preheated wok or deep saucepan, heat the remaining oil and stir-fry the garlic and ginger until fragrant. Stir in the chilli bean sauce, then add the oil and chilli flake mixture. Season with the pepper, sugar and vinegar. Turn off the heat and stir in the spring onions. Tip over the fish and serve immediately.

# pork & cos lettuce in egg & lemon sauce

## ingredients

### SERVES 4

4 pork loin steaks
salt and pepper
2 tbsp olive oil
bunch spring onions, white
      parts only, thinly sliced
1 cos lettuce, thinly sliced
      widthways
1 tbsp chopped fresh dill
225 ml/8 fl oz chicken stock
2 eggs
juice of 1 large lemon

## method

**1** Season the pork steaks with pepper. Heat the oil in a large, heavy-based frying pan, add the spring onions and fry until softened. Add the pork steaks and fry for 10 minutes, turning the steaks several times, until browned on both sides and tender.

**2** When the pork steaks are cooked, add the lettuce, dill and stock to the frying pan. Bring to the boil, cover and then simmer for 4–5 minutes or until the lettuce has wilted.

**3** Meanwhile, put the eggs and lemon juice in a large bowl and whisk together.

**4** When the lettuce has wilted, remove the pork steaks and lettuce from the frying pan with a slotted spoon, put in a warmed serving dish and keep warm in a low oven. Strain the cooking liquid into a measuring jug.

**5** Gradually add 4 tablespoons of the hot cooking liquid to the lemon mixture, whisking all the time. Pour the egg mixture into the frying pan and simmer for 2–3 minutes, whisking all the time, until the sauce thickens. (Do not boil or the sauce will curdle.) Season with salt and pepper. Pour the sauce over the pork steaks and lettuce and serve hot.

# stir-fried fresh crab with ginger

## ingredients

**SERVES 4**

3 tbsp vegetable or peanut oil

2 large fresh crabs, cleaned, broken into pieces and legs cracked with a cleaver

55 g/2 oz fresh ginger, julienned

100 g/3¹/₂ oz spring onions, chopped into 5-cm/2-inch lengths

2 tbsp light soy sauce

1 tsp sugar

pinch of white pepper

## method

**1** In a preheated wok or deep saucepan, heat 2 tablespoons of the oil and cook the crab over a high heat for 3–4 minutes. Remove and set aside.

**2** In the clean wok or deep saucepan, heat the remaining oil, then toss in the ginger and stir until fragrant. Add the spring onions, then stir in the crab pieces. Add the light soy sauce, sugar and pepper. Cover and simmer for 1 minute, then serve immediately.

# chirashi sushi with lobster & wasabi mayonnaise

## ingredients

**SERVES 4**

1 cooked prepared lobster

5 tbsp pickled ginger

1 quantity freshly cooked
   sushi rice

1/2 cucumber, cut into slices

1 ripe avocado, peeled, stoned
   and cut into slices

2 tsp wasabi paste

wasabi mayonnaise

2 tbsp Japanese mayonnaise

1 tsp wasabi paste, or to taste

## method

**1** Take the meat out of the lobster shell, keeping it in as large pieces as you can. If your lobster is whole, the best way to do this is to twist off the head and halve the body down the centre with a big sharp knife or cleaver. The claws will have to be smashed open to get at the meat. Cover them with a cloth and hit them hard with a rolling pin.

**2** Make the wasabi mayonnaise by mixing together the mayonnaise and wasabi.

**3** Chop 1 tablespoon of the pickled ginger very finely and mix it with the sushi rice.

**4** Divide the rice between 4 serving bowls. Arrange the lobster, cucumber and avocado on top of the rice, and spoon the wasabi mayonnaise into the gaps. Garnish each bowl with 1 tablespoon of the pickled ginger and 1/2 teaspoon of the wasabi paste.

# baby squid stuffed with pork & mushrooms

## ingredients

**SERVES 6–8**

400 g/14 oz baby squid

4 dried Chinese mushrooms, soaked in warm water for 20 minutes

225 g/8 oz pork mince

4 water chestnuts, finely chopped

1/2 tsp sesame oil

1 tsp salt

1/2 tsp white pepper

dark soy sauce and 1 red Thai chilli, chopped (optional), to serve

## method

**1** Clean the squid thoroughly, removing all the tentacles. Squeeze out any excess water from the mushrooms and finely chop, discarding any tough stems.

**2** Mix the mushrooms with the pork, water chestnuts, sesame oil, salt and pepper.

**3** Force the stuffing into the squid, pressing firmly but leaving enough room to secure each one with a cocktail stick.

**4** Steam for 15 minutes. Serve with a good soy sauce for dipping, adding the chilli, if you like.

# sweet chilli squid

## ingredients

**SERVES 4**

1 tbsp sesame seeds, toasted

2¹/₂ tbsp sesame oil

280 g/10 oz squid, cut into
strips

2 red peppers, thinly sliced

3 shallots, thinly sliced

85 g/3 oz mushrooms, thinly
sliced

1 tbsp dry sherry

4 tbsp soy sauce

1 tsp sugar

1 tsp hot chilli flakes,
or to taste

1 clove of garlic, crushed

freshly cooked rice, to serve

## method

**1** Place the sesame seeds on a baking sheet, toast under a hot grill and set aside.

**2** Heat 1 tablespoon of the oil in a frying pan or wok over a medium heat. Add the squid and cook for 2 minutes, then remove and set aside.

**3** Add another 1 tablespoon of the oil to the frying pan and fry the peppers and shallots over a medium heat for 1 minute. Add the mushrooms and fry for a further 2 minutes.

**4** Return the squid to the frying pan and add the sherry, soy sauce, sugar, chilli flakes and garlic, stirring thoroughly. Cook for a further 2 minutes.

**5** Sprinkle with the toasted sesame seeds, drizzle over the remaining sesame oil and mix. Serve on a bed of freshly cooked rice.

# stir-fried squid with hot black bean sauce

## ingredients

**SERVES 4**

750 g/1 lb 10 oz squid, cleaned and tentacles discarded

1 large red pepper, deseeded

115 g/4 oz mangetout

1 head pak choi

3 tbsp black bean sauce

1 tbsp Thai fish sauce

1 tbsp rice wine or dry sherry

1 tbsp dark soy sauce

1 tsp brown sugar

1 tsp cornflour

1 tbsp water

1 tbsp corn oil

1 tsp sesame oil

1 small fresh red Thai chilli, chopped

1 garlic clove, finely chopped

1 tsp grated fresh ginger

2 spring onions, chopped

## method

**1** Cut the squid body cavities into quarters lengthways. Use the tip of a small, sharp knife to score a diamond pattern into the flesh, without cutting all the way through. Pat dry with kitchen paper.

**2** Cut the pepper into long, thin slices. Cut the mangetout in half diagonally. Coarsely shred the pak choi.

**3** Mix the black bean sauce, fish sauce, rice wine, soy sauce and sugar together in a bowl. Blend the cornflour with the water and stir into the other sauce ingredients. Reserve until required.

**4** Heat the oils in a preheated wok. Add the chilli, garlic, ginger and spring onions and stir-fry for 1 minute. Add the pepper slices and stir-fry for 2 minutes.

**5** Add the squid and stir-fry over high heat for a further 1 minute. Stir in the mangetout and pak choi and stir for a further 1 minute, or until wilted.

**6** Stir in the sauce ingredients and cook, stirring constantly, for 2 minutes, or until the sauce thickens and clears. Serve immediately.

# squid & red peppers

## ingredients

**SERVES 4**

spice paste

2 tbsp vegetable or peanut oil

1 tbsp chilli oil with prawns

2 shallots, chopped

2–3 large fresh red chillies, deseeded and chopped

2 tbsp ground coriander

2 tbsp ground cumin

2.5-cm/1-inch piece fresh ginger, chopped

1 tbsp finely chopped lemon grass

3–4 coriander roots, chopped

1 tsp salt

1 tsp soft light brown sugar

stir-fry

2 red peppers, deseeded and diced

150 ml/5 fl oz plain yogurt

750 g/1 lb 10 oz squid, cleaned and sliced

juice of 1 lime

115 g/4 oz block creamed coconut, chopped

150 ml/5 fl oz hot water

## method

**1** Put all the ingredients for the spice paste into a food processor and process until chopped finely.

**2** Scrape the spice paste into a wok and stir-fry gently for 3–4 minutes. Add the red peppers and stir-fry for 1–2 minutes.

**3** Add the yogurt and bring to the boil. Add the squid and simmer for 2–3 minutes, then stir in the lime juice, coconut and water. Simmer for a further 1–2 minutes, until the coconut dissolves. Serve immediately.

# squid & red onion stir-fry

## ingredients

**SERVES 4**

450 g/1 lb squid rings
2 tbsp plain flour
$1/2$ tsp salt
1 green pepper
2 tbsp peanut oil
1 red onion, sliced
160-g/5$3/4$-oz jar black
    bean sauce

## method

**1** Rinse the squid rings under cold running water and pat dry with kitchen paper.

**2** Place the flour and salt in a bowl and mix together. Add the squid rings and toss until they are finely coated.

**3** Using a sharp knife, seed the pepper and slice into thin strips.

**4** Heat the peanut oil in a large preheated wok. Add the pepper and red onion to the wok and stir-fry for 2 minutes, or until the vegetables are just beginning to soften. Add the squid rings and cook for a further 5 minutes, or until the squid is cooked through.

**5** Add the black bean sauce to the wok and heat through until the juices are bubbling. Transfer to warmed bowls and serve immediately.

# salt & pepper squid wraps

## ingredients

**MAKES 6 PIECES**

4 tbsp plain flour
1 tsp Szechuan pepper or
    black pepper, crushed
1 tsp sea salt, crushed
12 squid rings, membranes
    removed, cut in half
vegetable oil, for frying
3 sheets of toasted nori
1/4 quantity freshly cooked
    sushi rice
4 tbsp Japanese mayonnaise

## method

**1** Mix the flour with the crushed Szechuan or black pepper and salt. Put the seasoned flour into a plastic bag with the squid and shake until the squid is thoroughly coated.

**2** Heat about 2 cm/3/4 inch of oil in a wok until it is very hot. Add the seasoned squid in batches and cook, stirring, for 1 minute, or until the coating is browned. Drain on kitchen paper to get rid of any excess oil.

**3** Fold a nori sheet in half lengthways, press along the fold and then tear it into 2 pieces. Lay a half-sheet smooth-side down on a work surface and place a heaped tablespoon of rice on the left. Lay 4 cooked squid halves on the rice and spoon over 2/3 tablespoon of the mayonnaise.

**4** Fold the bottom left-hand corner of the nori over the rice and filling, so that the folded edge forms a right angle with the bottom edge. Continue folding along that line to make a cone with a sharp point at the bottom. Place a drop of vinegared water on the underside of the join to seal it.

**5** Repeat with the rest of the ingredients to make 6 cones in total.

# rice with seafood & squid

## ingredients

**SERVES 4**

2 tbsp vegetable or peanut oil

3 shallots, chopped finely

2 garlic cloves, chopped finely

225 g/8 oz jasmine rice

300 ml/10 fl oz fish stock

4 spring onions, chopped

2 tbsp Thai red curry paste

225 g/8 oz baby squid,
cleaned and sliced thickly

225 g/8 oz white fish fillets,
skinned and cut into cubes

225 g/8 oz salmon fillets,
skinned and cut into cubes

4 tbsp chopped fresh
coriander

## method

**1** Heat 1 tablespoon of the oil in a wok and stir-fry the shallots and garlic for 2–3 minutes, until softened. Add the rice and stir-fry for 2–3 minutes.

**2** Add a ladleful of the stock and simmer, adding more stock as needed, for 12–15 minutes, until tender. Transfer to a dish, let cool and chill overnight.

**3** Heat the remaining oil in a wok and stir-fry the spring onions and curry paste for 2–3 minutes. Add the squid and fish and stir-fry gently to avoid breaking up the fish. Stir in the rice and coriander, heat through gently and serve.

# congee with fish fillet

## ingredients

**SERVES 6–8**

225 g/8 oz short-grain rice

3 litres/5¼ pints water

200 g/7 oz firm white fish fillet, flaked

2 tsp salt

½ tsp white pepper

175 g/6 oz lettuce, finely shredded

2 tbsp finely shredded spring onions

2 tbsp finely shredded fresh ginger

3 tbsp light soy sauce, to serve

## method

**1** Wash the rice and place in a large saucepan with the water. Cover and cook for about 2 hours, stirring regularly.

**2** Add the fish fillet, salt and pepper. Stir well, then return to the boil and cook for a couple more minutes.

**3** To serve, divide the lettuce, spring onions and ginger between large individual bowls. Pour the congee on top. Finally, sprinkle each bowl with 1–2 teaspoons of good quality soy sauce.

# seafood chow mein

## ingredients

**SERVES 4**

85 g/3 oz squid, cleaned

3–4 fresh scallops

85 g/3 oz raw prawns, peeled

1/2 egg white, lightly beaten

2 tsp cornflour, mixed to a
     paste with 2 1/2 tsp water

275 g/9 3/4 oz dried thin
     Chinese egg noodles

5–6 tbsp vegetable oil

2 tbsp light soy sauce

55 g/2 oz mangetout

1/2 tsp salt

1/2 tsp sugar

1 tsp Chinese rice wine

2 spring onions, shredded
     finely

a few drops of sesame oil

## method

**1** Open up the squid and score the inside in a criss-cross pattern, then cut into pieces about 2.5 cm/1 inch square. Soak the squid in a bowl of boiling water until all the pieces curl up. Rinse in cold water and drain.

**2** Cut each scallop into 3–4 slices. Cut the prawns in half lengthways if large. Mix the scallops and prawns with the egg white and cornflour paste.

**3** Cook the noodles in boiling water according to the packet instructions, then drain and rinse under cold water. Drain well, then toss with about 1 tablespoon of the oil.

**4** Heat 3 tablespoons of the oil in a preheated wok. Add the noodles and 1 tablespoon of the soy sauce and stir-fry for 2–3 minutes. Remove to a large serving dish.

**5** Heat the remaining oil in the wok and add the mangetout and seafood. Stir-fry for about 2 minutes, then add the salt, sugar, rice wine, remaining soy sauce and about half the spring onions. Blend well and add a little water if necessary. Pour the seafood mixture on top of the noodles and sprinkle with sesame oil. Garnish with the remaining spring onions and serve immediately.

# mixed seafood curry

## ingredients

### SERVES 4

1 tbsp vegetable or peanut oil

3 shallots, chopped finely

2.5-cm/1-inch piece fresh
galangal, peeled and sliced
thinly

2 garlic cloves, chopped finely

400 ml/14 fl oz canned
coconut milk

2 lemon grass stalks,
snapped in half

4 tbsp fish sauce

2 tbsp chilli sauce

225 g/8 oz uncooked jumbo
prawns, shelled

225 g/8 oz baby squid,
cleaned and sliced thickly

225 g/8 oz skinned salmon
fillet, cut into chunks

175 g/6 oz tuna steak,
cut into chunks

225 g/8 oz fresh mussels,
scrubbed and debearded

fresh Chinese chives,
to garnish

boiled rice, to serve

## method

**1** Heat the oil in a large wok and stir-fry the shallots, galangal and garlic for 1–2 minutes, until they start to soften. Add the coconut milk, lemon grass, fish sauce and chilli sauce. Bring to the boil, reduce the heat and simmer for 1–2 minutes.

**2** Add the prawns, squid, salmon and tuna and simmer for 3–4 minutes, until the prawns have turned pink and the fish is cooked.

**3** Add the mussels and cover with a lid. Simmer for 1–2 minutes, until they have opened. Discard any mussels that remain closed. Garnish with Chinese chives and serve immediately with rice.

# fish curry

## ingredients

SERVES 4

juice of 1 lime

4 tbsp fish sauce

2 tbsp Thai soy sauce

1 fresh red chilli, deseeded
    and chopped

350 g/12 oz monkfish fillet,
    cut into cubes

350 g/12 oz salmon fillets,
    skinned and cut into cubes

400 ml/14 fl oz coconut milk

3 kaffir lime leaves

1 tbsp Thai red curry paste

1 lemon grass stalk (white
    part only), chopped finely

225 g/8 oz jasmine rice, boiled

4 tbsp chopped fresh
    coriander

## method

**1** Combine the lime juice, half the fish sauce and the soy sauce in a shallow, non-metallic dish. Add the chilli and the fish, stir to coat, cover with clingfilm and chill for 1–2 hours, or overnight.

**2** Bring the coconut milk to the boil in a saucepan and add the lime leaves, curry paste, the remaining fish sauce and the lemon grass. Simmer gently for 10–15 minutes.

**3** Add the fish and the marinade and simmer for 4–5 minutes, until the fish is cooked. Serve hot with boiled rice with chopped coriander stirred through it.

# fish curry with rice noodles

## ingredients

**SERVES 4**

2 tbsp vegetable or peanut oil

1 large onion, chopped

2 garlic cloves, chopped

75 g/3 oz white mushrooms

225 g/8 oz monkfish, cut into
    cubes, each about
    2.5 cm/1 inch

225 g/8 oz salmon fillets,
    cut into cubes, each about
    2.5 cm/1 inch

225 g/8 oz cod, cut into
    cubes, each about
    2.5 cm/1 inch

2 tbsp Thai red curry paste

400 g/14 oz canned coconut
    milk

handful of fresh coriander,
    chopped

1 tsp soft light brown sugar

1 tsp fish sauce

115 g/4 oz rice noodles

3 spring onions, chopped

55 g/2 oz beansprouts

few Thai basil leaves

## method

**1** Heat the oil in a wok or large frying pan and gently sauté the onion, garlic and mushrooms until softened but not browned.

**2** Add the fish, curry paste and coconut milk and bring gently to the boil. Simmer for 2–3 minutes, then add half the coriander, the sugar and fish sauce. Keep warm.

**3** Meanwhile, soak the noodles for 3–4 minutes (check the packet instructions) or until tender, and drain well through a colander. Put the colander and noodles over a pan of simmering water. Add the spring onions, beansprouts and most of the basil and steam on top of the noodles for 1–2 minutes or until just wilted.

**4** Pile the noodles onto warmed serving plates and top with the fish curry. Sprinkle the remaining coriander and basil over the top and serve immediately.

# stir-fried rice noodles with marinated fish

## ingredients

**SERVES 4**

450 g/1 lb monkfish or cod,
  cubed
225 g/8 oz salmon fillets,
  cubed
2 tbsp vegetable or peanut oil
2 fresh green chillies,
  deseeded and chopped
grated rind and juice of 1 lime
1 tbsp fish sauce
115 g/4 oz wide rice noodles
2 tbsp vegetable or peanut oil
2 shallots, sliced
2 garlic cloves, chopped finely
1 fresh red chilli, deseeded
  and chopped
2 tbsp Thai soy sauce
2 tbsp chilli sauce
sprigs of fresh coriander,
  to garnish

## method

**1** Place the fish in a shallow, non-metallic bowl. To make the marinade, mix the oil, green chillies, lime juice and rind and fish sauce together and pour over the fish. Cover and chill for 2 hours.

**2** Put the noodles in a bowl and cover with boiling water. Leave for 8–10 minutes (check the packet instructions) and drain well.

**3** Heat the oil in a wok or large frying pan and sauté the shallots, garlic and red chilli until lightly browned. Add the soy sauce and chilli sauce. Add the fish and the marinade to the wok and stir-fry gently for 2–3 minutes until cooked through.

**4** Add the drained noodles and stir gently. Sprinkle with coriander and serve immediately.

# fish in coconut

## ingredients

**SERVES 4**

2 tbsp vegetable or peanut oil

6 spring onions, chopped
coarsely

2.5-cm/1-inch piece fresh
ginger, grated

2–3 tbsp Thai red curry paste

400 ml/14 fl oz coconut milk

150 ml/5 fl oz fish stock

4 kaffir lime leaves

1 lemon grass stalk, halved

350 g/12 oz skinned white fish
fillets, cut into chunks

225 g/8 oz squid rings and
tentacles

225 g/8 oz large cooked
shelled prawns

1 tbsp fish sauce

2 tbsp Thai soy sauce

4 tbsp chopped fresh Chinese
chives

boiled jasmine rice with
chopped fresh coriander,
to serve

## method

**1** Heat the oil in a wok or large frying pan and stir-fry the spring onions and ginger for 1–2 minutes. Add the curry paste and stir-fry for 1–2 minutes.

**2** Add the coconut milk, fish stock, lime leaves and lemon grass. Bring to the boil, then reduce the heat and simmer for 1 minute.

**3** Add the fish, squid and prawns and simmer for 2–3 minutes, until the fish is cooked. Add the fish and soy sauces and stir in the chives. Serve immediately with jasmine rice with fresh coriander stirred through it.

# spiced steamed fish

## ingredients

**SERVES 4–6**

2.5-cm/1-inch piece fresh
　ginger, finely grated
1 lemon grass stem
　(base only), thinly sliced
6 fresh red chillies, deseeded
　and coarsely chopped
1 small red onion, finely
　chopped
1 tbsp Thai fish sauce
900 g/2 lb whole fish, cleaned
2 fresh kaffir lime leaves,
　thinly sliced
2 fresh basil sprigs
freshly cooked rice and thin
　cucumber sticks, to serve

## method

**1** Place the ginger, lemon grass, chillies, onion and fish sauce in a food processor. Process to a coarse paste, adding a little water, if needed.

**2** Cut 3–4 deep slits crosswise on each side of the fish. Spread over the spice paste, rubbing it well into the slits. Place the fish in a dish deep enough to hold the liquid that collects during steaming. Sprinkle over the lime leaves and basil.

**3** Set up a steamer or place a rack into a wok or deep frying pan. Bring about 5 cm/2 inches of water to the boil in the steamer or wok.

**4** Place the dish of fish into the steamer or on the rack. Reduce the heat to a simmer, then cover tightly and steam the fish for 15–20 minutes, or until cooked through. Serve with freshly cooked rice and cucumber sticks.

# steamed yellow fish fillets

## ingredients

**SERVES 4**

500 g/1 lb 2 oz firm fish fillets,
   such as red snapper, sole
   or monkfish
1 red bird chilli
1 small onion, chopped
3 garlic cloves, chopped
2 coriander sprigs
1 tsp coriander seeds
1/2 tsp ground turmeric
1/2 tsp pepper
1 tbsp Thai fish sauce
2 tbsp coconut milk
1 small egg, beaten
2 tbsp rice flour
fresh red and green chilli
   strips, to garnish
stir-fried vegetables, to serve

## method

**1** Using a sharp knife, remove any skin from the fish and cut the fillets diagonally into 2-cm/ 3/4-inch wide strips.

**2** Place the bird chilli, onion, garlic, coriander and coriander seeds in a mortar and, using a pestle, grind to make a smooth paste.

**3** Transfer the paste to a bowl and add the turmeric, pepper, fish sauce, coconut milk and beaten egg, stirring to mix evenly. Spread the rice flour out on a large plate. Dip the fish strips into the paste mixture, then into the rice flour to coat lightly.

**4** Bring the water in the bottom of a steamer to the boil, then arrange the fish strips in the top of the steamer. Cover and steam for 12–15 minutes, or until the fish is just firm.

**5** Garnish the fish with the chilli strips and serve immediately with stir-fried vegetables.

# chirashi sushi with salmon

## ingredients

**SERVES 4**

8 large raw prawns, heads
removed

salt

1 tbsp sake

1 tbsp rice vinegar

250 g/9 oz sashimi-grade
salmon

7.5-cm/3-inch piece of
kombu, cut into thin strips

juice of 1 lemon

115 g/4 oz mangetout, tips
removed

1 quantity freshly cooked
sushi rice

55 g/2 oz lotus root, thinly
sliced

4 tbsp salmon roe

4 shiso leaves, to garnish

Japanese soy sauce, pickled
ginger and wasabi paste,
to serve

## method

**1** Insert a thin wooden skewer along the underside of each prawn to prevent it from curling during cooking. Place 2.5 cm/1 inch of water in a large pan and add a little salt and the sake. Bring to the boil, add the skewered prawns and simmer for 2 minutes or until they turn pink. Drain and cool.

**2** Peel each prawn, cut along the back of the body and scrape out the intestinal thread. Deepen the incision and carefully open the prawn into a flat butterfly shape. Sprinkle with the rice vinegar and place in the refrigerator until needed.

**3** Slice the salmon into 8-mm/1/3-inch thick strips, using a wet, very sharp knife and cutting across the grain. Wipe your knife on a damp cloth between each cut. Place in a bowl with the kombu strips and lemon juice. Set aside for 15 minutes, turning the fish once.

**4** Drop the mangetout into boiling salted water for 1 minute to blanch, then plunge into ice-cold water. Drain, then cut into strips.

**5** Divide the sushi rice between 4 serving bowls. To each bowl, add a quarter of the salmon, 2 cooked prawns, a quarter of the sliced mangetout and lotus root, and 1 tablespoon of the salmon roe. Garnish with a shiso leaf and serve with soy sauce, pickled ginger and wasabi paste alongside.

# classic sushi boat with salmon roe

## ingredients

**MAKES 8 PIECES**

1/3 quantity freshly cooked
   sushi rice
2 sheets of toasted nori, each
   cut into 4 strips lengthways
wasabi paste
8 tbsp salmon, trout, or flying
   fish roe
soy sauce and pickled ginger,
   to serve

## method

**1** Divide the rice into 8 equal batches. Wet your hands to stop the rice sticking, then shape each batch of rice into an oval. Carefully wrap a strip of nori round each oval of rice and trim off any excess. Place a drop of vinegared water on the underside of the join to seal it.

**2** Dab a little wasabi on top of each sushi boat and top with 1 tablespoon of the roe. Repeat with the rest of the ingredients. Serve with soy sauce, pickled ginger and more wasabi paste on the side.

# seared salmon sashimi with sesame & black pepper

## ingredients

**SERVES 4**

55 g/2 oz daikon (long white radish)

85 g/3 oz white sesame seeds

black pepper

400 g/14 oz sashimi-grade salmon

2 tsp peanut oil

4 shiso leaves

ponzu dipping sauce, to serve

## method

**1** Shred the daikon using the finest setting on a mandolin. Alternatively, cut it into long thin slices and then cut each slice along its length as finely as possible. Rinse, drain and then place in the refrigerator until needed.

**2** Crush the sesame seeds using a mortar and pestle, and spread over a large plate. Grind over plenty of black pepper and stir to mix.

**3** Trim the salmon fillet into a neat rectangle. Heat the oil in a frying pan until very hot. Sear the salmon for 1 minute on both sides and the edges, then remove from the pan.

**4** Lay the salmon on the sesame and pepper mixture and turn to coat evenly. Use a wet, very sharp knife to cut the seared salmon into 8-mm/1/3-inch thick oblongs, slicing across the grain. Wipe your knife on a damp cloth between each cut.

**5** Arrange the slices on 4 serving plates. Place a shiso leaf on each plate and top with a quarter of the shredded daikon. Serve with the ponzu dipping sauce.

# wraps with fresh tuna, salmon roe & shiso leaves

## ingredients

**MAKES 6 PIECES**

115 g/4 oz sashimi-grade tuna

3 sheets of toasted nori

1/4 quantity freshly cooked
   sushi rice

wasabi paste

6 shiso leaves, finely chopped

2 tbsp salmon roe

Japanese soy sauce, pickled
   ginger and wasabi paste,
   to serve

## method

**1** Trim the tuna and cut it into strips about 8 mm/1/3 inch thick, using a wet, very sharp knife and slicing across the grain. Wipe your knife on a damp cloth between each cut.

**2** Fold a sheet of nori in half lengthways, press along the fold and then tear it into 2 pieces. Put the half you are not using straight away back into the packet or cover it with clingfilm so that it does not dry out.

**3** Lay the half-sheet of nori smooth-side down on a work surface and place a heaped tablespoon of rice on the left-hand side. Dab the rice with a little wasabi paste. Top with a sixth of the tuna, then add a sixth of the chopped shiso leaves.

**4** Fold the bottom left-hand corner of the nori over the rice and filling, so that the folded edge forms a right angle with the bottom edge. Continue folding along that line to make a cone with a sharp point at the bottom. Place a drop of vinegared water on the underside of the join to seal it.

**5** Put 1 teaspoon of the salmon roe in the cone to garnish. Repeat with the rest of the ingredients to make 6 cones in total. Serve with soy sauce, pickled ginger and wasabi paste on the side.

# salmon, cucumber & pickled radish wraps

## ingredients

**MAKES 6 PIECES**

115 g/4 oz sashimi-grade salmon

3 sheets of toasted nori

1/4 quantity freshly cooked sushi rice

wasabi paste

1/3 cucumber, deseeded and cut into thin strips

55 g/2 oz takuan (pickled radish), cut into thin strips

Japanese soy sauce, pickled ginger and wasabi paste, to serve

## method

**1** Trim the salmon and cut into strips about 8 mm/1/3 inch thick, using a wet, very sharp knife and slicing across the grain. Wipe your knife on a damp cloth between each cut.

**2** Fold a nori sheet in half lengthways, press along the fold and then tear it into 2 pieces. Put the half you are not using straight away back into the packet or cover it with clingfilm so that it does not dry out.

**3** Lay a half-sheet of nori smooth-side down on a work surface and place a heaped tablespoon of rice on the left-hand side. Dab the rice with a little wasabi paste. Top with a sixth of the salmon strips, then add a sixth of the cucumber and takuan strips.

**4** Fold the bottom left-hand corner of the nori over the rice and filling, so that the folded edge forms a right angle with the bottom edge. Continue folding along that line to make a cone with a sharp point at the bottom. Place a drop of vinegared water on the underside of the join to seal it.

**5** Repeat with the rest of the ingredients to make 6 cones in total. Serve with soy sauce, pickled ginger and wasabi paste.

# salmon & scallops with coriander & lime

## ingredients

### SERVES 4

6 tbsp peanut oil

280 g/10 oz salmon steak, skinned and cut into 2.5-cm/1-inch chunks

225 g/8 oz scallops

3 carrots, thinly sliced

2 celery sticks, cut into 2.5-cm/1-inch pieces

2 orange peppers, thinly sliced

175 g/6 oz oyster mushrooms, thinly sliced

1 clove garlic, crushed

6 tbsp chopped fresh coriander

3 shallots, thinly sliced

2 limes, juiced

1 tsp grated lime rind

1 tsp dried red pepper flakes

3 tbsp dry sherry

3 tbsp soy sauce

cooked noodles, to serve

## method

**1** In a wok or large frying pan, heat the oil over a medium heat. Add the salmon and scallops and stir-fry for 3 minutes. Remove from the pan, then set aside and keep warm.

**2** Add the carrots, celery, peppers, mushrooms and garlic to the wok and stir-fry for 3 minutes. Add the coriander and shallots, and stir.

**3** Add the lime juice and rind, dried red pepper flakes, sherry and soy sauce and stir. Return the salmon and scallops to the wok and stir-fry carefully for another minute.

**4** Serve immediately on a bed of cooked noodles.

# pan-fried spiced salmon

## ingredients

SERVES 4

2.5-cm/1-inch piece fresh root
    ginger, grated
1 tsp coriander seeds,
    crushed
1/4 tsp chilli powder
1 tbsp lime juice
1 tsp sesame oil
4 salmon fillet pieces with
    skin, about 150 g/
    5 1/2 oz each
2 tbsp vegetable oil
stir-fried vegetables and
    freshly cooked rice,
    to serve
coriander leaves, to garnish

## method

**1** Mix the ginger, crushed coriander, chilli powder, lime juice and sesame oil together in a bowl.

**2** Place the salmon on a wide, non-metallic plate or dish and spoon the mixture over the flesh side of the fillets, spreading it to coat each piece of salmon evenly.

**3** Cover the dish with clingfilm and chill in the refrigerator for 30 minutes.

**4** Heat a wide, heavy-based frying pan or ridged griddle pan with the vegetable oil over high heat. Place the salmon in the hot pan, skin-side down, and cook for 4–5 minutes, without turning, until the salmon is crusty underneath and the flesh flakes easily.

**5** Serve the salmon immediately, with stir-fried vegetables and freshly cooked rice garnished with coriander leaves.

# barbecued tuna with chilli salsa

## ingredients

**SERVES 4**

4 tuna steaks, about
    175 g/6 oz each
grated rind and juice of 1 lime
2 tbsp olive oil
salt and pepper
green salad, to serve

chilli salsa
2 orange peppers
1 tbsp olive oil
juice of 1 lime
juice of 1 orange
2–3 fresh red chillies,
    deseeded and chopped
pinch of cayenne pepper

## method

**1** Rinse the tuna thoroughly under cold running water and pat dry with kitchen paper, then place in a large shallow non-metallic dish. Sprinkle the lime rind and juice and the oil over the fish. Season with salt and pepper, cover with clingfilm and marinate in the refrigerator for up to 1 hour.

**2** Preheat the barbecue. To make the salsa, brush the peppers with the olive oil and cook over hot coals, turning frequently, for 10 minutes, or until the skin is blackened and charred. Remove from the grill and cool slightly, then peel off the skins and discard the seeds. Place the peppers in a food processor with the remaining salsa ingredients and process to a purée. Transfer to a bowl and season with salt and pepper.

**3** Cook the tuna over hot coals for 4–5 minutes on each side until golden. Transfer to plates, and serve immediately with the green salad and the salsa.

# marinated tuna chirashi sushi

## ingredients

**SERVES 4**

350 g/12 oz sashimi-grade
   tuna
juice of 2 lemons
1 tbsp soy sauce
1 quantity freshly cooked
   sushi rice
4 tbsp finely chopped chives
4 tbsp pickled ginger
2 tsp wasabi paste
4 shiso leaves, to garnish
4 tsp white sesame seeds,
   toasted

## method

**1** Put the tuna into a bowl and pour the lemon juice and soy sauce over the top. Turn the tuna to coat, then place in the refrigerator and marinate for 30 minutes.

**2** Remove the tuna from the marinade and slice into 8-mm/1/3-inch thick strips, using a wet, very sharp knife and cutting across the grain. Wipe your knife on a damp cloth between each cut to keep the tuna strips neat.

**3** Divide the sushi rice between 4 serving bowls. Arrange the tuna slices on the rice and sprinkle the chives over the top.

**4** Add 1 tablespoon of pickled ginger and 1/2 teaspoon of wasabi paste to each bowl, garnish with a shiso leaf or two, and sprinkle with the toasted sesame seeds.

# tuna tataki hand rolls

## ingredients

**MAKES 6 PIECES**

1 tsp freshly ground black
    pepper
1 tbsp shredded fresh ginger
1 tbsp white sesame seeds
150 g/5$^{1}/_{2}$ oz very fresh tuna
    fillet
salt
2 tbsp vegetable oil
3 sheets of toasted nori
$^{1}/_{4}$ quantity freshly cooked
    sushi rice
$^{1}/_{2}$ cucumber, deseeded and
    cut into thin sticks
4 tbsp Japanese mayonnaise
wasabi paste

## method

**1** Mix together the black pepper, shredded ginger and sesame seeds. Rub the mixture all over the tuna, pressing the seeds on firmly. Season the tuna lightly with salt.

**2** Heat the oil in a frying pan until it is very hot. Cook the tuna for 4 minutes on each side, or until just cooked through. Remove from the frying pan, cool, then cut into thin slices.

**3** Fold a nori sheet in half lengthways, press along the fold and then tear it into 2 pieces. Lay a half-sheet smooth-side down on a work surface and place a heaped tablespoon of rice on the left. Lay a sixth of the tuna strips and cucumber sticks on the rice, then spoon over $^{2}/_{3}$ tablespoon of the mayonnaise and dot a little wasabi paste on top.

**4** Fold the bottom left-hand corner of the nori over the rice and filling, so that the folded edge forms a right angle with the bottom edge. Continue folding along that line to make a cone with a sharp point at the bottom. Place a drop of vinegared water on the underside of the join to seal it.

**5** Repeat with the rest of the ingredients to make 6 cones in total.

# spiced tuna in sweet-&-sour sauce

## ingredients

**SERVES 4**

4 fresh tuna steaks, about
500 g/1 lb 2 oz in total

1/4 tsp pepper

2 tbsp peanut oil

1 onion, diced

1 small red pepper, deseeded
and cut into short thin
sticks

1 garlic clove, crushed

1/2 cucumber, deseeded and
cut into short thin sticks

2 pineapple slices, diced

1 tsp finely chopped
fresh ginger

1 tbsp brown sugar

1 tbsp cornflour

1 1/2 tbsp lime juice

1 tbsp Thai fish sauce

300 ml/10 fl oz fish stock

lime slices and cucumber
slices, to garnish

## method

**1** Sprinkle the tuna steaks with pepper on both sides. Heat a heavy-based frying pan or ridged griddle pan and brush with a little of the oil. Arrange the tuna steaks in the pan and cook for 8 minutes, turning them once.

**2** Meanwhile, heat the remaining oil in a separate frying pan. Add the onion, pepper and garlic and cook gently for 3–4 minutes to soften.

**3** Remove the pan from the heat and stir in the cucumber, pineapple, ginger and sugar.

**4** Blend the cornflour with the lime juice and fish sauce, then stir into the stock and add to the pan. Stir over medium heat until boiling, then cook for 1–2 minutes, or until thickened and clear.

**5** Spoon the sauce over the tuna and serve immediately, garnished with slices of lime and cucumber.

# monkfish with lime & chilli sauce

## ingredients

### SERVES 4

4 x 115-g/4-oz monkfish fillets
25 g/1 oz rice flour
  or cornflour
6 tbsp vegetable or peanut oil
4 garlic cloves, crushed
2 large fresh red chillies,
  deseeded and sliced
2 tsp jaggery or soft light
  brown sugar
juice of 2 limes
grated rind of 1 lime
boiled rice, to serve

## method

**1** Toss the fish in the flour, shaking off any excess. Heat the oil in a wok and cook the fish on all sides until browned and cooked through, taking care when turning not to break it up.

**2** Lift the fish out of the wok and keep warm. Add the garlic and chillies and stir-fry for 1–2 minutes, until they have softened.

**3** Add the sugar, the lime juice and rind and 2–3 tablespoons of water and bring to the boil. Simmer gently for 1–2 minutes, then spoon the mixture over the fish. Serve immediately with rice.

# monkfish stir-fry

## ingredients

**SERVES 4**

2 tsp sesame oil

450 g/1 lb monkfish steaks, cut into 2.5-cm/1-inch chunks

1 red onion, sliced thinly

3 cloves garlic, chopped finely

1 tsp grated fresh ginger

225 g/8 oz fine tip asparagus

185 g/6 oz mushrooms, sliced thinly

2 tbsp soy sauce

1 tbsp lemon juice

lemon wedges, to garnish

cooked noodles, to serve

## method

**1** Heat the oil in a wok over medium-high heat. Add the fish, onion, garlic, ginger, asparagus and mushrooms. Stir-fry for 2–3 minutes.

**2** Stir in the soy sauce and lemon juice and cook for another minute. Remove from the heat and transfer to warm serving dishes.

**3** Garnish with lemon wedges and serve immediately on a bed of cooked noodles.

# spicy thai seafood stew

## ingredients

**SERVES 4**

200 g/7 oz squid, cleaned and
tentacles discarded
500 g/1 lb 2 oz firm white fish
fillet, preferably monkfish
or halibut
1 tbsp corn oil
4 shallots, finely chopped
2 garlic cloves, finely chopped
2 tbsp Thai green curry paste
2 small lemon grass stems,
finely chopped
1 tsp shrimp paste
500 ml/16 fl oz coconut milk
200 g/7 oz raw king prawns,
peeled and deveined
12 live clams in shells,
cleaned
8 fresh basil leaves, finely
shredded
fresh basil leaves, to garnish
freshly cooked rice, to serve

## method

**1** Using a sharp knife, cut the squid body cavities into thick rings and the white fish into bite-size chunks.

**2** Heat the oil in a large preheated wok. Add the shallots, garlic and curry paste and stir-fry for 1–2 minutes. Add the lemon grass and shrimp paste, then stir in the coconut milk and bring to the boil.

**3** Reduce the heat until the liquid is simmering gently, then add the white fish, squid and prawns to the wok and simmer for 2 minutes.

**4** Add the clams and simmer for a further 1 minute, or until the clams have opened. Discard any clams that remain closed.

**5** Sprinkle the shredded basil leaves over the stew. Transfer to serving plates, then garnish with whole basil leaves and serve immediately with rice.

# sweet-&-sour sea bass

## ingredients

**SERVES 2**

60 g/2¼ oz pak choi, shredded

40 g/1½ oz beansprouts

40 g/1½ oz shiitake mushrooms, sliced

40 g/1½ oz oyster mushrooms, torn

20 g/¾ oz spring onions, finely sliced

1 tsp finely grated fresh ginger

1 tbsp finely sliced lemon grass

2 x 90-g/3¼-oz sea bass fillets, skinned and boned

10 g/¼ oz sesame seeds, toasted

sweet-&-sour sauce

90 ml/3 fl oz unsweetened pineapple juice

1 tbsp sugar

1 tbsp red wine vinegar

2 star anise, crushed

6 tbsp tomato juice

1 tbsp cornflour, blended with a little cold water

## method

**1** Cut 2 x 38-cm/15-inch squares of baking paper and 2 x 38-cm/15-inch squares of aluminium foil.

**2** To make the sauce, heat the pineapple juice, sugar, red wine vinegar, star anise and tomato juice. Simmer for 1–2 minutes, then thicken with the cornflour and water mixture, whisking continuously. Pass through a fine sieve into a small bowl to cool.

**3** In a separate large bowl mix together the pak choi, beansprouts, mushrooms and spring onions, then add the ginger and lemon grass. Toss all the ingredients together.

**4** Put a square of greaseproof paper on top of a square of foil and fold into a triangle. Open up and place half the vegetable mix in the centre, pour half the sweet and sour sauce over the vegetables and place the sea bass on top. Sprinkle with a few sesame seeds. Close the triangle over the mixture and, starting at the top, fold the right corner and crumple the edges together to form an airtight triangular bag. Repeat to make another bag.

**5** Place on a baking sheet and cook in a preheated oven, 200°C/400°F/Gas Mark 6, for 10 minutes, until the foil bags puff with steam. To serve, place on individual plates and snip open at the table.

# chirashi sushi with smoked mackerel

## ingredients

**SERVES 4**

8 mangetout

5-cm/2-inch piece of daikon (long white radish)

1 quantity freshly cooked sushi rice

juice and zest of 1 lemon

2 spring onions, finely chopped

2 smoked mackerel, skin removed and cut into diagonal strips

1/2 cucumber, peeled and cut into slices

1 sheet of toasted nori, cut into thin strips

4 tbsp pickled ginger

2 tsp wasabi paste

## method

**1** Drop the mangetout into boiling, salted water for 1 minute to blanch, then plunge into ice-cold water to stop the cooking. Drain well.

**2** Shred the daikon using the finest setting on a mandolin or a very sharp knife. If you are using a knife, then cut the daikon into long, thin slices and cut each slice along its length as finely as you can. Rinse and then drain.

**3** Mix the sushi rice with the lemon juice and lemon zest.

**4** Divide the lemony rice between 4 serving bowls and sprinkle the spring onion over the top. Arrange the mackerel, cucumber, mangetout and daikon on top of the rice. Garnish with nori strips, and add 1 tablespoon of pickled ginger and 1/2 teaspoon of wasabi paste to each bowl.

# vegetarian

# omelette wraps with pickled radish & shiso

## ingredients

**MAKES 6 PIECES**

1/4 quantity freshly cooked
  sushi rice

wasabi paste

55 g/2 oz takuan (pickled
  radish), cut into thin strips

6 shiso leaves

### omelette wrappings

4 eggs

1 tsp caster sugar

2 tsp mirin

1 tsp Japanese soy sauce

1/4 tsp salt

3 tsp vegetable oil

## method

**1** First make the omelette. Gently whisk the eggs with the sugar, mirin, soy sauce and salt, taking care not to create large air bubbles. Strain into a jug.

**2** Pour 1 teaspoon of the oil into a tamago pan or frying pan, then heat over low to medium heat. Pour in 1/3 of the omelette mixture, tilting the pan to coat the base. When the omelette is almost set, flip it over and cook the other side. Turn it out onto a plate lined with kitchen paper and allow to cool. If using a round frying pan, trim to make a square shape. Cut the omelette in half, to make 2 wrappings.

**3** Place 1 piece of omelette on your chopping board. Spoon a heaped tablespoon of sushi rice onto the left-hand side. Dab a little wasabi over the rice. Place a sixth of the takuan strips and 1 shiso leaf over the rice.

**4** Fold the bottom left-hand corner of the omelette over the rice and filling, so that the folded edge forms a right angle with the bottom edge. Continue folding along that line to make a cone that ends in a point.

**5** Serve straight away while you use the rest of the ingredients to make the remaining rolls.

# omelette pouches with mushroom

## ingredients

**MAKES 6 PIECES**

15 g/$\frac{1}{2}$ oz butter

225 g/8 oz fresh mushrooms such as oyster or shiitake, sliced

$\frac{1}{4}$ quantity freshly cooked sushi rice

1 tbsp finely chopped flat-leaf parsley

pinch of cayenne pepper

6 long chives

Japanese soy sauce, pickled ginger and wasabi paste, to serve

### omelette wrappings

4 eggs

1 tsp caster sugar

2 tsp mirin

1 tsp Japanese soy sauce

$\frac{1}{4}$ tsp salt

4 tsp vegetable oil

## method

**1** Melt the butter in a small pan. When it is sizzling, add the sliced mushrooms and cook over high heat for 3–4 minutes until browned and reduced by half in volume.

**2** Remove the mushrooms with a slotted spoon and chop finely. Mix with the rice, chopped parsley and cayenne pepper.

**3** Now make the omelette wrappings. Gently whisk the eggs with the sugar, mirin, soy sauce and salt, taking care not to produce any large air bubbles. Strain into a jug.

**4** Pour $\frac{2}{3}$ teaspoon of the oil into a 15-cm/ 6-inch frying pan, then heat over low to medium heat. Pour in a sixth of the omelette mixture, tilting the pan to coat the base. When the omelette is almost set, flip it over and cook the other side. Turn out onto a plate lined with kitchen paper and allow to cool. Repeat until you have 6 thin omelettes.

**5** Transfer 1 omelette to your work surface and place a sixth of the mushroom and rice mixture in the centre. Gather up the 4 corners of the omelette and tie them together using a long chive. Repeat with the rest of the omelette wrappings. Serve with soy sauce, pickled ginger and wasabi paste.

# asparagus & omelette rolls

## ingredients

**MAKES 6–8 PIECES**

8 thin asparagus spears

4 eggs

1 tbsp water

1 tbsp mirin

1 tsp soy sauce

1/2 tbsp vegetable oil

ponzu dipping sauce, to serve

## method

**1** Lay the asparagus spears flat in a frying pan filled with simmering water and cook for 3 minutes or until tender. Cut into 9-cm/3½-inch lengths and set aside to cool.

**2** Whisk the eggs with the water, mirin and soy sauce. Heat the oil in a nonstick frying pan and pour in the egg mixture. Cook on one side until the top is just set, then lay the asparagus lengths in neat lines at one end of the pan.

**3** Shake the frying pan to loosen the omelette, then tip the pan away from you so that the omelette slides up the side. Using 2 chop-sticks, fold the omelette over the asparagus and then continue folding to make a roll.

**4** Lay a sheet of clingfilm over a rolling mat. Tip the omelette out onto the clingfilm. Roll it up, lifting away the mat and clingfilm as you go, and set aside to cool. This helps it to set in shape.

**5** Transfer the roll to a chopping board, seam-side down. Trim the ends and then cut the roll into 2-cm/3/4-inch pieces with a wet, very sharp knife. Turn the pieces on end and arrange them on a serving plate. Serve with the ponzu dipping sauce.

# asparagus & pepper rolls with tahini sauce

## ingredients

**MAKES 24 PIECES**

1/2 red pepper

4 very thin spears of asparagus

2 sheets of toasted nori

1/2 quantity freshly cooked
    sushi rice

tahini sauce

4 tsp tahini

1 tsp sugar

1 tsp Japanese soy sauce

1 tsp sake

## method

**1** Put the ingredients for the tahini sauce into a small bowl. Stir until the sugar dissolves.

**2** Place the pepper skin-side up under a hot grill until the skin blackens. Cool in a sealed plastic bag or box, then remove the skin and cut the flesh into thin strips. Blanch the asparagus spears in boiling water for 1–2 minutes, then dip into ice-cold water to stop the cooking. Drain.

**3** Fold a nori sheet in half lengthways, press along the fold and tear the sheet in half. Place a half-sheet smooth-side down on a rolling mat with one of the long sides towards you. With wet hands, spread a quarter of the rice over the nori, leaving a 1-cm/1/2-inch clear border along the furthest edge.

**4** Spread a line of tahini sauce across the rice at the end nearest to you. Top with a quarter of the pepper and add 1 asparagus spear.

**5** Pick up the nearest edge of the rolling mat. Slowly roll the mat away from you to wrap the nori around the filling. Press onto the clear border of nori to seal it. Transfer the roll to a chopping board and cut into 6 equal pieces using a wet, sharp knife. Repeat with the rest of the ingredients. Serve with the tahini sauce.

# pinwheel rolls with mushroom & spinach

## ingredients

**MAKES 24 PIECES**

200 g/7 oz spinach, stalks
    removed
1/2 tsp sesame oil
4 sheets of toasted nori
1 quantity freshly cooked
    sushi rice
wasabi paste
4 tsp pine nuts, toasted
Japanese soy sauce, pickled
    ginger and wasabi paste,
    to serve

spiced mushrooms
25 g/1 oz dried shiitake
    mushrooms, soaked in
    hot water for 30 minutes,
    then chopped finely, stems
    discarded
175 ml/6 fl oz dashi stock
1 tbsp mirin

## method

**1** First prepare the mushrooms. Place them in a pan with the dashi stock, bring to the boil and simmer for 15 minutes. Stir in the mirin and cool in the pan. Drain well.

**2** Wash the spinach and place in a pan with just the water that is clinging to the leaves. Cook for 2 minutes over medium heat to wilt. Press in a colander to squeeze out the water. Chop finely, then mix with the sesame oil.

**3** Place a nori sheet smooth-side down on a rolling mat so that one of the shorter sides is towards you. With wet hands, spread a quarter of the rice over the nori, leaving a 1-cm/1/2-inch clear border along the furthest edge.

**4** Dab a line of wasabi across the rice at the end nearest to you. Top with a quarter of the spiced mushrooms and place some of the sesame spinach alongside. Sprinkle with 1 teaspoon of the pine nuts.

**5** Slowly roll the mat to wrap the nori tightly around the filling, creating a pinwheel effect. Press the roll onto the uncovered border of the nori to seal it. Transfer the roll to a chopping board, seam-side down and cut it into 6 equal pieces using a wet, very sharp knife. Repeat with the rest of the ingredients. Serve with soy sauce, pickled ginger and wasabi.

# sesame-tofu chirashi sushi

## ingredients

**SERVES 4**

1 block firm tofu

2 red peppers, quartered and deseeded

1 sheet of toasted nori

1 quantity freshly cooked sushi rice

4 tbsp pickled ginger

2 tsp wasabi paste

2 tbsp finely chopped spring onions, green parts only, to garnish

pickled ginger and wasabi paste, to serve

### sesame marinade

1/4 tsp sesame oil

1 garlic clove, crushed

2-cm/3/4-inch piece fresh ginger, peeled and shredded

3 tbsp Japanese soy sauce

4 tbsp sake

1 tsp dark brown sugar

1 tsp red chilli flakes

## method

**1** Wrap the tofu in kitchen paper and place on a small chopping board. Put another chopping board on top and let stand for 30 minutes to squeeze out the excess water. Then cut the tofu into slices about 8 mm/1/3 inch thick, cutting across the block. Transfer the tofu slices to a small bowl.

**2** Place all the ingredients for the marinade in a bowl or jug and stir until the sugar dissolves. Pour the marinade over the tofu slices and carefully turn to coat. Place in the refrigerator for 20 minutes to marinate.

**3** Put the quartered peppers skin-side up under a hot grill until the skin blackens. Cool in a sealed plastic bag or box, then peel off the skin and cut the flesh into strips.

**4** Cut the nori sheet into squares measuring about 1 cm x 1 cm/1/2 inch x 1/2 inch.

**5** Divide the sushi rice between 4 serving bowls. Arrange the tofu slices on the rice and spoon a little of the marinade on top. Add a quarter of the pepper strips to each bowl, along with a few nori squares, 1 tablespoon of pickled ginger and 1/2 teaspoon of wasabi paste. Garnish with the chopped spring onions, and serve with pickled ginger and wasabi paste.

# oyster mushroom & fried tofu chirashi sushi

## ingredients

**SERVES 4**

2 sheets of abura-age (deep-fried tofu)

500 ml/18 fl oz dashi stock

4 tbsp sake

2 tbsp sugar

4 tbsp Japanese soy sauce

2 tbsp vegetable oil

450 g/1 lb fresh oyster or shiitake mushrooms, thinly sliced

1 quantity freshly cooked sushi rice

2 tsp white sesame seeds, toasted

Japanese soy sauce, pickled ginger and wasabi paste, to serve

## method

**1** Cut the fried tofu into thin strips. Place the dashi stock, sake, sugar and soy sauce in a pan, stir, then add the tofu strips. Cook over low heat for 15 minutes, uncovered, until the liquid has reduced by half. Drain well.

**2** Heat the oil in a frying pan. Add the mushrooms and cook, stirring, over medium to high heat for 2 minutes, until soft.

**3** Divide the rice between 4 serving bowls. Top with the seasoned fried tofu and the cooked mushrooms, and sprinkle with the toasted sesame seeds. Serve with soy sauce, pickled ginger and wasabi paste alongside.

# chirashi sushi with feta & sunblush tomatoes

## ingredients

**SERVES 4**

175 g/6 oz feta cheese

85 g/3 oz sunblush tomatoes in oil

handful of basil leaves, shredded, plus a few whole leaves to garnish

1 quantity freshly cooked sushi rice

55 g/2 oz baby spinach leaves

## method

**1** Drain the feta and cut it into small cubes. Slice the sunblush tomatoes into thin strips and pat with kitchen paper to remove any excess oil. Mix carefully with the feta and the shredded basil.

**2** Divide the sushi rice between 4 serving bowls. Arrange a quarter of the baby spinach leaves on each serving, and top with a mound of the feta and tomato mixture. Garnish each serving with whole basil leaves.

# green bean & tomato chirashi sushi

## ingredients

**SERVES 4**

140 g/5 oz very thin green beans

140 g/5 oz tomatoes on the vine

1 yellow pepper

1 quantity freshly cooked sushi rice

4 tsp white sesame seeds, toasted

Japanese soy sauce, pickled ginger and wasabi paste, to serve

## method

**1** Drop the beans into a pan of boiling water for 1–2 minutes to blanch. Plunge into ice-cold water to stop the cooking, then drain.

**2** Cut the tomatoes into thin slices, discarding the seeds.

**3** Cut the pepper into quarters, remove and discard the seeds, and cut into thin strips.

**4** Divide the sushi rice between 4 serving bowls. Arrange the blanched green beans, sliced tomatoes and pepper strips on the rice. Scatter the toasted sesame seeds over the top. Serve with soy sauce, pickled ginger and wasabi paste alongside.

# sweet rolled omelette sushi

## ingredients

**MAKES 10 PIECES**

1/2 sheet of toasted nori

1/2 quantity freshly cooked sushi rice

Japanese soy sauce, pickled ginger and wasabi paste, to serve

rolled omelette

6 eggs

1 tsp caster sugar

2 tsp mirin

1 tsp Japanese soy sauce

1/4 tsp salt

1–2 tsp vegetable oil

## method

**1** First make the omelette. Gently beat the eggs together with the sugar, mirin, soy sauce and salt, taking care not to create large air bubbles. Strain into a jug.

**2** Heat a tamago pan or frying pan over medium heat. Use a brush or folded piece of kitchen paper to oil the pan. Add a third of the egg mixture to the pan and tilt the pan to cover the bottom evenly. When the omelette has just set, fold it 4 times lengthways towards you, using a wooden spatula. Set aside, trimming it into an oblong if you have used a round frying pan.

**3** Repeat with another third of the egg mixture, but place the first folded omelette on top of the omelette in the pan before you wrap it up. Do the same with the rest of the egg mixture, so that you end up with 1 thick roll. Let cool, then cut crosswise into 10 slices.

**4** Cut the half-sheet of nori into 10 strips about 1 cm/1/2 inch wide and 7.5 cm/3 inches long.

**5** Make 10 rice blocks using a finger sushi mould or by hand and place them on a chopping board.

**6** Place a slice of rolled omelette onto each rice block. Wrap a nori strip neatly around each one, tucking the ends under the rice block to secure. Serve with soy sauce, pickled ginger and wasabi paste.

# asparagus &
# red pepper sushi

## ingredients

**MAKES 10 PIECES**

2 red peppers, quartered and deseeded

30 baby asparagus

1/2 sheet of toasted nori

1/2 quantity freshly cooked sushi rice

Japanese soy sauce, pickled ginger and wasabi paste, to serve

## method

**1** Place the quartered peppers skin-side up under a hot grill until the skin blackens. Cool in a sealed plastic bag or box, peel off the skin and cut the flesh into strips. Drop the asparagus into boiling water for 1–2 minutes to blanch, then dip into ice-cold water to stop the cooking.

**2** Cut the half-sheet of nori into 10 strips about 1 cm/1/2 inch wide and 7.5 cm/3 inches long.

**3** Wet a sushi mould to stop the rice from sticking. Arrange a layer of pepper strips over the bottom, leaving no gaps. Top with half of the sushi rice and press down with the lid.

**4** Lift off the sides of the sushi mould, holding down the lid with your thumbs as you do so. Turn the sushi out onto a chopping board so that the peppers are on top, and slice into 5 equal pieces using a wet, very sharp knife. Repeat, to make 10 pieces in total.

**5** Place 3 asparagus tips lengthways across the centre of the pepper and secure with a strip of nori, tucking the ends under the rice block to keep it neatly in place. Serve with soy sauce, pickled ginger and wasabi paste.

# spiced carrot sushi

## ingredients

**MAKES 10 PIECES**

1/2 quantity freshly cooked
    sushi rice
1 tsp shredded fresh ginger,
    squeezed to remove excess
    water, to garnish
2 tsp finely chopped spring
    onion, green parts only,
    to garnish
Japanese soy sauce, pickled
    ginger and wasabi paste,
    to serve

### spiced carrot

125 ml/4 fl oz dashi stock
2 tsp caster sugar
2 tsp Japanese soy sauce
1 large carrot, peeled and cut
    into large thin slices

## method

**1** First prepare the spiced carrot. Put the dashi stock, sugar and soy sauce into a small pan and set over low heat. Add the carrot slices and cook for 5–6 minutes, until tender but still retaining a little bite. Drain and cool.

**2** Wet the sushi mould to stop the rice from sticking. Cover the bottom with a layer of the spiced carrot. Top with half the sushi rice, then press down with the lid.

**3** Lift off the sides of the sushi mould, holding down the lid with your thumbs as you do so. Turn the sushi out onto a chopping board so that the carrot layer is on top, and slice into 5 equal pieces. Repeat with the rest of the ingredients to make 10 pieces in total.

**4** Top each sushi bar with a little shredded ginger and spring onion. Serve with soy sauce, pickled ginger and wasabi paste on the side.

# mediterranean pressed sushi

## ingredients

**MAKES 10 PIECES**

2 red peppers, quartered and
deseeded
100 g/3½ oz mozzarella, cut
into thin slices
handful of small basil leaves
4 sundried tomatoes in oil,
drained and cut into strips
olive oil, for brushing
½ quantity freshly cooked
sushi rice

## method

**1** Place the quartered peppers skin-side up under a hot grill until the skin blackens. Cool in a sealed plastic bag or box, peel off the skin and cut the flesh into strips.

**2** Wet the sushi mould to prevent the rice from sticking. Arrange the grilled pepper and mozzarella in wide, diagonal strips over the bottom of the sushi press, placing thinner strips of basil leaves and sundried tomatoes in between. Brush with oil, then cover with half of the sushi rice. Press down with the lid.

**3** Lift off the sides of the sushi mould, holding down the lid with your thumbs as you do so. Turn the sushi out onto a chopping board so that the layer of mozzarella and pepper is on top. Slice into 5 equal pieces using a wet, very sharp knife. Wipe your knife on a damp cloth between cuts to keep your sushi neat. Repeat, so that you have 10 pieces in total.

# fresh shiitake mushroom sushi

## ingredients

**MAKES 10 PIECES**

1 tbsp Japanese soy sauce
10 fresh shiitake mushrooms,
    stems removed
1/2 sheet of toasted nori
1/2 quantity freshly cooked
    sushi rice
Japanese soy sauce, pickled
    ginger and wasabi paste,
    to serve

## method

**1** Brush the soy sauce onto the mushrooms and cook under a hot grill for 1–2 minutes on each side, or until tender.

**2** Cut the half-sheet of nori into 10 strips about 1 cm/1/2 inch wide and 7.5 cm/3 inches long.

**3** Wet a finger sushi mould. Fill each section with sushi rice, working the rice into the corners without pressing too hard. Press down with the lid, then remove it and turn the neat blocks out onto a chopping board. Repeat so that you have 10 blocks.

**4** Alternatively, shape the rice by hand. Take a golfball-sized amount of rice in the palm of one hand, then gently press it into an oblong, using your palm and the fingers of your other hand. The block should be 5 cm/2 inches long and 2 cm/3/4 inch wide. Repeat to make 10 blocks and place on a chopping board.

**5** Place 1 grilled mushroom, skin-side down, on each rice block. Secure with a nori strip, tucking the ends under the rice block. Serve with soy sauce, pickled ginger and wasabi paste on the side.

# sweet tofu pouches

## ingredients

**MAKES 8 PIECES**

4 abura-age (deep-fried tofu)

175 ml/6 fl oz dashi stock

3 tbsp soy sauce

2 tbsp caster sugar

1 tbsp sake

1 tbsp sesame seeds, toasted

1/4 quantity freshly cooked
   sushi rice

## method

**1** Put the tofu into a bowl and pour boiling water over it to remove any excess oil. Drain and cool. Cut each piece in half and gently open out each half into a bag.

**2** Place the dashi stock, soy sauce, sugar and sake in a pan, stir and bring to the boil. Add the tofu bags and simmer for 10–15 minutes until almost all the liquid has been absorbed. Remove from the heat, drain and cool. Press any remaining liquid out of the bags with a clean tea towel (the bags should be moist but not wet).

**3** Gently mix the toasted sesame seeds with the sushi rice. Fill the bags with the rice mixture and fold over the tops to enclose them. Serve at room temperature.

# seasoned tofu

## ingredients

**SERVES 2**

300 g/10½ oz silken tofu, drained
4 tbsp vegetable oil
2 spring onions, finely sliced
½ fresh red chilli, finely sliced
1 tbsp Japanese soy sauce
1 tsp sesame oil

## method

**1** Place the tofu on a heatproof serving plate. Cut the block into cubes, but keep it intact.

**2** Heat the oil in a small pan over high heat until hot. Add the sliced spring onions and chilli, and wait until they begin to sizzle.

**3** Pour the hot oil mixture over the tofu, then sprinkle with the soy sauce and sesame oil. Serve as a block.

# stuffed aubergines

## ingredients

**SERVES 4**

8 small aubergines

2 tbsp vegetable or peanut oil

4 shallots, chopped finely

2 garlic cloves, crushed

2 fresh red chillies, deseeded
    and chopped

1 courgette, chopped coarsely

115 g/4 oz block creamed
    coconut, chopped

few Thai basil leaves, chopped

small handful of fresh
    coriander, chopped

4 tbsp Thai soy sauce

rice with chopped spring
    onions, to serve

sweet chilli sauce, to serve

## method

**1** Put the aubergines in a roasting pan and cook in a preheated oven, 200°C/400°F/Gas Mark 6, for 8–10 minutes, until just softened. Cut in half and scoop out the flesh, reserving the shells.

**2** Heat the oil in a wok or large frying pan and sauté the shallots, garlic and chilli for 2–3 minutes before adding the courgettes and aubergine flesh. Add the creamed coconut, herbs and soy sauce and simmer for 3–4 minutes.

**3** Divide the mixture between the aubergine shells.

**4** Return to the oven for 5–10 minutes, until hot, and serve immediately with rice and sweet chilli sauce.

# aubergine & mushroom stuffed omelette

## ingredients

### SERVES 2

3 tbsp vegetable oil

1 garlic clove, finely chopped

1 small onion, finely chopped

1 small aubergine, diced

$1/2$ small green pepper, deseeded and chopped

1 large dried shiitake mushroom, soaked, drained and sliced

1 tomato, diced

1 tbsp light soy sauce

$1/2$ tsp sugar

$1/4$ tsp pepper

2 large eggs

salad leaves, tomato wedges and cucumber slices, to garnish

dipping sauce, to serve

## method

**1** Heat half the oil in a large frying pan. Add the garlic and cook over high heat for 30 seconds. Add the onion and the aubergine and continue to stir-fry until golden.

**2** Add the pepper and stir-fry for a further 1 minute to soften. Stir in the mushroom, tomato, soy sauce, sugar and pepper. Remove from the pan and keep hot.

**3** Beat the eggs together lightly. Heat the remaining oil in a clean frying pan, swirling to coat a wide area. Pour in the egg and swirl to set around the pan.

**4** When the egg is set, spoon the filling into the centre. Fold in the sides of the omelette to form a square package.

**5** Slide the omelette carefully onto a warmed dish and garnish with salad leaves, tomato wedges and cucumber slices. Serve with a dipping sauce.

# spiced cashew nut curry

## ingredients

**SERVES 4**

250 g/8³/₄ oz unsalted cashew
 nuts
1 tsp coriander seeds
1 tsp cumin seeds
2 cardamom pods, crushed
1 tbsp corn oil
1 onion, finely sliced
1 garlic clove, crushed
1 small fresh green chilli,
 deseeded and chopped
1 cinnamon stick
¹/₂ tsp ground turmeric
4 tbsp coconut cream
300 ml/10 fl oz hot vegetable
 stock
3 dried kaffir lime leaves,
 crumbled
coriander leaves, to garnish
freshly cooked jasmine rice,
 to serve

## method

**1** Place the cashew nuts in a bowl, then cover with cold water and soak overnight. Drain thoroughly. Crush the seeds and cardamom pods in a mortar using a pestle.

**2** Heat the oil in a large frying pan. Add the onion and garlic and stir-fry for 2–3 minutes to soften but not brown. Add the chilli, crushed spices, cinnamon stick and turmeric and stir-fry for a further 1 minute.

**3** Add the coconut cream and the hot stock to the frying pan. Bring to the boil, then add the cashew nuts and lime leaves.

**4** Cover the pan, then reduce the heat and simmer for 20 minutes. Serve hot with jasmine rice garnished with coriander leaves.

# courgette & cashew nut curry

## ingredients

**SERVES 4**

2 tbsp vegetable or peanut oil

6 spring onions, chopped

2 garlic cloves, chopped

2 fresh green chillies,
    deseeded and chopped

450 g/1 lb courgettes, cut into
    thick slices

115 g/4 oz shiitake
    mushrooms, halved

55 g/2 oz beansprouts

75 g/3 oz cashew nuts,
    toasted or dry-fried

few Chinese chives, chopped

4 tbsp Thai soy sauce

1 tsp fish sauce

rice or noodles, to serve

## method

**1** Heat the oil in a wok or large frying pan and sauté the onions, garlic and chillies for 1–2 minutes, until softened but not browned.

**2** Add the courgettes and mushrooms to the wok and cook for 2–3 minutes until tender.

**3** Add the beansprouts, nuts, chives and both sauces and stir-fry for 1–2 minutes.

**4** Serve hot with rice or noodles.

# carrot & pumpkin curry

## ingredients

**SERVES 4**

150 ml/5 fl oz vegetable stock

2.5-cm/1-inch piece fresh galangal, sliced

2 garlic cloves, chopped

1 lemon grass stalk (white part only), chopped finely

2 fresh red chillies, deseeded and chopped

4 carrots, peeled and cut into chunks

225 g/8 oz pumpkin, peeled, deseeded and cut into cubes

2 tbsp vegetable or peanut oil

2 shallots, chopped finely

3 tbsp Thai yellow curry paste

400 ml/14 fl oz coconut milk

4–6 sprigs fresh Thai basil

25 g/1 oz toasted pumpkin seeds, to garnish

## method

**1** Pour the stock into a large saucepan and bring to the boil. Add the galangal, half the garlic, the lemon grass and chillies and simmer for 5 minutes. Add the carrots and pumpkin and simmer for 5–6 minutes, until tender.

**2** Meanwhile, heat the oil in a wok or frying pan and stir-fry the shallots and the remaining garlic for 2–3 minutes. Add the curry paste and stir-fry for 1–2 minutes.

**3** Stir the shallot mixture into the pan and add the coconut milk and basil. Simmer for 2–3 minutes. Serve hot, sprinkled with the toasted pumpkin seeds.

# onion, potato & red pepper curry

## ingredients

**SERVES 4**

2 tbsp vegetable or peanut oil

2 red onions, sliced

2 garlic cloves, chopped finely

2-inch piece fresh ginger, chopped finely

1 fresh red chilli, deseeded and chopped

1 tbsp Thai red curry paste

225 g/8 oz potatoes, cut into cubes, boiled for 5 minutes and drained

2 red peppers, deseeded and diced

300 ml/10 fl oz vegetable stock

1 tsp salt

4 tbsp chopped fresh coriander

## method

**1** Heat the oil in a wok and stir-fry the onions, garlic, ginger and chilli for 2–3 minutes. Add the curry paste and stir-fry over low heat for 2–3 minutes.

**2** Add the potatoes, peppers, stock and salt and cook for 3–4 minutes, until all the vegetables are tender. Stir in the coriander and serve immediately.

# thai yellow vegetable curry with brown basmati rice

## ingredients

**SERVES 4**

50 g/1³/₄ oz yellow pepper, deseeded
50 g/1³/₄ oz celery
50 g/1³/₄ oz baby corn
85 g/3 oz leek
100 g/3¹/₂ oz sweet potato
100 g/3¹/₂ oz pak choi
50 g/1³/₄ oz courgette
50 g/1³/₄ oz mangetout
300 ml/10 fl oz pineapple juice
200 ml/7 fl oz water
3 tbsp lime juice
2 tbsp cornflour
4 tbsp low-fat plain yogurt
4 tbsp chopped fresh coriander
150 g/5¹/₂ oz cooked brown basmati rice

### spice mix

1 tsp finely chopped garlic
¹/₄ tsp ground turmeric
1 tsp ground coriander
1 tsp finely chopped lemon grass
3 kaffir lime leaves
1 tsp finely chopped green chilli

## method

**1** To make the spice mix, pound all the spices to a fine paste using a mortar and pestle.

**2** To prepare the vegetables, cut the yellow pepper into 1-cm/¹/₂-inch squares, cut the celery, baby corn and leek into 5-mm/¹/₄-inch lengths, and cut the sweet potato into 1-cm/¹/₂-inch cubes. Shred the pak choi. Cut the courgette into 5-mm/¹/₄-inch cubes and slice the mangetout into thin strips.

**3** Put the pepper, celery, baby corn, leek, sweet potato, pineapple juice, water and the spice mix into a large saucepan with a lid and bring to the boil. Reduce the heat and skim the scum from the surface with a metal spoon. Cover and simmer for 15 minutes.

**4** Add the pak choi, courgette and mangetout and cook for 2 minutes. Add the lime juice, then gradually add the cornflour blended with a little cold water. Cook, stirring constantly, until thickened to the required consistency.

**5** Remove the curry from the heat and cool for 2–3 minutes. Stir in the yogurt. (Do not boil once the yogurt has been added or the curry will separate.) Stir in the fresh coriander and serve the curry with the rice.

# rice noodles with mushrooms & tofu

## ingredients

**SERVES 4**

225 g/8 oz rice stick noodles

2 tbsp vegetable oil

1 garlic clove, finely chopped

2-cm/³/₄-inch piece fresh
    ginger, finely chopped

4 shallots, thinly sliced

225 g/8 oz sliced shiitake
    mushrooms

100 g/3¹/₂ oz firm tofu
    (drained weight), cut into
    1.5-cm/¹/₂-inch dice

2 tbsp light soy sauce

1 tbsp rice wine or dry sherry

1 tbsp Thai fish sauce

1 tbsp smooth peanut butter

1 tsp chilli sauce

2 tbsp toasted peanuts,
    chopped

shredded fresh basil leaves

## method

**1** Place the rice noodles in a bowl, then cover with hot water and soak for 15 minutes, or according to the packet directions. Drain well.

**2** Heat the oil in a large frying pan. Add the garlic, ginger and shallots and stir-fry for 1–2 minutes, or until softened and lightly browned.

**3** Add the mushrooms and stir-fry for a further 2–3 minutes. Stir in the tofu and toss gently to brown lightly.

**4** Mix the soy sauce, rice wine, fish sauce, peanut butter and chilli sauce together in a small bowl, then stir into the pan.

**5** Stir in the rice noodles and toss to coat evenly in the sauce. Sprinkle with peanuts and shredded basil leaves and serve hot.

# vegetables with tofu & spinach

## ingredients

### SERVES 4

vegetable or peanut oil,
  for deep-frying
225 g/8 oz firm tofu, drained
  and cut into cubes
2 tbsp vegetable or peanut oil
2 onions, chopped
2 garlic cloves, chopped
1 fresh red chilli, deseeded
  and sliced
3 celery stalks, sliced
  diagonally
225 g/8 oz mushrooms, sliced
  thickly
115 g/4 oz baby corn,
  cut in half
1 red pepper, deseeded and
  cut into strips
3 tbsp Thai red curry paste
400 ml/14 fl oz coconut milk
1 tsp soft light brown sugar
2 tbsp Thai soy sauce
225 g/8 oz baby spinach
  leaves

## method

**1** Heat the oil for deep-frying in a frying pan and deep-fry the tofu cubes, in batches, for 4–5 minutes, until crisp and browned. Remove with a slotted spoon and drain on kitchen paper.

**2** Heat 2 tablespoons of the oil in a wok or frying pan and stir-fry the onions, garlic and chilli for 1–2 minutes, until they start to soften. Add the celery, mushrooms, baby corn and red pepper and stir-fry for 3–4 minutes, until they soften.

**3** Stir in the curry paste and coconut milk and gradually bring to the boil. Add the sugar and soy sauce and then the spinach. Cook, stirring constantly, until the spinach has wilted. Serve immediately, topped with the tofu.

# asian vegetables with yellow bean sauce

## ingredients

### SERVES 4

1 aubergine

salt

2 tbsp vegetable oil

3 garlic cloves, crushed

4 spring onions, chopped

1 small red pepper, deseeded
    and thinly sliced

4 baby corn cobs, halved
    lengthways

115 g/4 oz mangetout

200 g/7 oz green pak choi,
    coarsely shredded

425 g/14½ oz canned straw
    mushrooms, drained

115 g/4 oz beansprouts

2 tbsp rice wine or dry sherry

2 tbsp yellow bean sauce

2 tbsp dark soy sauce

1 tsp chilli sauce

1 tsp sugar

150 ml/5 fl oz vegetable stock

1 tsp cornflour

2 tsp water

## method

**1** Cut the aubergine into 5-cm/2-inch long thin sticks. Place in a colander, then sprinkle with salt and let stand for 30 minutes. Rinse in cold water and dry thoroughly with kitchen paper.

**2** Heat the oil in a frying pan or preheated wok. Add the garlic, spring onions and pepper and stir-fry over high heat for 1 minute. Stir in the aubergine pieces and stir-fry for a further 1 minute, or until softened.

**3** Stir in the baby corn cobs and mangetout and stir-fry for 1 minute. Add the pak choi, mushrooms and beansprouts and stir-fry for 30 seconds.

**4** Mix the rice wine, yellow bean sauce, soy sauce, chilli sauce and sugar together in a bowl, then add to the pan with the stock. Bring to the boil, stirring constantly.

**5** Slowly blend the cornflour with the water to form a smooth paste, then stir quickly into the pan and cook for a further minute. Serve immediately.

# egg-fried rice with vegetables & crispy onions

## ingredients

### SERVES 4

4 tbsp vegetable or peanut oil

2 garlic cloves, chopped finely

2 fresh red chillies, deseeded
   and chopped

115 g/4 oz mushrooms, sliced

55 g/2 oz mangetout, halved

55 g/2 oz baby corn, halved

3 tbsp Thai soy sauce

1 tbsp jaggery or soft light
   brown sugar

few Thai basil leaves

350 g/12 oz rice, cooked and
   cooled

2 eggs, beaten

2 onions, sliced

## method

**1** Heat half the oil in a wok or large frying pan and sauté the garlic and chillies for 2–3 minutes.

**2** Add the mushrooms, mangetout and baby corn and stir-fry for 2–3 minutes, then add the soy sauce, sugar and basil. Stir in the rice.

**3** Push the mixture to one side of the wok and add the eggs to the bottom. Stir until lightly set before combining into the rice mixture.

**4** Heat the remaining oil in another pan and sauté the onions until crispy and brown. Serve the rice topped with the onions.

# stir-fried ginger mushrooms

## ingredients

**SERVES 4**

2 tbsp vegetable oil

3 garlic cloves, crushed

1 tbsp Thai red curry paste

1/2 tsp ground turmeric

425 g/15 oz canned straw
    mushrooms, drained and
    halved

2-cm/3/4-inch piece fresh
    ginger, finely shredded

150 ml/5 fl oz coconut milk

40 g/11/2 oz dried shiitake
    mushrooms, soaked,
    drained and sliced

1 tbsp lemon juice

1 tbsp light soy sauce

2 tsp sugar

1/2 tsp salt

8 cherry tomatoes, halved

200 g/7 oz firm tofu

diced coriander leaves,
    for sprinkling

Thai fragrant rice, to serve

spring onion curls, to garnish

## method

**1** Heat the oil in a preheated wok or large frying pan. Add the garlic and cook for 1 minute, stirring. Stir in the curry paste and turmeric and cook for a further 30 seconds.

**2** Stir in the straw mushrooms and ginger and stir-fry for 2 minutes. Stir in the coconut milk and bring to the boil.

**3** Stir in the shiitake mushrooms, lemon juice, soy sauce, sugar and salt and heat thoroughly. Add the tomatoes and tofu and toss gently to heat through.

**4** Sprinkle the coriander over the mixture and serve hot with freshly cooked fragrant rice garnished with spring onion curls.

# egg fu yung

## ingredients

**SERVES 4–6**

2 eggs

1/2 tsp salt

pinch of white pepper

1 tsp melted butter

2 tbsp vegetable or peanut oil

1 tsp finely chopped garlic

1 small onion, finely sliced

1 green pepper, finely sliced

450 g/1 lb cooked rice, chilled

1 tbsp light soy sauce

1 tbsp finely chopped spring
   onions

150 g/5 oz beansprouts,
   trimmed

2 drops of sesame oil

## method

**1** Beat the eggs with the salt and pepper. Heat the butter in a frying pan and pour in the eggs. Cook as an omelette, until set, then remove from the pan and cut into slivers.

**2** In a preheated wok or deep saucepan, heat the oil and stir-fry the garlic until fragrant. Add the onion and stir-fry for 1 minute, then add the green pepper and stir-fry for a further 1 minute. Stir in the rice and, when the grains are separated, stir in the light soy sauce and cook for 1 minute.

**3** Add the spring onions and egg strips and stir well, then finally add the beansprouts and sesame oil. Stir-fry for 1 minute and serve.

# szechuan noodles

## ingredients

### SERVES 4

1 large carrot

250 g/9 oz dried thick Chinese
  egg noodles

2 tbsp peanut or corn oil

2 large garlic cloves, very
  finely chopped

1 large red onion, cut in half
  and thinly sliced

125 ml/4 fl oz vegetable stock
  or water

2 tbsp bottled chilli bean
  sauce

2 tbsp Chinese sesame paste

1 tbsp dried Szechuan
  peppercorns, roasted and
  ground

1 tsp light soy sauce

2 small pak choi or other
  Chinese cabbage, cut into
  quarters

## method

**1** Peel the carrot and cut off both ends, then grate it lengthways on the coarsest side of a grater to make long, thin strips. Set the carrot strips aside.

**2** Cook the noodles in a saucepan of boiling water for 4 minutes, or according to the packet instructions, until soft. Drain and rinse with cold water to stop the cooking, then set aside.

**3** Heat a wok or large frying pan over a high heat. Add the oil and heat until it shimmers. Add the garlic and onion and stir-fry for 1 minute. Add the vegetable stock, chilli bean sauce, sesame paste, ground Szechuan peppercorns and soy sauce and bring to the boil, stirring to blend the ingredients together. Add the pak choi quarters and carrot strips and continue stir-frying for 1–2 minutes, until they are just wilted. Add the noodles and continue stir-frying, using 2 forks to mix all the ingredients together. Serve the noodles when they are hot.

# hot-&-sour noodle salad

## ingredients

**SERVES 4**

350 g/12 oz dried rice
   vermicelli noodles
4 tbsp sesame oil
3 tbsp soy sauce
juice of 2 limes
1 tsp sugar
4 spring onions, finely sliced
1–2 tsp hot chilli sauce
2 tbsp chopped fresh
   coriander

## method

**1** Prepare the noodles according to the packet instructions. Drain, put in a bowl and toss with half the oil.

**2** Mix the remaining oil, soy sauce, lime juice, sugar, spring onions and chilli sauce together in a bowl. Stir into the noodles.

**3** Stir in the coriander and serve.

# sweet-&-sour vegetables on noodle pancakes

## ingredients

**SERVES 4**

115 g/4 oz dried thin cellophane noodles

6 eggs

4 spring onions, sliced diagonally

2¹/₂ tbsp peanut or corn oil

900 g/2 lb selection of vegetables, such as carrots, baby corn, cauliflower, broccoli, mangetout, mushrooms and onions, peeled as necessary and chopped into same-sized pieces

100 g/3¹/₂ oz canned bamboo shoots, drained

200 g/7 oz bottled sweet-and-sour sauce

salt and pepper

## method

**1** Soak the noodles in enough lukewarm water to cover and set aside for 20 minutes, or according to the packet instructions, until soft. Drain them well and use scissors to cut into 7.5-cm/3-inch pieces.

**2** Beat the eggs, then stir in the noodles, spring onions, salt and pepper. Heat a 20-cm/8-inch frying pan over a high heat. Add 1 tablespoon of oil and swirl it around. Pour in a quarter of the egg mixture and tilt the frying pan so it covers the bottom. Lower the heat to medium and cook for 1 minute, or until the thin pancake is set. Flip it over and add a little extra oil, if necessary. Continue cooking until beginning to colour. Transfer to a plate and keep warm in a low oven while you make 3 more pancakes.

**3** After you've made 4 pancakes, heat a wok or large, heavy-based frying pan over a high heat. Add 1¹/₂ tablespoons of oil and heat until it shimmers. Add the thickest vegetables, such as carrots, first and stir-fry for 30 seconds. Gradually add the remaining vegetables and bamboo shoots. Stir in the sauce and stir-fry until all the vegetables are tender and the sauce is hot. Spoon the vegetables and sauce over the pancakes.

# egg-fried rice with peas

## ingredients

**SERVES 4**

150 g/5$^1$/$_2$ oz long-grain rice

3 eggs, beaten

2 tbsp vegetable oil

2 garlic cloves, crushed

4 spring onions, chopped

125 g/4$^1$/$_2$ oz cooked peas

1 tbsp light soy sauce

pinch of salt

shredded spring onions,
    to garnish

## method

**1** Cook the rice in a saucepan of boiling water for 10–12 minutes until almost cooked, but not soft. Drain well, rinse under cold running water and drain thoroughly.

**2** Place the beaten eggs in a saucepan and cook over a low heat, stirring constantly, until softly scrambled. Remove the pan from the heat and set aside.

**3** Preheat a wok over a medium heat. Add the oil and swirl it around to coat the sides of the wok. When the oil is hot, add the garlic, spring onions and peas and sauté, stirring occasionally, for 1–2 minutes.

**4** Stir the rice into the mixture in the wok, mixing to combine. Add the eggs, soy sauce and salt to the wok and stir to mix in the eggs thoroughly.

**5** Transfer to serving dishes and serve garnished with the shredded spring onions.

# spicy tofu

## ingredients

**SERVES 4**

250 g/9 oz firm tofu, rinsed
   and drained thoroughly
   and cut into 1-cm/$\frac{1}{2}$-inch
   cubes
4 tbsp peanut oil
1 tbsp grated fresh ginger
3 garlic cloves, crushed
4 spring onions, thinly sliced
1 head of broccoli, cut into
   florets
1 carrot, cut into batons
1 yellow pepper, thinly sliced
250 g/9 oz shiitake
   mushrooms, thinly sliced
steamed rice, to serve

marinade
5 tbsp vegetable stock
2 tsp cornflour
2 tbsp soy sauce
1 tbsp caster sugar
pinch of chilli flakes

## method

**1** Combine all the ingredients for the marinade in a large bowl. Add the tofu and toss well to cover in the marinade. Set aside to marinate for 20 minutes.

**2** In a large frying pan or wok, heat 2 tablespoons of the peanut oil and stir-fry the tofu with its marinade until brown and crispy. Remove from the frying pan and set aside.

**3** Heat the remaining 2 tablespoons of peanut oil in the frying pan and stir-fry the ginger, garlic and spring onions for 30 seconds. Add the broccoli, carrot, yellow pepper and mushrooms to the frying pan and cook for 5–6 minutes. Return the tofu to the frying pan and stir-fry to reheat. Serve immediately over steamed rice.

# a firepot of mushrooms & tofu

## ingredients

**SERVES 4**

55 g/2 oz dried Chinese
  mushrooms
115 g/4 oz firm tofu, drained
2 tbsp bottled sweet chilli
  sauce
2 tbsp peanut or corn oil
2 large garlic cloves, chopped
1-cm/$\frac{1}{2}$-inch piece fresh
  ginger, peeled and finely
  chopped
1 red onion, sliced
$\frac{1}{2}$ tbsp Szechuan
  peppercorns, lightly
  crushed
55 g/2 oz canned straw
  mushrooms, drained
  weight, rinsed
vegetable stock or water
1 star anise
pinch of sugar
soy sauce, to taste
115 g/4 oz dried thin
  cellophane noodles

## method

**1** Soak the mushrooms in enough boiling water to cover for 20 minutes, or until soft. Cut the tofu into bite-sized chunks, coat with the chilli sauce and marinate.

**2** Just before you are ready to start cooking, strain the soaked mushrooms through a sieve lined with kitchen paper, reserving the soaking liquid. Heat the oil in a medium-size ovenproof casserole or large frying pan with a lid. Add the garlic and ginger and stir them around for 30 seconds. Add the onion and peppercorns and keep stirring until the onion is almost tender. Add the tofu, the soaked mushrooms and the canned mushrooms and stir carefully so the tofu doesn't break up.

**3** Add the reserved mushroom soaking liquid to the wok with just enough vegetable stock to cover. Stir in the star anise, a pinch of sugar and several dashes of soy sauce. Bring to the boil, then reduce the heat, cover and simmer for 5 minutes. Add the noodles, re-cover and simmer for a further 5 minutes, or until the noodles are tender. The noodles should be covered with liquid, so add extra stock at this point, if necessary. Use a fork or wooden spoon to stir the noodles into the other ingredients. Add more soy sauce, if liked.

# broccoli & mangetout stir-fry

## ingredients

**SERVES 4**

2 tbsp vegetable or peanut oil

dash of sesame oil

1 garlic clove, finely chopped

225 g/8 oz head of broccoli,
   cut into small florets

115 g/4 oz mangetout,
   trimmed

225 g/8 oz Chinese cabbage,
   chopped into 1-cm/$^1/_2$-inch
   slices

5–6 spring onions, finely
   chopped

$^1/_2$ tsp salt

2 tbsp light soy sauce

1 tbsp Shaoxing rice wine

1 tsp toasted sesame seeds,
   to garnish

## method

**1** In a preheated wok or deep saucepan, heat the oils, then add the garlic and stir-fry vigorously. Add all the vegetables and salt and stir-fry over a high heat, tossing rapidly, for about 3 minutes.

**2** Pour in the light soy sauce and Shaoxing and cook for a further 2 minutes.

**3** Transfer to a serving dish, garnish with the sesame seeds and serve hot.

# garlic spinach stir-fry

## ingredients

**SERVES 4**

6 tbsp vegetable oil

6 garlic cloves, crushed

2 tbsp black bean sauce

3 tomatoes, roughly chopped

900 g/2 lb spinach, tough
  stalks removed, roughly
  chopped

1 tsp chilli sauce, or to taste

2 tbsp fresh lemon juice

salt and pepper

## method

**1** Heat the oil in a preheated wok or large frying pan over a high heat, add the garlic, black bean sauce and tomatoes and stir-fry for 1 minute.

**2** Stir in the spinach, chilli sauce and lemon juice and mix well. Cook, stirring frequently, for 3 minutes, or until the spinach is just wilted. Season with salt and pepper. Remove from the heat and serve immediately.

# spicy vegetarian stir-fry

## ingredients

**SERVES 4**

3 tbsp vegetable oil

1/2 tsp turmeric

salt and pepper

225 g/8 oz potatoes, cut into
    1-cm/1/2-inch cubes

3 shallots, chopped finely

1 bay leaf

1/2 tsp ground cumin

1 tsp finely grated fresh ginger

1/4 tsp chilli powder

4 tomatoes, chopped coarsely

300 g/10 1/2 oz spinach
    (de-stalked), chopped
    roughly

125 g/4 1/2 oz fresh or frozen
    peas

1 tbsp lemon juice

cooked basmati rice, to serve

## method

**1** In a wok, heat 2 tablespoons of the oil and add the turmeric and a pinch of salt. Carefully add the potatoes, stirring continuously to coat in the turmeric. Stir-fry for 5 minutes, then remove from the wok and set aside.

**2** Heat the remaining tablespoon of oil and stir-fry the shallots for 1–2 minutes. Mix in the bay leaf, cumin, ginger and chilli powder, then add the tomatoes and stir-fry for 2 minutes.

**3** Add the spinach, mixing well to combine all the flavours. Cover and simmer for 2–3 minutes. Return the potatoes to the wok and add the peas and lemon juice. Cook for 5 minutes, or until the potatoes are tender.

**4** Remove the wok from the heat and discard the bay leaf, then season with salt and pepper. Serve with cooked basmati rice.

# crisp noodle & vegetable stir-fry

## ingredients

**SERVES 4**

peanut or sunflower oil,
  for deep-frying

115 g/4 oz rice vermicelli,
  broken into 7.5-cm/3-inch
  lengths

115 g/4 oz green beans,
  cut into short lengths

2 carrots, cut into thin sticks

2 courgettes, cut into thin
  sticks

115 g/4 oz shiitake
  mushrooms, sliced

2.5-cm/1-inch piece fresh
  ginger, shredded

1/2 small head Napa cabbage,
  shredded

4 spring onions, shredded

85 g/3 oz beansprouts

2 tbsp dark soy sauce

2 tbsp Chinese rice wine

large pinch of sugar

2 tbsp coarsely chopped fresh
  coriander

## method

**1** Half-fill a wok or deep, heavy-based frying pan with oil. Heat to 180–190°C/350–375°F, or until a cube of bread browns in 30 seconds.

**2** Add the noodles, in batches, and cook for 1¹/₂–2 minutes, or until crisp and puffed up. Remove and drain on kitchen paper. Pour off all but 2 tablespoons of oil from the wok.

**3** Heat the remaining oil over high heat. Add the green beans and stir-fry for 2 minutes. Add the carrot and courgette sticks, sliced mushrooms and ginger and stir-fry for a further 2 minutes.

**4** Add the shredded Napa cabbage, spring onions and beansprouts and stir-fry for a further minute. Add the soy sauce, rice wine and sugar and cook, stirring constantly, for 1 minute.

**5** Add the chopped coriander and toss well. Serve immediately, with the noodles.

# agedashi tofu

## ingredients

**SERVES 2**

150 ml/5 fl oz water

2 tsp dashi granules

2 tbsp shoyu (Japanese
　　soy sauce)

2 tbsp mirin

vegetable oil, for deep-frying

300 g/10½ oz silken tofu,
　　drained on kitchen paper
　　and cut into 4 cubes

2 tbsp plain flour

1 tsp grated fresh ginger

2 tsp grated daikon

¼ tsp kezuri-bushi shavings

## method

**1** Put the water in a pan with the dashi granules and bring to the boil. Add the shoyu and mirin and cook for 1 minute. Keep warm.

**2** Preheat a wok, then fill one-third full with oil, or use a deep-fryer. Heat the oil to 180–190°C/350–375°F, or until a cube of bread browns in 30 seconds. Meanwhile, dust the tofu cubes with the flour.

**3** Add the tofu pieces to the oil, in batches, and cook until lightly golden in colour. Remove, drain on kitchen paper and keep hot while you cook the remaining tofu cubes.

**4** Put 2 pieces of tofu in each of 2 bowls and divide the dashi stock between them. Top with ginger, daikon and kezuri-bushi.

# chinese vegetables & beansprouts with noodles

## ingredients

### SERVES 4

1.25 litres/40 fl oz vegetable
 stock
1 garlic clove, crushed
1-cm/$1/2$-inch piece fresh
 ginger, finely chopped
225 g/8 oz dried medium egg
 noodles
1 red pepper, deseeded and
 sliced
85 g/3 oz frozen peas
115 g/4 oz broccoli florets
85 g/3 oz shiitake mushrooms,
 sliced
2 tbsp sesame seeds
225 g/8 oz canned water
 chestnuts, drained and
 halved
225 g/8 oz canned bamboo
 shoots, drained
280 g/10 oz Napa cabbage,
 sliced
140 g/5 oz beansprouts
3 spring onions, sliced
1 tbsp dark soy sauce
pepper

## method

**1** Bring the stock, garlic and ginger to the boil in a large saucepan. Stir in the noodles, red pepper, peas, broccoli and mushrooms and return to the boil. Reduce the heat, cover, and simmer for 5–6 minutes, or until the noodles are tender.

**2** Meanwhile, preheat the grill to medium. Spread the sesame seeds out in a single layer on a baking sheet and toast under the preheated grill, turning to brown evenly – watch constantly because they brown very quickly. Tip the sesame seeds into a small dish and set aside.

**3** Once the noodles are tender, add the water chestnuts, bamboo shoots, Napa cabbage, beansprouts and spring onions to the pan. Return the stock to the boil, stir to mix the ingredients and simmer for a further 2–3 minutes to heat through thoroughly.

**4** Carefully drain off 300 ml/10 fl oz of the stock into a small heatproof jug and set aside. Drain and discard any remaining stock and turn the noodles and vegetables into a warmed serving dish. Quickly mix the soy sauce with the reserved stock and pour over the noodles and vegetables. Season with pepper and serve at once.

# oyster mushrooms & vegetables with peanut chilli sauce

## ingredients

**SERVES 4**

1 tbsp sesame oil

4 spring onions, sliced finely

1 carrot, cut into batons

1 courgette, cut into batons

1/2 head of broccoli, cut into
    florets

450 g/1 lb oyster mushrooms,
    thinly sliced

2 tbsp crunchy peanut butter

1 tsp chilli powder, or to taste

3 tbsp water

cooked rice or noodles,
    to serve

wedges of lime, to garnish

## method

**1** Heat the oil in a frying pan or wok until almost smoking. Stir-fry the spring onions for 1 minute. Add the carrot and courgette and stir-fry for a further 1 minute. Then add the broccoli and cook for 1 minute more.

**2** Stir in the mushrooms and cook until they are soft and at least half the liquid they produce has evaporated. Add the peanut butter and stir well. Season with the chilli powder. Finally, add the water and cook for a further minute.

**3** Serve over rice or noodles and garnish with wedges of lime.

# spicy noodles with mushroom egg rolls

## ingredients

### SERVES 4

2 tbsp vegetable or peanut oil

1 small onion, chopped finely

225 g/8 oz mushrooms,
    chopped

1 tbsp Thai red curry paste

1 tbsp Thai soy sauce

1 tbsp fish sauce

8 square egg roll skins

vegetable or peanut oil,
    for deep-frying

225 g/8 oz quick-cook noodles

1 garlic clove, chopped

6 spring onions, chopped

1 red pepper, deseeded and
    chopped

1 tbsp ground coriander

1 tbsp ground cumin

## method

**1** Heat 1 tablespoon of the oil in a wok and stir-fry the onion and mushrooms until crisp and browned. Add the curry paste, soy sauce and fish sauce and stir-fry for 2–3 minutes. Remove the wok from the heat.

**2** Spoon an eighth of the mixture across one of the egg roll skins and roll up, folding the sides over the filling to enclose it.

**3** Heat the oil for deep-frying in a wok and deep-fry the egg rolls, 4 at a time, until crisp and browned. Drain on kitchen paper and keep warm.

**4** Meanwhile, put the noodles in a bowl, cover with boiling water and set aside to swell.

**5** Heat the remaining oil in the wok and stir-fry the garlic, spring onions and red pepper for 2–3 minutes. Stir in the coriander and cumin, then drain the noodles and add them to the wok. Toss together and serve topped with the egg rolls.